Indigenous Women and Adult Learning

In contemporary educational research, practice and policy, 'indigenous women' have emerged as an important focus in the global education arena and the 2030 Sustainable Development Agenda. This edited book investigates what is significant about indigenous women and their learning in terms of policy directions, research agendas and, not least, their own aspirations.

The book examines contemporary education policy and questions the dominant deficit discourse of indigenous women as vulnerable. By contrast, this publication demonstrates the marginalisations and multiple discriminations that indigenous women confront as indigenous persons, as women and as indigenous women. Chapters draw on ethnographic research in Egypt, Ethiopia, India, Mexico, Nepal, Peru and the Philippines and engage with indigenous women's learning from the perspectives of rights, gender equality and cultural, linguistic and ontological diversity. The book investigates intergenerational and intercultural learning and indigenous women's agency and power in the face of complex and dynamic changing social, physical, economic and cultural environments. The grounded ethnographic chapters illustrate indigenous women's diverse historical and contemporary experiences of inequalities, opportunities and formal education and how these influence their strengths, learning aspirations and ways of learning, as well as their values, demands, desires and practices.

Chapters 1–6 and 8 in this book were originally published in a special issue of the journal *Studies in the Education of Adults*.

Sheila Aikman is Research Associate in the School of International Development, University of East Anglia, UK. She has carried out long-term educational ethnographic research in the Amazon region of Peru and specialised in the areas of gender equality, plurilingualism and intercultural education. She has worked in both academia (University of London and University of East Anglia) and international and national NGOs. She is a member of the UEA UNESCO Chair Team.

Anna Robinson-Pant is Professor of Education in the School of Education and Lifelong Learning, University of East Anglia, UK, and holds the UNESCO Chair for Adult Literacy and Learning for Social Transformation. She began her career in Nepal as a teacher educator, development planner and ethnographic researcher. Her current research interests are adult literacy, gender and sustainable development and the internationalisation of higher education.

Indigenous Women and Adult Learning

Edited by
Sheila Aikman and Anna Robinson-Pant

LONDON AND NEW YORK

First published 2021
by Routledge
2 Park Square, Milton Park, Abingdon, Oxon OX14 4RN

and by Routledge
52 Vanderbilt Avenue, New York, NY 10017

Routledge is an imprint of the Taylor & Francis Group, an informa business

Chapters 1–3 and 5–8 © 2021 Taylor & Francis
Chapter 4 © 2019 Rama Narayanan and Nitya Rao. Originally published as Open Access.

British Library Cataloguing in Publication Data
A catalogue record for this book is available from the British Library

ISBN 13: 978-0-367-51705-2

Typeset in Minion Pro
by Newgen Publishing UK

Publisher's Note
The publisher accepts responsibility for any inconsistencies that may have arisen during the conversion of this book from journal articles to book chapters, namely the inclusion of journal terminology.

Disclaimer
Every effort has been made to contact copyright holders for their permission to reprint material in this book. The publishers would be grateful to hear from any copyright holder who is not here acknowledged and will undertake to rectify any errors or omissions in future editions of this book.

Contents

Citation Information

The chapters in this book, except Chapter 7, were originally published in *Studies in the Education of Adults*, volume 51, issue 2 (August 2019). When citing this material, please use the original page numbering for each article, as follows:

Introduction
Indigenous women and adult learning: Towards a paradigm change?
Sheila Aikman and Anna Robinson-Pant
Studies in the Education of Adults, volume 51, issue 2 (August 2019), pp. 151–160

Chapter 1
Situating learning in the context of sustainability: Indigenous learning, formal schooling and beyond
Abeer Salem
Studies in the Education of Adults, volume 51, issue 2 (August 2019), pp. 161–179

Chapter 2
Declared 'literate': Subjectivation through decontextualised literacy practices
Amina Singh and Dipti Sherchan
Studies in the Education of Adults, volume 51, issue 2 (August 2019), pp. 180–194

Chapter 3
Indigenous knowledge, skills and action: Indigenous women's learning in the Peruvian Amazon
Sheila Aikman
Studies in the Education of Adults, volume 51, issue 2 (August 2019), pp. 195–212

Chapter 4
Adult learning for nutrition security: Challenging dominant values through participatory action research in Eastern India
Rama Narayanan and Nitya Rao
Studies in the Education of Adults, volume 51, issue 2 (August 2019), pp. 213–231

Chapter 5
Indigenous women's perceptions of the Mexican bilingual and intercultural education model
Ulrike Hanemann
Studies in the Education of Adults, volume 51, issue 2 (August 2019), pp. 232–249

Chapter 6

Exploring the informal learning experiences of women in a pastoral community in Ethiopia: The case of pastoral women in Karrayyu
Turuwark Zalalam Warkineh and Abiy Menkir Gizaw
Studies in the Education of Adults, volume 51, issue 2 (August 2019), pp. 250–267

Chapter 7

Negotiating indigenous identities within mainstream community livelihoods: Stories of Aeta women in the Philippines
Gina Lontoc
Studies in the Education of Adults, DOI 10.1080/02660830.2020.1763099

Chapter 8

Indigenous adult women, learning and social justice: Challenging deficit discourses in the current policy environment
Sushan Acharya, Catherine M. Jere and Anna Robinson-Pant
Studies in the Education of Adults, volume 51, issue 2 (August 2019), pp. 268–289

For any permission-related enquiries please visit:
www.tandfonline.com/page/help/permissions

Notes on Contributors

Sushan Acharya is Professor of Education in the Central Department of Education, Tribhuvan University (TU), Nepal, and a management committee member of the Open and Distance Education Centre. Her current research interests include family indigenous practices and intergenerational literacy and learning. She is interested in research and advocacy for gender equality and social inclusion, particularly in the education sector.

Sheila Aikman is a Research Associate in the School of International Development, University of East Anglia, UK. She has carried out long-term educational ethnographic research in the Amazon region of Peru and specialised in the areas of gender equality, plurilingualism and intercultural education. She has worked in both academia (University of London and University of East Anglia) and international and national NGOs. She is a member of the UEA UNESCO Chair Team.

Ulrike Hanemann is an independent professional in the field of education. Until 2017, she coordinated the adult literacy and basic education work at the UNESCO Institute for Lifelong Learning (UIL), Germany, involving research and capacity development in all world regions. Prior to joining UNESCO in 2011, she was a lecturer and advisor in teacher formation at the National Autonomous University of Nicaragua. Her current research interest focuses on the application of the lifelong learning principle to education for social transformation.

Catherine M. Jere is a Lecturer in Education and International Development at the University of East Anglia, UK. Her interests centre on exploring how institutional and social barriers to learning can be challenged and disrupted, working across research, evaluation, practice and teaching. She has led research into non-formal approaches to youth literacy, inclusion and gender equality in education in Malawi, and Southern Africa more widely. Prior to joining the UEA, she was a researcher and policy analyst with the UNESCO Education for All Global Monitoring Report.

Gina Lontoc is a Faculty Member in the Department of English, Faculty of Arts and Letters, and a Research Associate in the Research Centre for Social Sciences and Education (RCSSED) at the University of Santo Tomas, Philippines. She completed her PhD at the University of East Anglia, UK. Her research interests include sustainable livelihoods, adult literacy, indigenous people's education, language education and visual participatory methods.

Abiy Menkir Gizaw is Assistant Professor of Adult Education and Community Development and Executive Director for Community Services Technology Transfer and University-Industry Linkage at Bahir Dar University, Ethiopia. He has a background in sociology and social anthropology, linguistics, adult education and Lifelong Learning policy and management (Erasmus Mundus Scholarship); is Coordinator of the UNESCO Learning Cities Project in Bahir Dar and a member of the Global Network of Learning Cities (GNLC). His main research interests include adult literacy, crafts, indigenous and intergenerational learning and livelihood diversification.

Rama Narayanan is a freelance community nutritionist based in Chennai, India. She is the (retired) Chair of the Ford Foundation for Women and Food Security at the MS Swaminathan Research Foundation in Chennai. She has three decades of experience in helping communities and non-government organizations to integrate nutrition concepts in development programmes. Specialising in maternal and childcare services, she is interested in research and policy advocacy for mothers and young children.

Nitya Rao is Professor of Gender and Development at the University of East Anglia, UK. She has worked extensively as a researcher and advocate in the field of women's rights, employment and migration and education for over three decades. She has done fine-grained research on households and intra-household dynamics in diverse rural contexts to draw out implications for gendered wellbeing, empowerment and justice, with a particular focus on food, nutrition and health security and she has published extensively.

Anna Robinson-Pant is Professor of Education in the School of Education and Lifelong Learning, University of East Anglia, UK, and holds the UNESCO Chair for Adult Literacy and Learning for Social Transformation. She began her career in Nepal as a teacher educator, development planner and ethnographic researcher. Her current research interests are adult literacy, gender and sustainable development and the internationalisation of higher education.

Abeer Salem, PhD, is a researcher, programme developer and educator of diverse national and international experience in the fields of international development, communication, media, education and sustainability. She has researched and published on education for sustainability, sustainable communities, indigenous learning, indigenous entrepreneurship and education, media literacy, sustainability communication and environmental sustainability, as well as media literacy and education. She teaches at the October University for the Modern Sciences and Arts in Egypt.

Dipti Sherchan is a PhD student in the Department of Anthropology at the University of Illinois at Chicago, USA. Her research interest lies at the intersections of anthropology, art history and critical feminist studies. She is investigating the cultural politics of art institutions, nationalism and transnationalism in twentieth- and twenty-first-century Nepal. Her project proposes re-examining art worlds as culturally and politically salient ethnographic sites to explore issues of sovereignty, solidarity and belonging.

Amina Singh is an Adjunct Faculty Member at Kathmandu University, Nepal, teaching courses in research methodology. She has a decade of professional experience working as a consultant in the development sector conducting evaluations and assessments. In her current phase as an academic, she has research interests in higher education pedagogy, educational philosophy, leadership, adult learning and social change.

Turuwark Zalalam Warkineh is Assistant Professor of Adult Education and Community Development at Bahir Dar University, Ethiopia, and Coordinator of the UNESCO Chair for Adult Literacy and Learning for Social Transformation. She has been involved in various national adult education research studies as well as conducting research for an international IFAD-UNESCO project. Her research interests include adult literacy, informal learning, gender, intergenerational learning and indigenous knowledge systems.

Indigenous women and adult learning: Towards a paradigm change?

In contemporary educational research, practice and policy, 'indigenous women' have emerged as an important focus in the global education arena. This Special Issue investigates what is significant about indigenous women and their learning in terms of policy prescriptions, research agendas and not least indigenous women's own aspirations. The articles draw on the authors' ongoing research and experiences from diverse countries including Ethiopia, India, Mexico, Nepal and Peru. The articles engage with indigenous women's learning from the perspectives of rights, agency, power, gender equality and cultural, linguistic and ontological diversity. These are issues pertinent not only in these country contexts but reverberate across the field of adult education and women's learning in the UK and beyond.

This Introduction examines contemporary education policy to understand why there is a focus on indigenous women, and what such a focus contributes to promoting adult learning. It starts by questioning the global discourse of indigenous women as vulnerable and asks who are indigenous women? The articles demonstrate the kinds of marginalisations and discriminations indigenous women confront as indigenous persons, as women and as indigenous women, but they also point to women's agency and power in the face of complex and dynamic changing social, physical, economic and cultural environments. The grounded ethnographic nature of the research also emphasises the importance of recognising indigenous women, not as a homogeneous undifferentiated group or category. It illustrates their diverse positionalities emerging from their varying historical and contemporary experiences of inequalities, opportunities and formal education, as well as their learning desires, demands and practices.

Who are 'indigenous women'?

Given this diversity, what does it mean to be indigenous? As the Asian South Pacific Bureau for Adult Education (ASPBAE) notes there is no one single definition of indigenous. It refers to a collective who 'has been subject to colonisation, has rights to collective ownership of land, desires the maintenance and development of their own identities, language and religions and desires the freedom to determine their relationships with States in a spirit of co-existence, mutual benefit and respect' (2011, p.4). The UN Declaration on the Rights of Indigenous Peoples adopted in 2007 (Article 33) states that 'indigenous peoples have the right to determine their own identity or membership in accordance with their customs and traditions, but not at the expense of their rights to citizenship in the States in which they live'. Furthermore, indigenous peoples have the right to determine the structures and to select the membership of their institutions, and this includes education, in accordance with their own procedures. Indigenous peoples, then, have collective as well as individual rights, and their ability to realise these rights, which include living in a way they value within the states where they live, have been undermined by their experiences of colonisation. Across the globe, indigenous peoples suffer disproportionately from poverty, marginalisation, lack of adequate housing and income inequality. Social, economic and environmental change sweeping most countries today in the guise of 'development' or globalisation have destroyed or threaten indigenous modes of livelihood, such as fishing, hunting and gathering, livestock cultivation of small-scale agriculture (United Nations 2009).

However, the term 'indigenous' is highly contentious in many places and heavily loaded with historical and political tones that are problematic for many indigenous people. As a label it can be associated with 'backwardness' and being 'uncivilised'. For this reason many 'indigenous people' choose not to use the term. In some regions, for example in Latin America, the term has been widely adopted by the movement for rights and self-determination. There it identifies, and is used to self-identify, individuals and peoples who have been colonised since 16th century and continue to struggle within their nation states for recognition and rights as peoples. In the Philippines, where a strong indigenous movement exists, the term is associated with the indigenous movement for rights. In other countries, for example Nepal, Acharya *et al.* suggest that although at one level there is a consensus among indigenous people (known as *Adivasi* or *janajati*[1]) and movements regarding the definition 'questions arise around whether the term can still hold if an individual becomes more economically, educationally, socially and geographically mobile'. So it becomes important to ask whether indigenous is a label being applied to individuals externally and what associations it brings, or whether it is an identity that is self-determined. Two of the articles in the SI (see articles by Singh and Sherchan, and Narayanan and Rao) do *not* use the term indigenous, reflecting the problematic nature of term. Whether the term indigenous is used or not, the articles in this SI address important issues of recognition, respect and rights and questions of alternative knowledges, ways of knowing and learning and challenges of intergenerational and intercultural learning.

While we have chosen to use the term indigenous for this SI, we are acutely aware of its complexities and limitations. First, there is the question of self-identification and individuals' and communities' right and power to decide themselves who is or is not indigenous, particularly in the context of rapidly increasing mobility and socio-economic change; secondly there is the way that when applied externally the term can be used to label and stigmatise; and thirdly within the field of international development, 'indigenous woman' is often used as a category to highlight a group perceived to be vulnerable, hitherto invisible and underserved by mainstream education (including the 2030 Sustainable Development Agenda). In terms of who is indigenous, we authors of this SI are not indigenous and it is not our intention to speak on behalf of indigenous women. Our intention, rather, is to challenge the ways that the category of 'indigenous women' is susceptible to homogenising and stigmatising indigenous women. We aim to increase the visibility of indigenous women, to help document their situations and problematise approaches to their education. We also aim to celebrate their achievements and recognise their rich diversity: their diverse gendered relationships within their indigenous and national communities; diverse economic and class situations both rural and urban with many living precarious lives in urban slums or in environmentally degraded rural communities; and diverse formal education experiences from no schooling to PhDs and professional qualifications.

Indigenous women and discrimination and marginalisation

Where data does exist, they reveal a pattern of persisting disparities between indigenous peoples and the non-indigenous population in all the regions of the world and across all sectors, not only in education. As the United Nations (2017) notes, the education sector mirrors and condenses the history of abuse and discrimination suffered by indigenous peoples but it also offers ways of combatting the discrimination. Gender-based discrimination also influences the patterns of exclusion and inclusion for indigenous women; evidence clearly demonstrates that many indigenous women face serious problems on a daily basis, ranging from extreme poverty, dispossession and discrimination to human rights abuses such as killings, torture and rape (IWGIA 2000). Indigenous women are, therefore, among the most marginalised groups globally and experience a 'double repression' as indigenous peoples oppressed by dominant groups within their nation states and as women, who may face repressive attitudes within their countries and repressive practices in their indigenous societies (Winding and Kampbel 2016, p. 4).

What, then, is the nature of the current focus on indigenous women within the field of education? In the statements and articles of the SDGs, to which 193 countries are signatories, indigenous peoples are specifically mentioned. The Education Goal (SDG 4) of ensuring inclusive and equitable education and lifelong learning for all by 2030 firmly places indigenous peoples within a category of 'the vulnerable' alongside persons with disabilities, refugees and poor children in rural areas. It expresses a concern to 'eliminate gender disparities in education and ensure equal access to all levels of education and vocational training for the vulnerable, including persons with disabilities, indigenous peoples and children in vulnerable situations' (https://sustainabledevelopment.un, see also Archarya *et al.*, this Issue). The acquisition of knowledge and skills for sustainable development and sustainable lifestyles, human rights, gender equality, promotion of a culture of peace and non-violence, global citizenship and appreciation of cultural diversity and of culture's contribution to sustainable development are the cornerstones of an inclusive and equitable quality education (https://progress of Goal 4//2016). This then is a way for indigenous peoples and indigenous women in particular to overcome their vulnerability.

This goal raises the question of in what way are indigenous women considered 'vulnerable'? Identified as persons lacking formal education and by implication, lacking in the qualities of a modern citizen education, schooling and non-formal education programmes have been tailored to aid their inclusion and assimilation. In the worst cases, entire peoples experienced forced removal of their children and/or their enrolment in residential schools, where widespread abuse of indigenous children was practised. In less blatant ways, schooling for indigenous children in many places continues to have 'a profoundly lasting and damaging impact on indigenous culture, heritage and language' (United Nations 2017, p.4). It is indigenous culture, heritage, oral language traditions and institutions with their own forms of teaching and learning that sustain indigenous values, economies, and sustainable development. But an ignorance of these systems and the integrity of indigenous women's knowledge has led to a disruption of the transmission of languages, cultural values and practices (see for example Aikman, this Issue; Aikman 2012). Viewed as lacking in learning, skills and knowledge, this deficit approach then labels indigenous women as vulnerable and renders them a target for national policies and global goals which impose external notions of 'sustainable development' and equitable and quality education and learning.

Changing discourses: from vulnerability to empowerment

As the articles in the SI demonstrate, 'indigenous women' is not a homogeneous category and it can obscure diverse ways in which indigenous women engage with and respond to experiences of inequalities and discrimination. Their diversity is embedded in their individual and collective historical and contemporary experiences of inequalities, discrimination and marginalisation, their experiences of formal education and their freedoms and capabilities to draw on their indigenous cosmologies and learning to give value and meaningfulness to their indigenous identities. The knowledges, skills and learning and forms of sustainable development that indigenous women value are themselves diverse.

Changing relationships and engagement with national and global societies over time and across generations influence the learning indigenous women value and how they shape their demands for new learning. The articles in this Special Issue offer insights into contemporary challenges facing indigenous women as individuals, as members of an indigenous people and as active members of indigenous organisations and demonstrate something of the complexity and diversity of indigenous women's learning. They explore what is happening in the name of adult learning and lifelong learning, with a view to setting out challenges to what Robinson-Pant and Rao (2006) have identified as a deficit approach to reaching and including women through adult education. As the Special Rapporteur in her assessment of the current status of UN Declaration of the Rights of Indigenous Peoples (UNDRIP) states: 'racism and discrimination are prevalent mindsets and attitudes that prevent the establishment of equal relationships between indigenous peoples' and require a 'paradigm change' (cited in IWGIA 2018, p. 9–10).

Indigenous women's learning has been put under the spotlight with the rise of international human rights standard-making and the intersection between three rights-making agendas: the international coalescence around education and its role in national and global development through the Declaration of Education For All (1990), the Dakar Framework for Action (2000) and the subsequent Sustainable Development Goals; the series of global meetings to embed and expand on the 1979 Convention on the Elimination of All Forms of Discrimination Against Women (CEDAW) and the work of the Commission on the Status of Women (CSW), leading to a new awareness of the need to address girls' and women's education and tackle inequality, poor quality and learning outcomes; and thirdly the rise of the indigenous movement at national, regional and global levels culminating in the Declaration on the Rights of Indigenous Peoples (UNDRIP) in 2007. This Declaration calls for attention to the rights and needs of indigenous women, effective measures to ensure continuing improvements in their economic and social rights, full protection and guarantees from all forms of violence and discrimination and reaffirms and applies the right to education to the specific historical, cultural, economic and social circumstances of indigenous peoples (see articles 21 and 22).

Much of the education analysis of indigenous women's learning needs has focussed on their supposed educational deficit and their vulnerability. Examination of inequalities within the education field has also tended to focus on the economic inequalities that indigenous women experience, how these influence their access, and their children's access, to and participation in education programmes (UNESCO 2018). The education-focussed SDG continues to prioritise children, especially girls, and schooling, to the neglect of adult learning, with little to say about learning and knowledge outside of the formal education system. This runs the risk of continuing to portray indigenous women as passive victims, devoid of their own agency, decision-making and self-determination.

However, there is a discernible shift in the discourse in the field of education, influenced by the development of gender rights and indigenous rights. There are calls for indigenous women's active engagement in education from the Special Adviser on Gender Issues and Advancement of Women and the Secretariat of the UN Permanent Forum on Indigenous Issues (United Nation 2010, p. 3). They aim to improve gender relations within indigenous societies and society more widely and 'facilitate indigenous women participating fully in all areas of their lives, whether in their home or in the public arena'. The Fifth International Conference on Adult Education in 1997 was concerned that adult education become part a larger political agenda and integral to national development agendas (Cited in ASPBAE 2011, p.xxx). A decade on from the adoption of UNDRIP, the Commission on the Status of Women has begun to consider indigenous women's empowerment and 'full exercise of their indigenous and collective rights, in accordance with their world vision and includes the right of each people to freely choose their economic, social and cultural development' (Cited in IWGIA 2018). At the same time, the Ministerial Declaration – an outcome of the annual High Level Political Forum (HLPF), and Review process in 2017 for the 2030 Agenda for the SDGs – made reference to indigenous peoples including 'the need to empower indigenous peoples', and to include them in 'appropriate national plans and measures to implement social protection systems' (IWGIA 2018, p. 592). 2019 has been declared the International Year of Indigenous Languages in efforts to celebrate, promote and protect indigenous languages, the ongoing loss of which is the complex knowledges and cultures they foster are increasingly being recognised as 'strategic resources for good governance, peacebuilding, reconciliation, and sustainable development. More importantly, such losses have huge negative impacts indigenous peoples' most basic human rights' (https://www.un.org/development/desa/dspd/2019/01/2019-international-year-of-indigen-ous-languages/).

While discourses are changing and indigenous women use their learning to actively influence and shape global rights agendas through their own organisations (see articles in this Special Issue by Aikman, Acharya *et al.* and Narayanan and Rao), they continue to experience profound discrimination and marginalisation not only economically but culturally and socially but in relation to their languages, world views and philosophies. In what ways are the diverse learning needs, demands and values of indigenous women being heard in local, national and global fora and what kinds of responses are they getting?

Indigenous adult learning: what is the difference?

The distinction between adult learning for indigenous women and indigenous adult learning is central to this Special Issue. Our starting point and main concern is not only access and inclusion for minority groups in mainstream adult learning programmes (the focus of SDG4, as indicated earlier in this introduction). Rather, we set out to explore what is distinctive about indigenous learning practices, knowledges and skills as a basis for re-visiting adult learning debates. We recognise also that 'indigenous learning' has different meanings which are often confused: first, as learning processes (which may include learning systems) and how indigenous women learn – 'learning as a verb'; and secondly, the learning which results, the different kinds of knowledges with which women engage (Rogers 2013).

Inevitably, indigenous education has often been defined in terms of what it is not – and particularly in opposition to formal education and schooling. Introducing the term 'knowledge heritage', Parajuli and Rai (2019) discuss the 'elitist and global values' informing the development of formal education in Nepal, as well as the rigidity of the curriculum. Similarly, Salem (in this Issue) contrasts indigenous learning in Egypt with the 'packaged' and standardised forms of knowledge underpinning formal education. In their research with the Karrayu pastoral community in Ethiopia, Warkineh and Menkir found that formal education (including state-run non formal adult education programmes) was defined as that 'brought by outsiders' and that government providers considered this as conveying 'science-proven' knowledge.

Our concern is not, however, just about the different ways in which women learn literacy or other skills within a formal programme, but also about the hidden curriculum with its focus on learning 'the rules of the state' (Althusser 1971). In Singh and Sherchan's account which draws on Althusser, we see how the Nepal state literacy programme has helped to reinforce and construct the dominant discourse around who is literate or not, and is part of a 'system differentiation' based on who attended or did not attend the course. The issue here is not just about how indigenous learning differs, but about how the adult literacy programme is constructing Thakali women learners as homogenous and perpetuating stereotypes about this specific indigenous group. As the authors ask, 'what does non formal education do to indigenous women?' A similar question is posed by Lontoc, who explores how Aeta women (in the Philippines) position themselves in relation to adult learning programmes. The Aeta women in her study explained the importance of learning new skills and knowledge to enhance their agricultural practices and combat social as well as economic marginalisation.

What emerges in these accounts is the problematic relationship between indigenous learning and schooling (including non-formal adult literacy programmes). Formal education is viewed by many of the authors, and the communities with whom they research, as a threat, 'destroying culture' (Warkineh and Menkir) through privileging contrasting values, knowledges and practices. What is also lost is the time and opportunities for young people to learn indigenous livelihood skills with their elders – as they spend so many hours of the day in school or formal programmes. As an elderly woman in Salem's case study of a Bedouin community commented, 'I realised that what 'life' taught them exceeded what I see other girls learned in school'.

The relationship between formal and informal learning, as Salem suggests, can be considered as 'complementary or contradictory'. The tensions identified in all these case studies suggest that the relationship is inevitably 'contradictory' and this is related to the imposition of formal learning/curriculum on indigenous communities (see earlier section regarding colonisation). The focus on education systems can mean that learning and education, informal and formal, are often conflated in debates. This is where we need to look outside the education sector to understand more about what 'indigenous learning' means; thus several of the articles here focus on the health and agriculture sectors.

Colley *et al.* (2003) have highlighted the limitations of defining informal learning only in relation to formal learning, and the assumption that there is only one kind of informal learning. Recently, there has been greater exploration into how people engage in different kinds of informal learning in everyday life or formal institutions (see Rogers 2013, Robinson-Pant 2016). Peer learning, intergenerational learning and experiential learning are some of the concepts used in this Special Issue to investigate the different kinds of relationships and practices involved in indigenous learning. Warkineh and Menkir suggest that 'all indigenous learning is intergenerational' but that the reverse does not necessarily hold true. Through an in depth exploration of midwifery in this indigenous pastoral community in Ethiopia, they identify the different skills that women learn through giving birth and helping others give birth and also the beliefs which inform these practices. A woman cannot become a midwife until she herself has given birth – linking to the ideas of 'experiential learning' – though she will begin to learn about these practices from older women long before this stage.

Indigenous women and education: the challenges and opportunities

The example of indigenous midwifery raises issues about how to bring together modern medicine with indigenous knowledge, given the strong discourse in this Ethiopian rural context that hospital deliveries are isolating and alienating experiences for women. The health sector illustrates all too clearly the possible dangers of taking a romanticised and external approach to indigenous knowledge without also a critical perspective. Again, this could be related to the tendency to polarise Western and indigenous knowledge in development discourse, rather than seeking to develop a space where synergies could be explored and indigenous women's own voices and knowledge listened to. Narayan and Rao's case study gives insights into how this can be achieved through 'a bottom-up, collective process, contextually and spatially embedded' approach to nutrition education. Significantly, this residential learning programme in India was based on indigenous learning practices – recognising the importance of the collective, yet also facilitating a process of dialogue, reflection, action and learning which led to women and men deconstructing gender norms.

Looking at the characteristics of indigenous adult learning outlined above, and what emerges clearly from all the articles, is that indigenous knowledge is not static and indigenous women's lives are being lived in contexts of huge upheaval and change. 'Traditional' knowledge and skills have always been dynamic and as Tom *et al.* (2019, p. 5) note 'rooted in key cultural precepts and practices and refined over generations'. What the articles in this Special Issue share is the valuing of collective as well as individual learning, in addition to prioritising informal, experiential and intergenerational learning. Given the strongly defined gender roles and boundaries in several of the indigenous communities researched here, such learning often comes across as gender differentiated. This is where our focus on indigenous women is important as it questions whether indigenous women's learning can become men's too? As the example of the nutrition learning programme in India illustrates, it is also possible to transform gendered approaches to indigenous learning.

Turning to the provision of education *for* indigenous women and the common starting assumption that they are 'doubly vulnerable' (see earlier), the providers' focus has often been (as for many other groups of women) on catching up with men – whether in relation to literacy, leadership skills or access to languages of power. For instance, some of the indigenous women's movements in Nepal have implemented programmes to support women to take up political roles both at local and national levels which include soft skill development (Acharya *et al.*). Hanemann discusses an intercultural bilingual programme in Mexico which set out to enhance gender equality through promoting the language rights and resources of indigenous women, alongside increasing access to a dominant language, Spanish. Whereas women had instrumental reasons for learning to read Spanish, such as being able to travel alone, they saw indigenous literacy instruction as strongly connected to intergenerational learning – 'we don't want to lose the culture, the language, the food, the way of walking of our grandparents, so that there is a memory of what those will leave behind who are already old … '

So, what can such approaches offer to wider debates about quality adult education and new ways of thinking about adult learning? Starting from where women are now - building on their specific knowledges and skills, and engaging with their aspirations for learning - are well-recognised principles of adult education. What is less common is the attempt to combine a rights-based and instrumental/functional approach to adult learning – rather than seeing this as a choice between contradictory aims (empowerment versus economic progress). Within this context, the interconnection of indigenous and gender rights is explicitly recognised by several of the case studies here. The focus on intergenerational and experiential learning has the potential to make the specific community central to knowledge construction - rather than implementing a curriculum based on a notion of useful generalised knowledge. Such approaches can help to shift notions of teaching and learning: viewing learning as embedded in indigenous women's ontologies and teaching as a situated practice of scaffolding learning. Addressing the tensions around how and when to engage with 'outsider' knowledge and languages may be a more pressing and visible concern in the programmes reviewed in this Special Issue but is an equally important issue for mainstream programmes to consider too.

Towards a paradigm change?

This Special Issue emerged from discussions amongst the contributors about the commonly found invisibility of indigenous women within research on indigenous education and within debates on adult education. Several of us have long been critiquing 'deficit' models of education (see Aikman and Robinson-Pant 2016, Aikman 2012), challenging mainstream education provision for indigenous groups (see Dyer and Aikman 2012) and raising issues around gender equality and women's empowerment (Rao and Cagna 2018). Based on research in very different countries in South and South East Asia, Africa and South America, the kinds of questions that we are asking were about quality education and learning, gender equality, social justice, participation, cultural and linguistic diversity, change and social movements. As ethnographers, we were struck by the lack of methodological innovation or diversity in relation to the research conducted in many of these contexts. As Singh and Sherchan point out in the context of Nepal, most of the research on Thakali women has been conducted by 'non-native (and few native) male researchers', with the result that even when Thakali women are discussed, 'they are mentioned briefly as anecdotes but never form the core voice of the research inquiry'. Aikman's article draws on long term ethnography with the aim of giving attention to one particular group of indigenous woman in order to trace the forms and kinds of knowledge they have valued and continued to value over their lifetimes. It highlights how indigenous women's learning needs and values change over generations as the social, cultural and economic context changes. But it also demonstrates indigenous women's agency in the face of radical and destructive environment and social change.

Based on ethnographic and participatory approaches to research, the papers in this Special Issue recognise voice, ownership of knowledge and the ethics of representation as key issues in research with/on indigenous women. The authors all adopt a social practice or situated approach (Street 1984, Barton *et al.* 2000), viewing literacy and learning as embedded in and shaped by social relations and recognising many literacies and diverse literacy practices, rather than only focussing on the dominant literacy associated with schooling (Street 1995). In this respect, the papers differ from the common starting point of education 'for' sustainable futures (Ng'asike 2019, Lagunas 2019) and a focus on formalised learning programmes and institutions, as they foreground informal learning. The aim of this Special Issue is to shift attention to indigenous women's lives and experiences of learning – including in the context of mainstream literacy and development programmes.

In this Introduction we have attempted to 'unsettle' dominant discourses about who indigenous women are, their knowledges and learning, their demands and aspirations. The individual articles provide evidence to challenge generalised prescriptions of global policy and to embrace the diversity and complexity of indigenous women's lives and the learning they can offer us. Rather than homogenising indigenous women into a category characterised by learning deficits and vulnerabilities, this Special Issue looks towards working with indigenous women as empowered and knowledgable actors who are seeking further learning which will support them in their aims to achieve self-determined and sustainable futures. We hope this Special Issue can contribute to a further step towards developing a 'situated' and rights-based approach to research and policy on adult learning with indigenous women.

Note

1. Leading indigenous scholars coined the term Janajati to find a common term to identify population outside of the Hindu caste hierarchy (Neupane, 2012): 'Generally the words Janajati (nationality) and Adivasi (the indigenous people) are used as synonyms. Of course, Janajati is related to social composition and Adivasi has its relation with time period' (Gurung *et al.* as cited by Neupane, 2012). These days the two terms are used interchangeably in Nepal and both refer to indigenous people (ibid.).

Acknowledgements

We thank Professor Alan Rogers and Professor Nitya Rao for their helpful comments and suggestions on a draft of this Introduction.

Disclosure statement

No potential conflict of interest was reported by the authors.

ORCID

Anna Robinson-Pant (iD) http://orcid.org/0000-0003-3989-2272

References

Aikman, S., 2002. Women's oral knowledge and the poverty of formal education in the SE Peruvian Amazon. *In*: C. Sweetman, ed. *Gender, development and poverty*. Oxford: Oxfam Publishing, 41–49.

Aikman, S., 2012. Interrogating discourses of intercultural education: from indigenous Amazon community to global education forum. *Compare*, 42(2), 235–257.

Aikman, S., and Robinson-Pant, 2016. Challenging deficit discourses in education and development. *Compare*, 46(2), 314–334.

Althusser, L., 1971. Ideology and ideological state apparatus. *In*: B. Brewster (Trans.) *Lenin and philosophy and other essays*. London: Monthly Review Press, 170–186.

ASPBAE. 2011. Quality adult education benchmarks for indigenous education. Discussion Paper, Asian South Pacific Association for Adult and Basic Education, Mumbai, India.

Barton, D., Hamilton, M., and Ivanic, R., 2000. *Situated Literacies: reading and writing in context*. London: Routledge.

Colley, H., Hodkinson, P., and Malcolm, J., 2003. *Informality and formality in learning*. London: Learning and Skills Research Centre.

Dyer, C., and Aikman, S., 2012. Education and Inclusion: examining the narratives. *Compare* 42 (2), 177–185.

IWGIA, 2000. Policy indigenous women. International Policy Document, manuscript. International Work Group for Indigenous Affairs, Copenhagen.

IWGIA, 2018. *Yearbook 2018*, International Work Group for Indigenous Affairs, Copenhagen.

Lagunas, R. M., 2019. Nahuatl in Coatepec: Ideologies, practices and management for linguistic and cultural continuance. *International review of education*, 65(1), 67–86.

Ng'asike, J. T., 2019. Indigenous knowledge practices for sustainable lifelong education in pastoralist communities of Kenya. *International review of education*, 65(1), 19–46.

Parajuli, M. N., and Rai, I. M., 2019. Knowledge heritage in women's everyday practices: Missing aspects of Nepal's modern education, Working Paper, Kathmandu University School of Education.

Rao, N., and P. Cagna., 2018. Feminist Mobilisation, Making Claims and Policy Change: an introduction. *Development and Change*, 49 (3), 708–713.

Robinson-Pant, A., 2016. *Learning knowledge and skills for agriculture to improve rural livelihoods*. Paris: IFAD/UNESCO.

Robinson-Pant, A., and Rao, N., 2006. Adult education and indigenous people: addressing gender in policy and practice. *International journal of educational development*, 26, 209–223.

Rogers, A. 2013. The Classroom and the Everyday: The Importance of Informal Learning for Formal Learning. http://pages.ie.uminho.pt/inved/index.php/ie/issue/view/1/showToc

Street, B. V., 1984. *Literacy in theory and practice*. Cambridge: Cambridge University Press.

Street, B. V., 1995. *Social literacies: critical approaches to literacy in development, ethnography and education*. London: Longman.

Tom, M. N., Huaman, E. S., and McCarty, T., 2019. Indigenous Knowledges as vital contributions to sustainability. *International review of education*, 65(1), 1–18.

UNESCO 2018. Migration, Displacement and Education, Building Bridges not Walls. Global Education Monitoring Report 2019, UNESCO, Paris.

United Nations. 2009. *The State of the World's Indigenous Peoples I*. Department for Social and Economic Affairs, New York.

United Nations. 2010. *Gender and Indigenous Peoples' Education* Briefing Note No. 3, UN Permanent Forum on Indigenous Issues, New York.

United Nations. 2017. *The State of the World's Indigenous Peoples III*, Education. Department for Social and Economic Affairs, New York.

Winding, D., and Kampbel, E.-R., 2016. *Indigenous Women Workers; with case studies from Bangladesh, Nepal and the Americas*. Geneva: International Labour Office.

Sheila Aikman

Anna Robinson-Pant ⓘ

Situating learning in the context of sustainability: Indigenous learning, formal schooling and beyond

Abeer Salem (iD)

ABSTRACT
This paper focuses on learning by a group of Bedouin women in a community in eastern Egypt. It discusses the dynamic nature of indigenous learning, and the adaptability of its patterns and content. It describes how its patterns may yield to modern learning systems, and how traditional knowledge and livelihoods may be lost in the process. It gleans ideas on how traditional and formal learning can meet, situating learning in the larger context of sustainability.

Introduction

Learning in indigenous communities is a unique experience. The diverse learning patterns, the elements to be learned and the ways of learning are very distinctive to the particulars of each of these communities. The diversity of local and traditional knowledge stems from the fact that this knowledge is based on the immediate and ever-changing realities of the community and corresponds to its uniqueness. Hence, indigenous ways of learning are as varied and diverse as indigenous communities are, varying in both place and time. The more we know and learn about indigenous people and indigenous knowledge, the more we realise the diversity of this knowledge; it is hard to generalise from each local community.

While the diversity of indigenous knowledge may be a resultant of a variety of different reasons, the relationship between learning and the immediate environment a community lives in is key to determining the kind of needed knowledge in a particular locale. It is plausible to think that this holds true especially in communities that live very close to the land and who depend on the immediate environment for their livelihoods like Bedouins, for example, to whom the environment is an important aspect of their life experience. Therefore, whilst learning is related to and based on the social, cultural and environmental contexts in these communities, all contextual changes will affect and reflect on the patterns of learning as well. Indigenous communities as they steer their way through social, cultural and environmental change, navigate through different learning content, approaches and patterns. Hence, in each of these communities, a new mix of learning – a hybrid mixing the new and the traditional – emerges.

This paper focuses on the ways of learning by a group of Bedouin women[1] in a community in eastern Egypt; on why and what they learn within their context. It discusses the dynamic nature of indigenous learning, and the adaptability of its patterns and content to serve the needs of the learner and the community. It examines how, in the context of change, some patterns of indigenous learning may yield and give way to new systems of learning, and how traditional knowledge and livelihoods may be lost in the process. Given the porous boundaries defining age-relevant learning in this community, this paper discusses life-long learning as a defining feature of learning in Bedouin communities rather than age-specific learning. It seeks to contribute to our understanding of the dynamics of learning for Bedouin women and help us glean ideas on where and how traditional and formal learning and education can meet, situating learning in the larger context of sustainability. Sustainability is defined as the sum of locally embedded and thriving communities that are interlinked, interrelated and are mutually engaged in healthful relationships.

The findings analysed in this paper are part of a study I conducted on several communities in Egypt that live close to nature. I utilised a multiple case study design that employs an eclectic data collection strategy, drawing information from semi-structured in-depth interviews, focus groups, group discussions and conversations (Salem 2013). I supplemented the results of that study with observations and information gleaned from further interviews, discussions and conversations with Bedouin community members during subsequent visits over 5 years after completion of the study. Being a female Egyptian outsider, we communicated in Arabic although Bedouin is their main language. Their proficiency in Arabic and my limited knowledge of Bedouin enabled us to communicate and engage in meaningful discussions. Meetings with women took place in their homes, or in the workspaces where they sell their embroidery, or during the tea breaks through their herding trips.

The communities that contributed to the larger study live close to nature and have their lives defined by the environment in which they live. Their distinctive lifestyles, therefore, require a set of skills, knowledge and capabilities that are not readily available to them through formal education, but are available through informal mechanisms of socialisation including elders, other community members, informal learning and lived experience. For example, Bedouin community members who contributed to this study have declared that they learned about climate change and its effect on their livelihoods through sheer observation of the changes in their immediate environment. This is only one example of the kind of knowledge learned through traditional ways. One of the objectives of the larger study was to glean what kind of knowledge, vision, ideas and insights these communities can contribute to our thinking for the future.

The conceptual framework for the larger study is informed by insights from different disciplines, theories and schools of thought. These include theories of development, sustainability, learning, environmental identity, local-based knowledge, place, creativity, complexity, living systems and associated concepts.

Theoretical underpinnings

Indigenous learning is closely related to the question of sustainability. The basic theoretical underpinnings of the field denote how the emergence of formal (modern) education (schooling) has affected the variety and diversity of learning practices around the world. It denotes education as a process that occurs at a distance from reality and the context within which it occurs. These also define attributes of indigenous education revealing alternative approaches to learning that stress those variables that are largely missing from the modern learning patterns and practices.

Formal education is largely criticised for producing modernised individuals and thus transforming society into a decontextualised version. In terms of time, place and content, schooling does not correspond to the needs of communities where livelihoods are closely related to the land (Krätli 2001, Birch *et al.* 2010, Suliman *et al.* 2017). Moreover, the idea that education can provide better livelihoods is being questioned by Indigenous communities (Aikman 2002) underscoring the importance of contextual relevance and diversity (Rivière 2009). In Africa, for example, a call for relevant education is echoed while emphasising the importance of local knowledge for real development (Hoppers 2000, Nyamnjoh 2004, Venter 2004, Nsamenang 2005, Breidlid 2009, Shizha 2010, Aikman 2011, Higgs 2012, Nsamenang and Tchombe 2011, Darko 2014).

In contrast, the richness of indigenous education is reflected in its affiliation with nature and with life itself. Education in indigenous communities reflects a pathway that allows for development and transformation; it is a journey to become fully human (O'Sullivan and Taylor 2004). Indigenous African education, for example, plays a vital role in the transmission of values that Africans consider to be essential in understanding and experiencing the fullness of life. Education, hence, is not a process or institution separate from everything else in life. There is no distinction between formal or informal education. The term *education* is a Western concept that does not speak to the traditional African reality, in which the entire community is continually engaged in learning and teaching. In traditional Africa, learning begins very early in life, soon after birth, and continues to old age. The whole of life is a process of learning to become fully human, to attain personhood (Tedla 1992). Traditional education is communal, where the whole community is not only the teacher but also the classroom (Semali 2002).

Indigenous Indian education is described as equivalent to breathing in life or to be with life. Community and social relationships are among the foundations of indigenous education. Ultimately, the goal of a right and true education is to become *complete* as a man or as a woman, to become fully alive and a realised human being in a harmonious relationship with one's inner and outer worlds (Cajete 2004).

Sterling presents another view on education as conducive to sustainability, as essentially transformative, constructive and participatory. This is another major departure from the model of modern education as transmissive and as one of social reproduction and maintenance, towards a vision of continuous co-evolution where both education and society are engaged in a relationship of mutual transformation – one which can explore, develop and manifest sustainability values (Sterling 2001).

The different views of education reflect a continuum of learning approaches that may be considered contradictory but may be considered complementary as well. These views perhaps represent the evolution of our understanding of learning and its role in society. It is reasonable, therefore, to discuss attributes that make indigenous education quite distinct from formal education.

The pedagogy–andragogy nexus: life-long learning

The relationship between children's learning (outside of formal school) and adult learning is complex in indigenous communities for various reasons. One of the salient features of learning in Bedouin communities is that the boundaries that mark the end of children's learning and the beginning of adult learning are mostly blurred and overlapping. Learning continues throughout people's lives; it barely has a starting point or an endpoint. This entails life-long learning as a basic premise of learning in this Bedouin community. Problem solving as one of the main characteristics of adult education (Knowles *et al.* 2005) can be found in both children's and adult learning in this community. This also applies to experiential education (Kolb 1984), while being a central concept in adult education, it is a basic component of learning for all ages in Bedouin communities.

Teaching and learning

Different kinds of learning are an outcome of organic learning processes. Cultural learning from observing and opting in (Rogoff *et al.* 2014), social learning through watching other people model various behaviours (Bandura 1971) and non-intentional and unconscious learning through application and experience, which constitutes the foundation of most of what is learnt in any learning situation (Rogers 2014). This learning is much deeper and longer lasting than many other kinds of learning and it happens continuously; and while seemingly vague and chaotic, it constitutes the basic tenets of indigenous learning (Rogers 2016). These different types of learning denote a somewhat similar process where the learner observes, listens, asks questions, experiments and implements accordingly.

Indigenous ways of learning are not focussed on the idea of imparting or transmitting knowledge like formal teaching. From an indigenous learning perspective, teaching takes away some agency from the learner, so it is done very cautiously when needed and is regarded as an integral part of the knowledge conveyed; not as a separate mechanism for conveyance of information and knowledge (Margolin 2005). In these communities, learning happens regularly during daily activities, where teaching is embedded in its largest sense, not as a specific separate activity. Fathers and mothers teach through their own performance of activities and tasks, peers teach through collective activities, elders teach through storytelling, and nature teaches through its features, power and prowess.

Routes to indigenous learning

The routes of learning for indigenous people denote their distinctive ways of learning and describe how they learn, not what they learn. These are indigenous learning systems (ILSs), peer learning, experiential learning (Rogers 2016) and the natural environment. These four routes to learning are provided in this paper as a frame of analysis and should not conceal the fluid nature of learning in these communities.

ILSs are the common culturally organised events and practices designed to help younger members of the community to learn. This entails conscious or semi-conscious learning, often intentional on the part of the provider, and includes elements such as rituals, clothing and stories. These systems draw upon kinship networks as well as family and household, teaching many things from household practices to environmental knowledge, and discussion of world and community events. While learning through ILS is mainly through elders, some learning occurs through friends and peers. Learning from experience is a route to learning that comprises much of what is learned in indigenous communities. It is experiential, unconscious, unintentional learning, creating tacit funds of knowledge and banks of skills. This learning experience is situated, socioculturally constructed and localised (Rogers 2016).

Why Bedouin women?

Focusing on Bedouin women reveals many realities that are relevant to their lives but may not be readily noticed due to the conservative nature of these communities. Women are important players in Bedouin communities (Abu-Lughod 1985, Briggs *et al.* 2003, Cole 2003, Bastawisi 2008, Ahmed 2010), and the significance of the role of women in these communities may be largely overlooked. Women's role in ensuring their community's sustainability is indispensable whether during times of stability or in times of change. As much as socialisation is considered a woman's role, she also steps out to assume a big role in mitigating and adapting to community level changes whether economic, environmental and cultural. These roles require learning starting from a very young age and this is continued throughout their lives, as their roles alter and expand to include new responsibilities, and as changes affect their communities.

In Bedouin communities, women develop their skills in anticipation of change in proactive, non-reactionary ways (Briggs *et al.* 2003). Coupled with their knowledge of their immediate environment, they play a significant role in sustaining the community in turbulent times and uncertain circumstances, when women exhibit flexibility and an ability to learn and cope with new situations; perhaps the most salient of which are economic and environmental changes. The balance between maintaining continuity and embracing change defines a main aspect of women's contribution to the sustainability of their communities

Relevant to women's roles is women's power (Bastawisi 2008) – the power that emanates not only from women's ties with and influence on family, relatives and extended circles of relationships in the community including in laws; but also from participation in activities that are considered to be a woman domain such as herding, and producing products, tools, utensils and means for storage of food stuffs. While not all of these activities, except herding, are direct livelihood activities, the ability of women to play these roles enables men to wander about in search of other livelihoods activities far away from home (Bastawisi 2008). Women's power in Bedouin communities is mostly covert, strongly affecting decisions that are apparently considered a male domain of power like marriage decisions for girls in the family (Abu-Lughod 1993). Yet women exhibit the power of dissent and resistance in some communities through composing poems and songs in defiance of undesirable decisions or situations they cannot change (Abu-Lughod 1990, 1993).

Context and community

Al Qemam[2] is a small semi-settled community of Bedouins located in the south Sinai desert where they have lived for more than 1400 years (Bastawisi 2008, De Jong 2011). It consists of some 1500 families. While there are some modern features like a school and a health care facility, it is very traditional in its customs and practices. The main livelihoods activities of the inhabitants are horticulture, herding goats and sheep, tourist guiding for mountain climbing, trekking and selling locally made goods to tourists (Bastawisi 2008).

The patterns of learning for both men and women are closely linked to two main factors – the roles that they play in the community, and the changes which come about in the community through internal and external influences. While the need to learn varies in its particulars from child to adult learning, the general socio-cultural influences surrounding the learner have a large impact on what and how they learn. These influences propose a certain set of learnings that elders ensure that younger generations receive.

In this community, women are described as the keepers of old medicine, the original storytellers and the master herders. The main herbal healer, an elderly man who lives in the mountains near the village, claims that the basics for his healing skills were gleaned from older women healers in the tribe; on which he built his own knowledge and created new formulas. Women have historically provided support to their families in different ways including herding, orchard gardening and producing dairy products (Perevolotsky 1981, Bastawisi 2008). As changes occurred in the community, women embraced new learnings and activities. Women are prepared for engagement in these developing roles through life-long learning and from daily experiences.

Like most Bedouin communities, this community holds to an oral informal law which they describe as a comprehensive set of rules that governs everything in their lives, regulating rights, duties and disciplinary actions. This law mandates ways to judge wrongdoings and issue punishments for crimes including harassment of women, lying, stealing and cursing. It includes rules about passing through the lands of other tribes to the rights of every individual (human and non-human) in the tribe (Salem 2013).

The informal law secures each woman's right to voice opinions regarding matters that affect her or issues about which she is knowledgeable. Although learning as a requirement for girls is not mentioned in the informal law, a woman's right to voice an opinion reflects the girls' right to learn. This connects between voicing an opinion and the right to learn is obvious and necessary, according to the community members, since sound opinion entails knowledge and learning. Regarded as a responsibility, not a privilege, this right requires solid understanding of the community's norms, tradition and culture which enables women the capability of giving sound advice and opinion. Girls learn the law in various ways as they go through different phases in their lives.

Patterns of learning

Since learning in indigenous communities is mostly a response to needs as they emerge, women and young girls are geared towards learning what helps them accomplish their basic roles in society. Girls' roles can be described according to the age: one to 8 years, 9 to 12 years, 13 years until marriage which can be around the age of 19 (Bastawisi 2008).

Maintaining the household

Household needs can be considered the most important of all needs in this as in all Bedouin communities. Women's informal learning is directly linked to these activities. Girls learn how to help with all the physical tasks related to the upkeep of the household unit as soon as they are old enough (Briggs *et al.* 2003).

In contrast with young boys, young girls (6–8 years) are given simple responsibilities at home like feeding chicken and collecting chicken eggs. Girls accept these tasks willingly and accomplish them even if they go to school (Bastawisi 2008). They learn these tasks both through direct instruction by the older females in the family and by observing and imitating their mothers and elder sisters. As they grow up, different tasks are increasingly delegated to them. This kind of learning reflects unconscious learning, as a young woman who collects herbs for income explains, 'Some things I learned alone, no one taught me. I just looked at how my mother did it'.

Household duties extend beyond the basic chores of the domestic sphere to necessitate going outside. As girls grow older into the age group (9–12), herding becomes one of the main tasks, reflecting the family's trust in the girl's ability to walk far away from home. Herding is a woman's domain and is undertaken as a responsibility at the same time with herb collection (Bastawisi 2008), as well as fetching water.

Sustaining the norms and values of the community

In Bedouin communities, women are the guardians of social norms and morality; they are responsible for socialising children into Bedouin society (Abu-Lughod 1985) and for upholding tradition, values and customs. To be able to do this, they become well versed in the cultural norms, rules, ethics and the informal law and how to implement them.

In this community, women's gatherings are significant venues for early socialisation for boys and girls in the community. Women meet at each other's homes, bring their children with them and talk about various issues and happenings in the community. Girls and boys learn many of the values of the community from these gatherings. Men's gatherings are an important venue for socialisation for men, but they are not as inclusive as women's gatherings, young boys and girls are not allowed to attend men's gatherings (Bastawisi 2008). Moreover, socialisation means not only transmitting social norms and values to the younger generation, but also sustaining and guarding the values of the community through the acknowledged right of women to voice their opinion on any issues occurring in the community. Women reach this level of authority by being prepared through the different phases of their lives through informal and experiential learning about the traditions, culture, values and customs of the community. Women have the power of discipline and correction in most cases. According to two older women who have grand-children, '*It is we who teach our children everything about our ways and values and the right ways to do things. Men engage in upbringing the children only when there is a huge problem and only when we bring it to their attention*'.

Contributing to household livelihoods

Women in Bedouin communities have a shared responsibility for making some financial contribution to the family, finding ways to improve existing livelihood practices and increasing access to economic opportunities, like participation in herding and cultivation as mentioned earlier. Women also contribute through non-monetary means through exchange of produce, eggs, fruits with others in the community, as well as exchanging services like knitting for others, caring for the sick or the children of other families as needed (Bastawisi 2008).

Contribution to family income can also be through their ability to collect medicinal plants and selling them to traditional healers in the community. The young woman who collects herbs for income explained how she uses the money she gets from collecting herbs to pay for her daughter's medicine and physiotherapy: '*I have collected herbs since I was young; this helps me now with treating my daughter. Every once in a while, I collect herbs, dry them and sell them to healers in the community. I also learned how to package them for the healers for selling. I make more money this way*'. An elderly female head of a family explained how her skills in collecting and drying herbs was one of the main sources of income that helped her raise her family of eight children: '*My husband died, and I had to raise my children and support my family. Collecting and drying herbs was a main source of income that helped me pull through this phase*'.

Currently, and since the booming of tourism, women and girls contribute to the income of the family through their skills in embroidery.

Creating and nurturing a family

The expected role of wife and mother is still the most revered for girls in this community. For this, she needs to learn certain skills: how to care for a home, carry out domestic chores and other activities mentioned above. Older women teach newly wedded brides everything about their new roles as brides and take a big role in maintaining good relationships and strong ties with the new family (Bastawisi 2008). Marriage responsibilities traditionally began with weaving a hair home to live in when married. Hair homes are made of long goat hair, woven into four or five carpet-like sheets that are then combined to form a tent. An important characteristic of these hair homes is that the animal hair does not allow rain to get inside the tent; raindrops run over the hair outside, not inside the hair home. This responsibility is symbolic and requires about six months of hard work (Salem 2013).

Pathways to learning

Although girls in Bedouin communities were not historically engaged in formal education, they learned in a variety of ways. Ways of learning in this community reveal specific attributes that are markedly different from formal learning in schools, which may not be generalised across all indigenous communities.

Gatherings for oral story telling are one example of ILS and one of the most important ways of teaching values, norms, and identifying proper and improper behaviours, among other things, in traditional communities. Besides being a medium for learning through generations, storytelling was one way of teaching girls what their role is in their community, and what to expect their roles to be in future. Stories also teach about how things were different in the past.

Storytelling in this community is mostly carried out by older women and grandmothers who retell the stories to young girls and boys. Two women who never attended school remember what old gatherings were like: 'We used to gather around our great grandmother and listen to the tales. Many of them were scary as they told about ogres that ate young children and so on. But we learned that we do not go astray in certain places surrounding us'. The lessons in the tales are so deep that they are still effective: 'Even when we got older we still fear the places where ogres can be according to the tales'.

Bedouin tribes have different ways of teaching younger community members herding and shepherding. In this Bedouin community, the process of passing on the skills for herding is for younger girls (age 7–10 years) to accompany older girls (16–22 years). Herding is a non-ceremonial rite of passage for girls denoting transition to adulthood (Bastawisi 2008). Other Bedouin tribes have different ILS for herding, where older men in the community pass on relevant knowledge like the best places for the goats to graze, and the types and properties of the different plants in the area to the young (Ahmed 2010).

Herding also demonstrates peer learning. During herding trips, younger girls learn much from their older peers. They explore their surroundings and their place in it, they learn where to find the water, recognise and differentiate between the different herbs, and learn which herbs are found in which areas. They also experiment with herbs to find out their uses on their hair or skin. They learn participation, how to make choices and how to accept group decisions. In other words, they learn team work and a certain level of democracy. The girls sing along the way, play the flute which echoes through the hills, making it a happy activity which inspires even younger girls to want to join when they are older, they spend some time knitting, sewing and making embroidery while herding, they also drink tea and exchange stories as they sit around watching the goats wander about. Herds may range from 50 to 100 goats; girls learn how to count them to make sure none is lost. They give their goats names and train the goats to respond to them as they call out when they need to move to another spot or go home. Girls agree on the next day's spot by rotation, so that each of them gets to choose for one day. The choice is respected by other girls; they all abide by the choice made (Bastawisi 2008).

El Naj is a seasonal activity that represents an ILS. It is basically a re-living of the old style of Bedouin life. It is a time when families from different tribes travel to places where herbs flourish because of relative abundance of rain and let their goats graze. Families spend time together, exchanging ideas and life experiences between the different groups. A young woman who goes with her family annually commented, '*El Naj is an old activity... we still do it to revive the old ways of living. If we do not do it and anything happens here to the water or the food we have, we will not be able to live. El Naj reminds us of how we used to live long time ago. We go and collect sticks for the fire and we make* farasheeh *(a kind of bread); we collect grass [for the animals to eat], we walk with the goats... we remember our old ways*'.

This activity also represents a form of peer learning. Women and girls benefit from these gatherings as they stay around the place where the tents are built, while men go hunting or trekking. During the *Naj* time, which can amount to four months, the women and girls mingle with others from other tribes and exchange their experiences and information. '*The young ones who did not experience this life we used to have learn from us how to live it, this is how they learn our old ways. If a girl's hand is not dry, she will not be able to pull out the grass from the land*', says a mother of three young girls who never went to school, reminiscing about older days when girls were strong and explaining that girls need to be strong and used to working to be able to do the things they need.

The natural environment is considered a learning source for this community located in a mountainous area. The continual mutual contact and impact results in a strong and direct relationship between desert women, the surrounding natural resources and environment. It is a historical relationship defined within the context of division of labour and gender roles (Bastawisi 2008). One woman who stopped going herding upon marriage and soon went back to herding afterwards explains what can be learned from mountains and the joy of herding, '*We learn patience from climbing the mountains around here. We know what patience is and we experience it as we climb the mountains and as we take the goats to graze. When you are half way climbing a mountain, you look up and realise you need to be patient and have will power and drive to complete your way up. Or when you go out with a herd and walk around until you find a good spot for them to eat. Then you move to another place after a while. Then you count them and call out for the ones who are missing. You find yourself talking to them. You spend a whole day with them. You learn a lot from them*'.

Climate change is learned through observing the surrounding environment. The elders in the community know that some plants have started to disappear due to the change of the weather and that the number of cats and foxes increased in relation to this disappearance. They recite the names of trees that were in the land a long time ago and describe how they were replaced with other trees over the years.

Learning from nature includes acknowledging the value of natural elements, like water. For a desert community like this one, water is precious. Gemeia, the youngest of three sisters explained why they care for the water they collect for the family: '*When you walk for hours to bring some water for your family, you are very careful not to waste it. You exert every effort to get each drop of water you use, you can't misuse it. Nature teaches us this'.*

Learning from experience is embedded in most learning situations in this community. Much of the women's and girls' learning is experiential, unconscious learning, creating tacit funds of knowledge and banks of skills (Rogers 2016). They use trial and error experimentation to learn how to do new things or cope with new situations (Briggs *et al.* 2003). Children learn counting and many other things while herding livestock, entirely unintentionally - the smell, shape and behaviour of the sheep and goats. They also learn the shape, smell, touch and feel of herbs. From their engagement in household practices, they learn much from observation of others and practising domestic tasks. Working in the tourist market, women learn through observation and watching others, and through experimenting with new products. It is their experience that has enabled these women to understand the markets they deal with, to realise which items sell more quickly and which items are slow to sell. Om Youssef, who sells embroidered scarves, and who is one of the pioneers in the business commented while inspecting some of her scarves, *'People from England like these colours more than these'.*

The nature of learning in the community

The specific attributes of the nature of learning in this community are markedly different from formal learning in schools and may not be generalisable across all indigenous communities. These ways of learning reveal that learning is mutually reinforcing and holistic.

If we take *herding* in this Bedouin community as an example, we find that it is an activity taught by practice and accumulated *experience*; it is reinforced as an important task in the oral tales, part of the *ILS*, and through *peer learning* since elder girls teach it to younger ones. This kind of reinforcement helps inculcate, not only the activity, but the rules and values associated with it. It can also be argued that each of these ways of learning appeals to more than one sense which helps further inculcate it not only in the minds (reasoning) but also in the hearts (emotions) of the girls. Peer learning, for example, appeals to the feelings of community, the emotional bond that binds peers; the ILS appeal more to the reasoning, and experience appeals to the other senses like touch, smell, and sight. Indigenous learning is not solely cognitive, like memorising or rote learning; it is holistic.

Modern changes in the community

This community, like all communities, was subject to substantial changes that required adaptation. Accelerated change started as far back as 1967 with the advent of tourism (Hobbs and Tsunemi 2007, Gilbert 2013). Tourism resulted in increased settlement, which resulted in increased community services, the diffusion of new technology, and the introduction of formal schooling among other changes.

The booming and later decline of tourism affected the community deeply. The advent of new economic opportunities brings in its wakes several changes including the abandonment of original livelihoods (Aikman 2002). Tourism left a deep mark on this community as its boom provided a lucrative economic opportunity markedly different from the prevalent traditional opportunities at the time. The drastic increase in the inflow of income from tourism resulted in the decline of nourishment of traditional ways of livelihoods like orchards and herding. Additionally, flourishing tourism resulted in a loss of interest in some of the local environmental knowledge relevant to everyday living as it seemed to be of limited use to younger generations at the time (Hobbs 2001). With the later decline of tourism, the ancestral knowledge relevant to orchard cultivation, herding and herbal healing seemed to regain prominence; albeit with a lag in knowledge and in practice.

Improving handicrafts for economic gain has been an important activity for girls and women in the community that started with tourism. Women in this community initially developed their skills in embroidery through informal learning but they were called upon to maximise these skills to be able to sell embroidered items to tourists who came to visit the area. Local initiatives were strengthened and broadened in scope by government and non-government organisations, local and international. This led to the emergence of local enterprises led by women in the community. Sabiha, for example, was trained through one of the development projects implemented in the community, after which she developed her own local enterprise. She got some 50 women together, out of the potentially productive 800 women in the community to help them capitalise on their authentic skills in embroidery to produce handmade products; she trains the women, who then train the girls, on improving and perfecting their sewing, finishing and other skills to ensure the quality of the products. She inspects the products and holds workshops where women who excel in a certain aspect of the work train others and help them understand faulty production and practise how to do it well. They make the products under her supervision and she sells them. '*Most girls learn, at some point in their lives, how to knit and use beads, etc. The quality of their work is not good for selling. They need to be trained for better finishing and quality*'. Sabiha commented.

Tourism provided the necessary conditions for settlement for this community: a stream of tourists and income (Perevolotsky *et al.* 1989). Life conditions after settling improved when new life support systems like electricity and readily available water started to be givens. Settlement, however, has affected the community in a way that is contrary to their original lifestyle. Herding in the same surrounding areas resulted in pressure on land use. Although vegetation was preserved to a certain extent owing to traditional practices (Hobbs *et al.* 1998, Gilbert 2013), while wildlife has been drastically affected (Hobbs *et al.* 1998).

Modern changes led to the abandonment of orchard gardening which used to be one of the major responsibilities of women in this community. Girls learned about cultivation through helping their mothers in the various chores of cultivation and caring for the orchards including watering, placing cloth bag-like fittings over grape vines, picking out wild grass and carrying it back to feed the sheep and goats, among others (Bastawisi 2008). This learning has gradually decreased as the interest in cultivation dwindled owing to the more immediate income from tourism about 60 years ago (Perevolotsky *et al.* 1989). Other abandoned tasks include cutting the wool of sheep and spinning it into thread to knit woollen clothes for young children for the long and freezing winter. An elderly woman who did not send her daughters to school describes this activity: *'In my time, we used to learn how to spin using a wooden stick. Girls now do not learn this as before. Very few do'*. She asks her daughter to bring the wooden stick used as a spinning tool and demonstrates how she used to do it.

Technology has had a profound effect on the community. Television, for example, has largely replaced oral story telling as an amusing and educational pastime, and more importantly, as an enduring ILS that lasted for many years. It has also introduced the women and girls to new practices and new interests, for example, to new ways of dressing, Gemeia commented *'we started noticing and comparing what other girls are wearing and what we are wearing when we started to watch TV. We never compared before, we all dressed alike'*. Interestingly, although TV has diminished the value of oral tales in this community, television is not regarded as a good source of information: *'We call it* talaf el zouhoun, *not television'*, commented one Bedouin father of three, with a play on words which literally mean destroying the brains, referring to the quality of the content of TV which is largely regarded as empty and lacking in purpose.

The effect of new technology and social media on girls is especially noted. Most women and girls have mobile phones, some of them smart phones. Through social media, users are given immediate and extensive access to information and borderless learning which is not place- or language-bound. Social media has also opened a non-traditional channel for connections outside the immediate community. The advent and expansion of social media has affected this community deeply in both negative and positive ways. Om Youssef commented, *'Young girls now can make [social media] accounts with fake names and know things that are inappropriate for them to know'*. Inappropriate in this context can refer to a wide range of learnings, including different ways of clothes, types of information and gender issues. Nonetheless, social media has also helped women and girls to get acquainted with styles of life around the world and learn useful things such as different ways of cooking, taking care of babies and children, and other maternal and family matters. It also helps with marketing needlework. The latter is seen as positive by the women in this community.

The paradox of formal education

The effect of formal education in this community gives mixed signals. Formal education is promoted as a development plan, as a safeguard from possible future risks. It is publicised as the guarantee that provides employment and secures girls' future more than the security provided by husbands and family. These ideas are not consistent with traditional ideas that promote the original roles and relationships of girls and women within the context of the community and its values. Hence, formal education divided the community: some view it as something to aspire for to the benefit of their children, convinced with the messages promoting its value; others view it as a threat.

With the introduction of formal schooling, the general understanding was that girls would not give up their original tasks and responsibilities to attend school, but women in particular viewed the hours spent in school as a threat since it would prevent their girls from spending time herding, which would negatively affect their goats that are their biggest asset (Bastawisi 2008). The threat perspective seems to have materialised since formal schooling has affected some of the community's cultural and livelihood practices. It has affected the perceived importance and value bestowed to some aspects of informal learnings in the community. The changing patterns of herding is a case at hand where mothers currently do it rather than their daughters. 'Now older women and mothers go herding, young girls even when not in school, they stay at home and do the household duties and their school homework. My daughter is in school now, so I go herding instead', commented Om Saleh during a herding trip. The diminishing interest in informal learning for girls is partly due to the lack of sufficient time to do both, while the belief that formal learning is more important in terms of providing more livelihoods opportunities in the future is very strong.

There is also an awareness of a gap of knowledge owing to the nature of the formal school provision available, a feeling that the formal schooling system is unable to provide many of the benefits that the informal systems of learning provide. The elderly woman who uses the wooden stick to spin explained that, although she used to regret that she could not afford to send her girls to school, 'I realised that what "life" taught them exceeded what I see other girls learned in school'. And as one of the mothers who went back to herding because her daughter goes to school commented, while she used to view school as more important than herding, regrets that much was lost by attending school: 'Now I do it instead of my daughter, but when she grows up and has her own daughters, she will not be able to do it. She will not know how'.

Meanwhile, the community's experience with formal schooling did not deliver the anticipated results, leaving some community members feeling that its promises were not delivered. OmYoussr, who pursues handicraft activities, commented on her experience with formal education, saying, 'I studied all the way up to Thanaweya Amma [the examination for the national General Secondary Education Certificate] and I got very high grades. I could not go to University because it was not appropriate in my time to travel and live alone. But my younger sister did. She delayed getting married. She now has a higher degree. What is the use of a higher degree when there are no jobs here?'

Learning and sustainability

Learning is an omnipresent feature and function of life. The intricate linkage between knowledge, learning and community needs is key for survival in indigenous communities. This necessitates questioning aspects and functions of learning in these communities: Does formal learning and the kind of knowledge it conveys contribute to the sustainability of these communities or accentuate their dependency? What functions does indigenous learning serve for the community and what is being lost to adopting formal ways of learning? Can formal learning and indigenous ways of knowing be reconciled for the ultimate benefit of indigenous communities? These questions are very pertinent ones when discussing the impact of learning and the long term effect of education in indigenous communities.

The relevance of education

The prevalent discrepancy between the kind of education provided in schools and the actual needs of specific local communities is at the core of the question of sustainability. The prevalent Western educational paradigm is detached from the intrinsic cultural identities, the immediate environment, the needs and specific aspirations of indigenous communities everywhere. The relationship – or rather, the disconnect – between education and livelihoods is a serious concern that must be addressed in the context of sustainability. This constitutes an even more pressing concern for indigenous communities where knowledge and livelihoods that have historically supported these communities are eroded due to the infiltration of modernity, with its lures and its acclaimed benefits.

In this community, formal education did not create jobs but affected the practice of traditional livelihoods negatively. Herding, as discussed in this paper, is an example of a traditional livelihood activity that is being gradually abandoned by girls despite being acknowledged as important by community members. This situation creates a livelihoods gap where old activities are eroded, and new ones are not created, which begs the question whether formal schooling can support the learning of traditional livelihood activities, through inclusion into curricula. Meanwhile, the fact that the knowledge associated with herding cannot be sustained in isolation from its practice as part of daily life should be stressed.

Moreover, since women's learning is closely related to their roles in the community, where women undertake many responsibilities and fulfil many duties, it is important to highlight the diversity of knowledge needed by Bedouin women compared to the standardised pattern and system of formal education. The direct relevance and immediacy of what women learn is important; women learn what is directly relevant to their lives, to their place and to their community. They implement what they learn immediately. The feeling of self-worth in this case is different from the feeling of self-worth that is inherent in formal education. The former relates to the level of engagement of women in their community, the latter seems to relate more to becoming a bystander, an onlooker, who awaits a future formal job that is distant from the community's daily needs and activities, hence alienating women. This alienating role of formal education can have a distancing effect on educated women in these communities.

Relevance also relates to how formal education can bear discriminately on girls when access to formal schools require travel or being away from home for extended periods of time, in which case boys will have better chances. Meanwhile, indigenous learning can also be criticised for confining girls and women to roles that are predetermined by the community. Striking a balance that ensures both individual and community needs would be the optimal learning situation.

Informal, formal and beyond

Finding ways whereby informal and formal ways of learning can be mutually beneficial and capitalised on is a difficult task. Ideas include finding ways to make formal learning more relevant to the learner's life as in informal learning, helping learners recognise the unconscious learning in informal learning for scrutiny and evaluation, and helping people unlearn what have been learnt informally if deemed harmful (Rogers 2014). Other ideas stem from further understanding of how informal ways of learning affect learners' minds and finding ways that can enhance formal teaching. It is proposed that indigenous languages and cultures makes adapting to modern learning like mathematics, for example, difficult. Deeply embedded native meanings, language and vocabulary make it hard to understand the unfamiliar, like mathematical equations (Barton and Frank 2001). Other ideas include ways to include indigenous knowledge into large scale development plans and informal learning settings (May and Aikman 2003).

Learning, creativity and diversity

When learning is packaged as a standardised form that treats all learners as equals, how does this contribute to individual growth or change in a creative way? Or to allow diversity?

Creativity is a given mode of problem solving, an innate ability to adapt, change, transform and survive. Creativity is developed through successive trials at discovering new things, without fear of making mistakes and is undertaken with wholehearted interest. Learning in schools aims at accumulating knowledge that is learnt by repetition which hampers creativity and diminishes originality (Bohm 1996, Csikszentmihalyi 1996). Creativity is acquired through training of the mind to seek newness and originality. A creative state of mind is hence more relevant to the indigenous ways of learning since dealing with emerging needs and the tendency to improvise while attempting to respond to these needs can be viewed as giving recurrent possibilities for creativity. However, even indigenous patterns of learning can also hamper creativity if excessive control and restriction of exploration is pursued and too much conformity is enacted.

Meanwhile, the part played by formal schooling in the growth and development of the individual would seem to be at odds with creativity, diversity and life-long learning as main principles of sustainability. While learning is considered a main contributor to change and growth at the personal level and while each person lives her entire life constructing a universe of meaning and making sense of herself and her world (Jarvis 2004), formal education, as a standardised form of learning, contributes to developing a sense of self that is not entirely accommodative of personal differences. Modern education plays a significant role in limiting variety and decreasing diversity.

Conclusion

Indigenous learning is diverse and takes many different shapes and forms. This paper only scratches the surface of ways of learning that have beneficially served indigenous communities and sustained them for many years. Valuing indigenous ways of learning is increasingly becoming a necessity as it could mean the only tested and tried means for sustainability for communities that have thrived using this knowledge for many generations. There must be ways whereby the ultimate learning situation can be sought, one that fosters their ability to engage in their community, preserving the community's identity, while allowing for new ideas and learnings to enhance creativity and experimentation.

This study of learning among a group of indigenous Bedouin women and girls shows that, instead of being seen as poor, weak and limited in roles, many of these women have a good deal of power and scope for decision-making. They play a large part in indigenous learning and have considerable control over the tools for learning. They are innovative and capable of adapting to new situations. But their informal learning patterns would seem to be under threat from the more formal education of schools. There are indications that some basic indigenous activities are being increasingly abandoned by girls and young women. Besides reflecting a loss in an authentic ILS, thiks abandonment creates generations of younger women not fully adept at a main livelihood activity that has historically supported this community and sustained its livelihoods.

Notes

1. This article is focussed on learning of Bedouin women. It does not discuss the details on gendered differences in men's and women's learning and lives.
2. All names are pseudonyms.

Acknowledgments

The author would like to acknowledge the support of Dr Alan Rogers in the conceptualisation of this paper.

Disclosure statement

No potential conflict of interest was reported by the author.

ORCID

Abeer Salem http://orcid.org/0000-0001-9231-9497

References

Abu-Lughod, L., 1985. A community of secrets: the separate world of Bedouin women. *Signs: Journal of women in culture and society*, 10(4), 637–657.
Abu-Lughod, L., 1993. *Writing women's worlds: Bedouin stories*. LA: University of California Press.
Abu-Lughod, L., 1990. The romance of resistance: tracing transformations of power through Bedouin women. *American ethnologist*, 17(1), 41–55.
Ahmed, M.T., 2010. *Ecosystems and human well-being: El Maghara, Northern Sinai, Egypt*. United Nations Environment Program. Nairobi: Earthprint.
Aikman, S., 2011. Educational and indigenous justice in Africa. *International journal of educational development*, 31(1), 15–22.
Aikman, S., 2002. Women's oral knowledge and the poverty of formal education in the SE Peruvian Amazon. *Gender & development*, 10(3), 41–50.
Bandura, A., 1971. *Social learning theory*. NY: General learning Press.

Barton, B. and Frank, R., 2001. Mathematical ideas and indigenous languages. *Sociocultural research on mathematics education: an international perspective.* Mahwah, NJ: Lawrence Erlbaum Associates, 135–140, 135–149.

Bastawisi, I., 2008. Women in desert communities: women of the Jebaleya tribe. *Studies in folkloric arts*, Vol. 16. Cairo, Egypt: Ministry of Culture.

Birch, I., *et al.*, 2010. *Towards education for Nomads: community perspectives in Kenya.* London. UK: International Institute for Environment and Development.

Bohm, D., 1996. *On creativity.* NY: Routledge.

Breidlid, A., 2009. Culture, indigenous knowledge systems and sustainable development: a critical view of education in an African context. *International journal of educational development*, 29(2), 140–148.

Briggs, J., *et al.*, 2003. Changing women's roles, changing environmental knowledges: evidence from Upper Egypt. *The geographical journal*, 169(4), 313–325.

Cajete, G.A., 2004. A Pueblo story for transformation. *In*: Edmund O'Sullivan and Marilyn Taylor, eds. *Learning toward an ecological consciousness: selected transformative practice.* New York (NY): Palgrave Macmillan, 103–113.

Csikszentmihalyi, M., 1996. *Creativity: flow and the psychology of discovery and invention.* NY: Harper Perennial.

Cole, D.P., 2003. Where have the Bedouin gone?. *Anthropological quarterly*, 76(2), 235–267.

Darko, I.N., 2014. Environmental stewardship and indigenous education in Africa: looking beyond euro-centric dominated curricula. *Emerging perspectives on 'African development': speaking differently.* New York, NY: Peter Lang.

De Jong, R. E., 2011. A grammar of the Bedouin dialects of central and southern Sinai. *Handbook of oriental studies. The Near and Middle East.* Leiden, the Netherlands: Koninklijke Brill NV.

Gilbert, H., 2013. Bedouin overgrazing' and conservation politics: challenging ideas of pastoral destruction in South Sinai. *Biological conservation*, 160, 59–69.

Higgs, P., 2012. African philosophy and the decolonisation of education in Africa: some critical reflections. *Educational philosophy and theory*, 44(2), 37–55.

Hobbs, J. and Tsunemi, F., 2007. Soft sedentarization: Bedouin tourist stations as a response to drought in Egypt's Eastern Desert. *Human ecology*, 35(2), 209–222. Retrieved from http://www.jstor.org/stable/27654182

Hobbs, J., Grainger, J., and El-Bastawisi, I., 1998. Inception of the Bedouin Support Programme in the St. Katherine Natural Protectorate, Sinai, Egypt. *Mountain research and development*, 18(3), 235–248.

Hobbs, J., 2001. Exploration and discovery with the Bedouin of Egypt. *Geographical review*, 91(1/2), 285–294.

Hoppers, W., 2000. Nonformal education, distance education and the restructuring of schooling: Challenges for a new basic education policy. *International review of education/ Internationale Zeitschrift fr Erziehungswissenschaft/ Revue Inter*, 46(1/2), 5–30.

Jarvis, P., 2004. *Adult education and lifelong learning: theory and practice.* NY: Routledge.

Knowles, M., Holton, E., and Swanson, R., 2005. *The adult learner: the definitive classic in adult education and human resource development.* USA: Elsevier.

Kolb, D. A., 1984. *Experiential learning: experience as the source of learning and development.* Englewood Cliffs, NJ: Prentice-Hall.

Krätli, S., 2001. *Education provision to nomadic pastoralists: a literature review.* UK: Institute of Development Studies.

Margolin, M., 2005. Indian pedagogy: a look at traditional California Indian teaching techniques. *In*: M. Stone and Z. Barlow, eds. *Ecological literacy: educating our children for a sustainable world.* San Francisco, CA: Sierra Club Books, 67–79.

May, S. and Aikman, S., 2003. Indigenous education: addressing current issues and developments. *Comparative education*, 39(2), 139–145.

Nyamnjoh, F.B., 2004. A relevant education for African development-some epistemological considerations. *Africa development. Senegal, CODESRIA*, 29(1), 161–184.

Nsamenang, A. B., 2005. *The intersection of traditional African education with school learning.* *In*: L. Swartz, C. De la Rey, and N. Duncan, eds. *Psychology: an introduction.* Cape Town, South Africa: Oxford University Press, 327–337.

Nsamenang, A. B. and Tchombe, T. M., 2011. Handbook of African educational theories and practices. A generative teacher education curriculum. Bamenda, Cameroon: Presses Universitaires dAfrique.

O'Sullivan, E. and Taylor, M.M., 2004. *Learning toward an ecological consciousness: selected transformative practices.* NY: Palgrave Macmillan.

Perevolotsky, A., 1981. Orchard agriculture in the high mountain region of Southern Sinai. *Human ecology*, 9(3), 331–357.

Perevolotsky, A., Perevolotsky, A., and Noy-Meir, I., 1989. Environmental adaptation and economic change in a pastoral mountain society: the case of the Jabaliyah Bedouin of the Mt. Sinai region. *Mountain research and development*, 9(2), 153–164.

Rivière, F., ed. 2009. *Investing in cultural diversity and intercultural dialogue.* Vol. 2. Paris, France: UNESCO.

Rogers, A., 2014. *The base of the Iceberg: informal learning and its impact on formal and non-formal learning.* *In*: Regina Egetenmeyer, ed. Study guides in adult education. Opladen, Germany: Barbara Budrdich Publishers

Rogers, A., 2016. Learning and indigenous peoples, unpublished paper presented at workshop on indigenous learning. December 2016. http://totald.org.uk/images/downloads/LEARNING%20AND%20INDIGENOUS%20PEOPLES%20draft%20(002).pdf

Rogoff, B., Najafi, B., and Mejía-Arauz, R., 2014. Constellations of cultural practices across generations: indigenous American heritage and learning by observing and pitching. *Human development*, 57(2–3), 82–95.

Salem, A., 2013. *Negotiating sustainability: reclaiming ecological pathways to bio-cultural regeneration in Egypt.* Dissertation (PhD). Prescott College for the Liberal Arts, the Environment and Social Justice. ProQuest Dissertations Publishing.

Semali, L.M., 2002. Community as classroom: (re)valuing indigenous literacy. *In*: L.M. Semali and J.L. Kincheloe, eds. *What is indigenous knowledge? Voices from the academy.* NY: Routledge.

Shizha, E., 2010. The interface of neoliberal globalization, science education and indigenous African knowledges in Africa. *Journal of alternative perspectives in the social sciences*, 2(1), 27–58.

Sterling, S., 2001. *Sustainable education: revisioning learning and change.* 1st ed. Devon, UK: Green Books Ltd.

Suliman, M., Shah, M., and Ullah, I., 2017. Addressing the issue of nomadic communities children educational exclusion through mobile tent schools in Malakand, Pakistan. *Imperial journal of interdisciplinary research (IJIR)*, 3(3), 540–546.

Tedla, E., 1992. Indigenous African education as a means for understanding the fullness of life: Amara traditional education. *Journal of black studies*, 23(1), 7–26.

Venter, E., 2004. The notion of ubuntu and communalism in African educational discourse. *Studies in philosophy and education*, 23(2/3), 149–160.

Declared 'literate': Subjectivation through decontextualised literacy practices

Amina Singh (iD) and Dipti Sherchan

ABSTRACT

The concepts of adult literacy and adult education have been predominantly framed by the discourse of development in Nepal whereby literacy programmes are designed to combat illiteracy with the purpose of promoting the socio-economic and human development in the country. In this effort, certain groups of women and ethnic minorities have been homogenously categorised as 'illiterate' and constituted as target groups for such basic and functional literacy programmes. This process of subjectivation through literacy programme works to impose feelings of inadequacy among the participants of the literacy programme, which further invalidates their own experience and situated knowledge. This article illustrates this process of subjectivation and resistance to it while challenging the idea of a homogenous 'Thakali women' through the personal narratives of Thakali women and their experiences of engaging with the discursive practices of literacy. In doing so, the article argues that the decontextualised approach to literacy further erases the socio-cultural, economic and historical context within which the individuals form their experiences and knowledge and hence, the need for culturally contextualised literacy practices that account for lived experiences and knowledge.

Introduction

Literacy has been regarded as an important driver of human development. In the global policy discourses, the assumed relationship between women, literacy and development has shifted over the years with evolving and nuanced understandings of these three constructs. Despite these conceptual developments, it appears literacy is still narrowly conceived in instrumental terms when it comes to the implementation of adult literacy programmes. In Nepal, the concepts of adult literacy and adult education have been predominantly framed by the discourse of development whereby literacy programmes are designed to combat illiteracy with the purpose of promoting the socio-economic and human development in the country.

There have been numerous critiques of the reductionist approaches to literacy, where literacy outcomes are conceived in numbers and people are segregated into binary categories of illiterate and literate; men and women; rural and urban, and so forth (Robinson-Pant 2004, Chopra 2011). Such critiques also examine and discuss the problematic assumptions underlying notions of what constitutes being 'illiterate' as well as the gendered assumptions about how literacy is supposed to benefit men and women that are found to shape the literacy practices. What had been missing in such critiques of narrow conceptions of literacy were the perspectives of the individuals and groups who get targeted for these programmes. How do the individual participants understand themselves as targeted subjects of such literacy programmes? What are the people's understanding and assumptions about literacy and how did they find it relevant? What are their experiences of engaging or perhaps not engaging with such programmes?

A growing body of ethnographic studies on literacy has added new perspectives, constructs and frameworks to understand and explore literacy. This has also led to the emergence of what has been termed as 'New Literacy Studies' (NLS) (Street 2003) that conceptualises literacy as a social practice (Street 1984). An important insight drawn from ethnographic studies has been the understanding of the gendered nature of literacy practices and the contradictions between the objectives of the literacy programme and the subjective understanding and needs of the women who are expected to participate in these programmes (Robinson-Pant 2001). An ethnographic study (Prins 2008) in El Salvador examining a Freirean-inspired literacy programme suggested that while such literacy practices generated some psychosocial benefits for the women, they were deemed inadequate to actually shift the gendered power relations in the communities.

Through this article, we aim to contribute to this on-going conversation on adult literacy practices using personal narratives of Thakali[1] women who have been deemed 'illiterate' and hence constituted as 'target' subjects by the national literacy programme in Nepal. The narratives are drawn from an ethnographic study conducted by co-author Dipti Sherchan in Ghasa Village of Mustang district within the local indigenous Thakali community in 2014 as part of her Master's dissertation. During the two and half months stay in the village, Dipti had talked to more than thirty Thakali women to explore how they had experienced the presence or absence of education in their lives and their views on the ongoing literacy programme. From among these different narratives, in this article, we closely examine two such narratives that illuminate diverse subjective experiences and encounters with the literacy programme.

The timing of the study in 2014 is of significance as the national literacy programme was part of the three years (2012–2015) Literate Nepal mission (LINEM) with the aim to achieve literacy rates of at least 75% among 15 years and above group by 2015. In this article, we borrow Robinson-Pant's question (2004, p. 28) to frame our inquiry, '*How does the dominant development discourse construct "illiterate women" and how do the "illiterate" women themselves interact with this discourse*'? (Emphasis original). Here, we aim to explore these questions although slightly rephrased; how does the discourse of 'Literate Nepal Mission' construct the 'literate women' and how do the Thakali women interact with this discourse? In our analysis, we employ Althusser's (1971) notion of subjection as well as Butler's (1997) understanding of processes of subjectivation with the purpose to illuminate the process of construction of the 'literate women' along with the subjective experiences of two participants in interacting with the LINEM programme.

The literate Nepal mission: Declaring a 'literate' Nepal

The report of Nepal National Education Planning Commission (NNEPC 1956) states that adult literacy initiatives first began in 1953 with the aim of teaching adults to read and write and to do basic arithmetic. At that time, the national literacy rates were estimated to be at 2%. In 2006, the '10-Year Literacy/Non-formal Education Policy Framework' was developed to unite all the varied adult literacy and adult education programmes under a national policy framework. As a result, the Government of Nepal (GoN) launched the nationwide National Literacy Campaign (NLC) in 2008– 2009 and later on continued the campaign from 2012 to 2015 under the banner 'Literate Nepal Mission' (LINEM) with the aim to achieve literacy rates of at least 75% among 15 years and above group by 2015. At the beginning of the mission, the Annual Household Survey of 2012/2013 (GoN 2016) showed the adult literacy rates (age 15+) to be at 62.2% with literacy rates among men to be 75.2% and among women to be 51.9%. This meant that in order to achieve the goals of LINEM by 2015, women had to be the main target group of the campaign.

The status report on the NLC (GoN 2016) reports that in the year 2015/2016, a total of 29 districts had been declared 'fully literate' with Mustang among the list. The report states that in order to identify the illiterates and literates, literacy has been defined as the 'ability to read and write in any language with understanding and the ability to do simple arithmetic calculations' (GoN 2016, p. 11). The report also indicates variations in literacy rates among different ethnicities and castes with the Thakali group among the top 10 ethnic/caste groups to have the highest literacy rates in Nepal. Of the total participants who attended the literacy programmes in the year 2015/2016, 95.4% were women (GoN 2016, p. 29).

Another recent report on the literacy campaign explains that the LINEM programme took the approach of 'each one teach one' with daily two hour classes held 6 days a week over a period of four months with the sole purpose of meeting the literacy targets by 2015 (UNESCO 2017, p. 13). Among the issues and challenges in implementation of the LINEM programme, the report raises concern over the adequacy of the programme duration of four months and whether it was a sufficient length of time for participants to acquire the level of competency to be declared as literate. Another concern raised in the report is the variations in evaluation of the literacy achievements of participants by the literacy facilitators in order to test and certify participants as literate. It appeared in the study that some of the literacy facilitators were unaware of the standard evaluation methods prescribed and hence, employed their own methods to make an assessment of the literacy competency and make recommendations for certification to the District Education Offices.

Reviewing these reports indicate that the emphasis of the LINEM programme has been on achieving these statistical targets within a solely numerical result-based framework shaped by the development agenda. While the measures used to demarcate the illiterate from the literate are deemed as objective, the reports discussed earlier indicate that the 'declaration' of being literate may be based on varied methods of assessments conducted by the literacy facilitators. This seems to indicate that the 'power' to declare an individual 'literate' lied in the hands of the individual literacy facilitators. The disaggregated data presented in the status report on the NLC (GoN 2016) report to show variations in literacy levels between men and women; different ethnic and caste groups and across different geographic regions of the country do not further explain why or how these variations exist. There is also no attempt to explore or even acknowledge the possible variations within a particular ethnic or caste group, ignoring gendered differences within a group. What it seems here is that the recent adult literacy programme conducted to declare Nepal as a 'literate' nation has only done just that; discursive constitution of individual citizens as 'literate' to declare the entire district as being 'literate' with the prospect of eventually declaring Nepal as a 'literate' nation. However, there is much more happening through such seemingly innocuous declarations which will be further explored in this article.

On Thakali women

The Thakali ethnic group is among the 59 different indigenous nationalities in Nepal that are officially recognised by the GoN. According to the National Foundation for Development of Indigenous Nationalities (NFDIN) Act of 2002, the term 'Indigenous Nationalities' has been defined as 'a tribe or community as mentioned in the schedule having its own mother language and traditional rites and customs, distinct cultural identity, distinct social structure and written or unwritten history'(NFDIN 2003, p. 32). In this sense, the Thakali community is regarded among the indigenous nationalities that have been living in Nepal. According to the population monograph of Nepal (Volume II), Central Bureau of Statistics (2014) report, 73.1% of the female population from Thakali community is literate, which is a comparatively higher rate of literacy compared to that of women from other ethnic groups. These statistics, however, represents the literacy rate of female population above the age of 5 without a disaggregation of how many adult females are literate. The Thakali women have been described as having 'business acumen and marketing abilities' of which the Thakali community hold a distinct pride in (Tamang 2010, p.162). There is a general stereotypical discourse on how women from indigenous communities are considered more vocal, outspoken, and thereby, more 'empowered' than women from non-indigenous communities, especially from Brahmin and Chhetri castes. The social norms of sexuality and control over economy are some of the major areas where these distinctions are pointed out. The fact that Thakali women run hotels and have considerable power and control over the economy through this business has been used as an argument to portray Thakali women as empowered. However, like any other category, the heterogeneity among the Thakali women often goes ignored. The notion of heterogeneity, which is understanding that 'all women are not created or constructed equal' allows us to look at the experiences of different Thakali women in a pluralistic manner (Tong 2009).

One of the reasons that such dimensions remain unexplored in ethnographic studies of Thakali community is perhaps because of the 'male bias' that exists in the research inquiry tradition in Nepal. Despite the contestable population of around 13,000 only, the Thakali community is probably one of the most studied ethnic groups in Nepal (Turin 1997). In many of these academic research works, Thakali culture, rituals and practices are described and discussed at length. However, the narratives of the Thakali women are mostly absent from these accounts. Most of the research has been conducted by non-native (and few native) male researchers. There are academic works conducted by female researchers, focusing on women from other communities but there is no significant corpus of work on Thakali women that can be referred to in order to understand their version of the 'Thakali' experience and culture. Most of the literature on Thakali communities is predominantly influenced by male-narratives on the historical myths and lineages in Thakali community. Even when Thakali women are discussed in these works, they are mentioned briefly as anecdotes but never form the core voice of the research inquiry.

In the context of the LINEM programme, the Thakali women have been subsumed under the category 'women' where the only differentiation made is on the basis of their 'literacy status' as defined by the programme. As a woman, you are either 'literate' or 'illiterate' and the programme is interested in the latter group to achieve the goals of the programme. This article thus centres on the experiences of the Thakali women from Ghasa, Lower Mustang on how they encountered the literacy programme.

Declared 'literate'

To illustrate the process of subjectivation and the constitution of 'literate' subjects we start with an account by Dipti from her ethnographic study that illustrates the performative declarations that transform the 'illiterate' into 'literate' through a ceremony:

> On 4th July 2014, a 'Total Literate Mustang' programme was being held at a school hall in Lete VDC as part of the 'Total Literate Nepal' programme. About 20 women and few men were present in the programme as 'literate' participants. They were part of the adult literacy programs that ran in the Mustang region and would go on to receive acknowledgement in the programme. The audience mostly comprised of villagers and students from the school. I had accompanied around eight Thakali women from Ghasa who would be receiving the certificates of being literate along with other women from the women's group in the village. Earlier during a conversation with one of the participants, Santoshi *mhom* (grandmother) had mentioned, 'we will have to give a *test* and write our names in front of the people'. Early morning at around 8 am, the women from Ghasa village had gotten ready, put on their best clothes (sarees and not the traditional Thakali attire), and got on the local bus for about an hour of bumpy ride to Lete where the programme was being held. The programme itself was uneventful with few speeches and felicitations but the attraction of the programme was when the women were asked to come to the podium and sign their names on a white board. They formed a line and gradually wrote their names and when one of the women, who was from a Dalit caste, was called upon to give a speech, she said a few lines, laughed and left the podium. One of the participants was Kanchi *mhom*[2], a 60-year-old Thakali woman who ran a small tea-shop in the bus-stop area in Ghasa, who was excited to be a part of the programme. She was one of the oldest members from her village to be 'declared literate' (Sherchan 2014).

Declaration ceremonies, such as the one described above are an important part of the LINEM programme where each district has to be declared as being 'fully literate'; meaning there is no one left between the age of 15 and above who is 'illiterate' as deemed by the State. As mentioned earlier in this article, the status report on the NLC (GoN 2016) informs that along with Mustang district, 28 other districts were declared 'fully literate' in the year 2015/2016. Althusser (1971) discusses how ideology and the ideological State apparatuses are applied to produce subjects through teaching 'know-how' in forms 'which ensure *subjection to the ruling ideology* or the mastery of its "practice"'(p. 133, emphasis original). He gives examples of the process of subjection in reproduction of labour power through ideological State apparatus by asking 'What do children learn at school'? His point is, through this subjection, the learners not only learn the skills (literacy skills in our case above) but also the 'rules' of the State and become subjects through submission to these rules while also mastering the practice of them at the same time.

The process of subjection with the ultimate goal to declare the nation as 'literate' is linked to the ideological apparatus framed by the neoliberal ideology. The ideology of a 'literate nation' requires individuals to be hailed as 'literate' subjects whose 'subjecthood' is guided by the neoliberal framework. Within this ideological framework, literacy is a desirable and generic skill that is deemed necessary to become 'responsible' productive citizens of a literate nation. For this to work, the neoliberal 'literate' subject must be obvious as in recognisable. Individuals must internalise what it means to be 'literate' and take up this subjecthood as 'free-thinking' individuals and master the practice of the literate as scripted by the discourse. It is through this 'process of responsibilization' (Kelly 2001) that the neoliberal subjects get discursively constituted as responsible, informed and choice-making individuals participating in literacy programmes. This subjection also works to produce a sense of deficiency among those who fail or refuse to acquire literacy placing the 'blame' on the individuals rather than any structural issues that may hinder their participation. This point will be further elaborated in reading the personal experiences of literacy.

The performativity of writing one's name on the white board in front of the villagers and students is an important part of the process of constitution of the literate subject. Here, 'performativity' is understood as 'a set of processes that produce ontological effects... that work to bring into being certain kinds of realities... that lead to certain kinds of socially binding consequences' (Butler 2010, p. 147). There are also other material artefacts that also work in the constitution of the literate subject; the 'formal' wear – the saree (*and not the traditional Thakali wear*) and the certificate. It is through this discursive material performativity of writing their names on the white board that the individuals get constituted as literate individuals and get recognised as such. Butler's account of 'subjectivation'[3] building on the work of Althusser and Foucault provides the theoretical perspective to further unpack this phenomenon of the constitution of the 'literate' subject. Butler explains that:

> Subjection is, literally, the *making* of a subject, the principle of regulation according to which a subject is formulated or produced. Such subjection is a kind of power that not only unilaterally *acts* on a given individual as a form of domination, but also *activates* or forms the subject. Hence, subjection is neither simply the domination of a subject nor its production, but designates a certain kind of restriction *in* production. (Butler 1997, p. 84; emphasis original)

There are a few important points made by Butler that are useful in our attempt to further explore how the LINEM programme constitutes 'literate' subjects. First, the discourse of the 'Literate Nation' and the design of LINEM programme offer the 'principles of regulation' according to which the subject is to be produced. This is not to say that the LINEM programme externally uses its power of domination targeting individuals for subordination. Foucault (1977) explains that these individuals are instead formed as subjects through discursively constituted 'identity' as literate. The Thakali women while 'becoming literate' are also subjected to relations of power through the discourse. In this sense, the second point to be noted is that the discourse of LINEM is *productive* in that it works to constitute and constrain subjects as being 'literate' but does not *determine* the subject. This point of subjection being constitutive but non-determining is important to imagine possibilities for agency of the subjects, which will be revisited later in the article. Through the use of discourse, power offers the condition as well as the constraints of the possibilities of the subject. These conditions of possibilities are not only offered by the discourse alone, but also embedded in the mutually constitutive performative acts; in the above case writing one's name on the white board. A third point emphasised by Butler (1997) is the importance of recognition and iterability of the subject. To be constituted as a literate subject, one has to perform in ways to make themselves recognisable as being 'literate'. Each performative act of writing one's name on the board done by the women here both reiterates the 'literate' while making each individual 'intelligible' as being 'literate' and thus 'declared literate'.

The process of subjectivation and the constitution of 'literate' subjects as illustrated above indicate the continued dominance of what is referred to as the 'autonomous' model (Street 2003) of literacy in Nepal. As indicated above, the subjection 'designates a certain kind of restriction *in* production' (Butler 1997, p. 84) of the 'literate' in such a way that is limiting and highly reductive. A marker of being literate has been reduced to being able to write one's name on the board in the Nepali language. This limited utilitarian approach to literacy is deemed problematic as it ignores social differences among the women and the varied cultural and geographical context within which these different women live their lives. Despite the discourse in the policy documents of understanding literacy as more than being able to read and write, this reductive practice of literacy ignores the idea of how literacy practices shape the individual's interactions with the world around them and that it may vary from one context to another. In doing so, it also ignores other forms of literacies and existing knowledge's among the Thakali women who are deemed as 'illiterate' and thus targets of the LINEM programme.

Experiencing 'Literacy'

In this section of the article, we go into exploring how the Thakali women experienced the discourse of 'literacy' through the different narratives of two Thakali women. We will continue to employ Butler's ideas of subjectivation and performativity in the analysis of these narratives in exploring how do these Thakali women interact with the discourse of literacy. We start by the story of Kanchi *mhom*, who was mentioned earlier in the excerpt of the declaration ceremony.

Kanchi *mhom*, runs a small tea-shop on the edge of the newly established bus-park area which has a constant flow of travellers, pilgrims, and villagers. There is a line of wooden box-styled restaurants run by Thakalis and non-Thakalis targeted specifically at the passengers that get off the local buses. Kanchi *mhom*'s shop sees little business, few cups of tea and petty purchases on a normal day. Her regular source of income is her home-made local *raksi* (alcoholic beverage) and snacks she prepares for the police-men stationed at the entrance of the village. Her husband left her with a one-year-old son after two years of their marriage so she went back to her parental house. Having brought her son up and gotten him married, she now lives on her own in a one-roomed house built of corrugated iron sheets and wooden scaffolding. The hut has been loosely separated into a store room, a kitchen area, a shop area and a sleeping area. Kanchi *mohm* shares:

> I have studied till grade four. My brother used to know how to do accounts although he had also only studied till grade four. His education was supported by the Subbas. There was no one in the village to send me to the school. I would ask my brothers to teach me but they would say they haven't studied well enough to teach me. My father used to read Ramayana so he had an old copy of the book. He taught us a little bit from the book. I used to study those letters, memorize them, and practice writing them; I had a lot of desire to study. If there were schools like nowadays. (Interview Transcript, Sherchan 2014)

Kanchi *mhom* was part of the adult literacy programme that was run in Ghasa village by a school teacher for few months. However, she did not have time to study properly because she had to run her shop and her eyes were weak. She had requested the teacher to teach her separately but that was not possible so she attended few of the classes and studied on her own. When asked why she wanted to attend the adult literacy class, she said,

> People forced me to… They tell the ones who have not studied to take the class. They say that it is important to know how to write one's name, or how to use mobile phones. Since they said so, I also decided to take the class but I told them that I could not manage in the evening. So I studied myself from home. I learnt some on my own by reading one page a day. If I don't work then I won't be able to earn my living. (Interview Transcript, Sherchan 2014)

The principle of regulation in constituting 'illiterate' subjects here is to distinguish between those who have attended formal education and those who have not. In this sense, the notion of education seems to be understood as being synonymous with the concept of literacy. This *system of differentiation* (Foucault 1982) between the 'illiterates' and 'literates' created by the State is what allowed the literacy educators to approach someone like Kanchi *mhom*, identify her as 'illiterate' and insist that she participate in the literacy programme. This differentiation works to create a subjective feeling of 'lacking' or deficiency among those who have not attended formal schooling and thus producing desire for formal education as experienced by Kanchi *mhom*. While constituting and constraining subjects as 'illiterate', this offers possibilities for the individuals to be identified and the choice to become candidates for adult literacy programmes. Although we could say Kanchi *mhom* did not feel that she had any agency in making that choice and felt coerced to participate. The literacy programme was made mandatory in the village for women who had not gone to schools and at times, even burdensome given it interfered with her daily life.

Following the discourse, Kanchi *mohm* understood being 'literate' as being able to write one's name and use mobile phones. Moreover, the skills that she possesses like her ability to handle the finances of her shop, run the household, make *raksi* to earn a living and the capacity to self-learn remain unacknowledged not only by others but also by herself. Hence, the subjectivation of the literacy discourse constitutes the individual, Kanchi *mohm* as 'illiterate' erasing her 'entrepreneurial' self, her business acumen and other socio-cultural markers that may have signified her otherwise, other than being 'illiterate'. She becomes 'illiterate' despite the fact that as single woman through her own local knowledge and practices, she has quite successfully managed to earn a living and live an independent life. This subjectivation makes it possible for her to construct her sense of self in particular ways. Kanchi *mhom* views herself as being unable to not only recognise the letters but also to use technology. These inabilities are ingrained in how she perceives herself in relation to other people in the village. She is an active person who is a member of the women's group in the village, runs a shop on her own and attends to social duties at the same time; however, her construction of self is heavily influenced by the sense of lack or her struggle to be literate.

This sense of deficiency produced through the constitution of the 'illiterate' seems to have a productive effect making her *decide* to take the classes. Kanchi *mohm* says, 'I also decided to take the class but I told them that I could not manage in the evening. So I studied myself from home'. As mentioned earlier in this article, the literacy practice of LINEM constitutes and constrains Kanchi *mohm* but it does not *determine* her as a subject in the literacy practice. While the requirement for the programme is to attend the 2 hour evening classes and be 'taught' by the educator, Kanchi *mohm* subverts that requirement and learns on her own at home. While being constituted and constrained by how she is deemed as illiterate, working towards becoming 'literate' she works within the boundaries of possibilities determined by the literacy programme but still learns literacy on her own terms. In that sense, while being subjectivated by the literacy discourse, Kanchi *mohm* exercises her agency that also resists the discursive practice that is creating her possibilities of being as a 'literate' subject. She challenges *the very idea that one has to be 'taught' formally inside a classroom to become literate*. This is so because the 'conditions of possibility are embedded not in discourse alone, but in mutually constitutive social acts' (Davies 2006, p. 426). The very process that constitutes Kanchi *mohm* as an illiterate engaging her in the literacy practice to become literate, offers possibilities for performative agency (Butler 2010).

In contrast to Kanchi *mhom*'s narrative, Juni *mhom* did not attend the adult literacy programme in the village. She is 72 years old, lives with her elder sister in a traditional Thakali house, and is mostly involved in agriculture. Juni *mhom* is unmarried and according to her, she did get a lot many marriage proposals but she never felt inclined to accept one. It is not uncommon for women to remain unmarried in Thakali culture. Despite her age, she is active in a lot of manual tasks like farming, taking care of the cattle, carrying fodder and wood and cooking. She has had series of unfortunate accidents and has even undergone breast cancer treatment. When asked about whether she had gone to school or not, she replied,

> I haven't studied… from an early age, I started working in the fields. I learnt from observing others. Nowadays, people do not want to be involved in agriculture… What can one do by wishing to study? At this age, my eyes have given up on me. I have heard that *raatri*[4] school has been introduced in the village but then I will soon die. They were saying that those who do not know how to sign won't be given their old age pension. But my eyes don't support me anymore so how am I supposed to study. So I told them it is fine if they don't give me the money. (Interview Transcript, Sherchan 2014)

A recurring theme in both Kanchi *mhom* and Juni *mhom*'s narrative is this idea that if they are unable to sign their names, they are ineligible to receive their old age pension. Such a policy does not exist, however, when asked around, people explained that it was said in order to 'motivate' the women to learn to write their names. This hints to the influence of the literacy educators in producing particular understandings of literacy. However, such interpretation with implementing an adult literacy programme at the expense of causing misunderstandings has worked to produce an alternative 'regime of truth' within the discourse of literacy. It has led the participants to believe that the literacy programme is a step towards ensuring that they receive their old age pension, undermining perhaps the normalising aims of the literacy discourse. Here, another discursive 'truth' has appeared that works in the constitution of the 'literate' subject, which also shapes the ideas behind the rationale for literacy. This perspective seems to be helpful in making sense of Juni *mohm*'s outright resistance to the literacy programme, however, in doing so, has she managed to evade the pervasiveness of power that works to constitute her as a subject?

Juni *mohm*'s resistance to the programme is not just due to her age but because unlike Kanchi *mhom* whose livelihood is dependent on the small shop, Juni *mhom* has sizable pieces of land from her brothers as well as herself which produces both cash crops and grains like buckwheat, maize, paddy, and so on. She also owns cattle. Moreover, she lives with her elder sister and has other close relatives so the support system that she has is bigger than that of Kanchi *mhom*'s. In the work of Mary C. Cameron, she explores the intersections of caste and gender between the so-called lower caste and higher caste Hindu communities and presents 'the complexity of social and material relations within which low-caste people act and live' (Cameron 1998, p. 271). A similar approach can be applied to looking at social and material relations within the community of Thakali women instead of across communities not only because of the heterogeneity but also hierarchies that are not explicit but are embedded within. For example, the different women who participated in this ethnographic study are all from Ghasa village and belong to the same Thakali community; however, they all have different social and economic locations. Kanchi and Juni *mhoms*' economic and social standing become important markers in the distinct individual experiences and how they individually chose to engage with the literacy programme.

To make sense of Juni *mohm*'s engagement with the literacy programme through resistance and 'non-engagement', we again turn to Butler's application of the Foucauldian idea of formation of subjects. Following Foucault, Butler (1997) argues that the subject reiterates its subjection through the very act of resistance. The fact that Juni *mohm* resisted and chose not to participate in the literacy activities becomes the constitutive social act confirming her subjectivation as an 'illiterate' who will not be paid the pension. Butler explains:

> ... in Foucault the possibility of subversion or resistance appears (a) in the course of a subjectivation that exceeds the normalizing aims by which it is mobilized ... or (b) through convergence with other discursive regimes, whereby inadvertently produced discursive complexity undermines the teleological aims of normalization. (Butler 1997, p. 92–93)

During the course of the implementation of the literacy programme, another discourse generated as a tool of motivation seems to exceed (or perhaps re-constitutes) the 'normalizing aims' of the literacy programme, which was to constitute a functional literate to build a literate Nation. For Juni *mohm* and others, the purpose of literacy and becoming 'literate' was reconstituted as 'being eligible' for pension, which not only undermines but severely restricts the aims of normalisation according to the literacy discourse. Juni *mohm's* possibilities for resistance seems to have been marked by this discursive constitution of the literate subject as one being able to receive pension as she was also being constituted as an 'economically able' subject by another discursive regime. In her narrative, Juni *mohm* constructs herself as one who could resist as she did not need to rely on the pension and she was not bothered about being 'deemed' illiterate. In Juni *mohm's* narrative, one can also hear enactment of performative agency. She says, 'I haven't studied ... from an early age, I started working in the fields. I learnt from observing others. Nowadays, people do not want to be involved in agriculture ...'. In those words, Juni *mohm* also presents an alternative account of *learning and knowledge*, learning through observation and practice working in the fields. In her localised context, for Juni *mohm* this learning is more practical than learning to read and write as she asks, 'What can one do by wishing to study'?

Conclusion: Decontextualised literacy practices

The approach underlying the above literacy programme practiced in Nepal as recent as 2015/2016, referred to as the 'autonomous' model of literacy (Street 2003), may declare the individual as being literate/illiterate, but the approach does not take into account the socio-cultural and economic conditions of the individual. Using a universal one-dimensional measure of literacy, the approach completely erases any existing knowledge and other forms of literacy grounded in the cultural/traditional practices of the diverse population in Nepal. This approach assumes 'illiteracy' (as measured and defined by the LINEM programme) as an impediment for economic progress and human development and 'literacy' as a necessary condition towards achieving those development goals. The policy and practice of literacy, including the various post-literacy interventions based on neoliberal perspective of human capital theory, completely ignore the deep-rooted problems of structural inequalities, discrimination and social exclusion as causes of poverty and injustice in our society (Regmi 2015). Trying to solve this problem of poverty through a universal one-dimensional measure of literacy only works to exacerbate the problem by reproducing these problematic structures.

Thus, the autonomous model of literacy with a purely utilitarian function shaped by the neoliberal development paradigm functions in ways to inadvertently reproduce any inequalities and exclusion in the society (Duckworth and Brzeski 2015).

What this means is that the seemingly neutral and objective perspective of literacy is not really devoid of any ideological influence. The literacy practices, even the evidently ideology-free functional literacy practices, work to provide the discursive space through which individuals get constructed as 'illiterate' while producing the necessary 'subjects' for the literacy practices to take place. This is not to hold the deterministic view that the individuals passively take on the identity of 'illiterate' or even 'literate' without agency. Instead, in the process of this subjectivation (Butler1997) the discourse also offers possibilities for the subjects to act as agents in resistance to the dominant discourse that works to constitute them as 'illiterate'. This is evident in how Kanchi *mohm* subverts the literacy practices by choosing to study on her own instead of attending the regular classes and Juni *mohm* exercises her agency (although confined) in deciding not to attend the literacy programme at all.

Acharya (2004, p. 7) asserts, '… imparting knowledge and skills to women alone and taming them to be more responsible for the household as well as for themselves will not help achieve the goal of gender justice. Most literacy programs of Nepal have been unable to internalize this knowledge'. This is the case because in Nepal even today as we have seen above, the approach to literacy that targets women is informed by the dominant development discourse that still holds onto the essentialist perspective of 'woman' and 'womanhood'. The problems and politics of ignoring differences among women (Tamang 2010) and treating all women as a homogeneous group through a uniform 'one size fits all' approach has been raised frequently. Such approaches often design their literacy programmes completely ignoring the contextual realities and everyday literacy needs as well as the existing local knowledge of the diverse groups of women. Similarly, Rao and Robinson-Pant (2006) draw attention to the gender-blind approach within indigenous adult education programmes that are informed by the rights-based agenda. In either approach, the socio-economic realities of everyday life and experiences of the women from indigenous and other minority groups are left ignored in design and implementation of the literacy programme.

The points made above have been further illustrated through the narratives on the experience of literacy by the Thakali women that are devoid of the existing cultural and historical discourse on Thakali women. On the one hand, they are considered more empowered compared to other women, more specifically Hindu non-ethnic women; however, the literacy discourse replaces this discourse to group them with all others as one homogeneous group of 'women'. While erasing all other differences and individual capacities and knowledge, not just among women in general, but also within the heterogeneous group of *Thakali* women, the literacy discourse works to create two broad groups, thus constituting the 'illiterate' and the 'literate'. This decontextualises the individual, which is a result of the process of normalisation and the discursive effect of being constituted as 'illiterate'. The practice of literacy as illustrated above indicates that even today, the image of 'uneducated women, [which were constructed] in political and development discourse as holding back the country' is held as a legitimate narrative on the identity of women in Nepal (Skinner and

Holland 2009, p. 299). This dominant portrayal of the monolithic mass of 'uneducated rural women' also continues to ignore the differences among women and the everyday realities they face.

The standardised practices of literacy in the simplistic functional terms without consideration for local contexts and existing knowledges, also work to decontextualise the literacy practice itself. As seen in the discussion of the narratives above, the Thakali women do not behave as passive individuals to be subjectivated by this literacy discourse. In the process of subjectivation and normalisation as 'illiterates' and 'literates', the individuals also exercise their performative agency in particular ways. In doing so, they manage to subvert some of the standardising acts and processes of the literacy practice, thus undermining the force of the normalisation.

The critique of the current practice of literacy discussed in this article has a few implications. First, there needs to be a recognition of the limitations of the current literacy practices to achieve the goals of economic prosperity and human development. If literacy and education are to be considered as means to achieve development in Nepal, there needs to be a careful analysis as well as acknowledgement of the historical and socio-cultural roots to the economic disparities in the first place instead of simplistic assumptions that the problem exists simply due to 'lack of literacy skills'. Second, if literacy and education are to address the structural problems of inequalities and exclusion, there needs to be a practice of literacy that is grounded in their every reality including their own local languages and culture. This is important specially for those belonging to indigenous groups in Nepal who till now have been forced to adopt the standard *Khas* Nepali with no regard to the possibilities of other kinds of literacies they may have. In Freirean terms, literacy should be a tool for people to not just *read the word but also to read the world* in order to transform it (Freire and Macedo 1987). In the current context of Nepal, there is some space for optimism towards a more localised practice of literacy with the political restructuring to a federated structure and movement towards more localised forms of literacy and educational practices including use of mother tongue. However, how this shift may happen will be dependent on how education will be conceptualised in the current emergent policy discourse; either as a way for social change and empowerment or only as an economic investment. This is yet to be seen and realised.

Disclosure statement

No potential conflict of interest was reported by the authors.

Notes

1. The Thakali people are one of the many indigenous nationalities residing in Nepal; considered an elite minority in terms of population and economic status, with distinct geo-political and cultural ties to the Thak region of the northeastern Nepal. The term 'Thakali' will be further explained later in the article.
2. *mhom* is the Thakali word for grandmother
3. Butler (1997) uses the word 'subjection' and 'subjectivation' interchangeably to refer to the same phenomenon.
4. The adult literacy classes are also referred to as *raatri* or night school.

ORCID

Amina Singh (iD) http://orcid.org/0000-0002-0100-3604

References

Acharya, S., 2004. *Democracy, gender equality and women's literacy: experience from Nepal.* Kathmandu, Nepal: UNESCO.

Althusser, L., 1971. Ideology and ideological state apparatus. *In:* B. Brewster (Trans.) *Lenin and philosophy and other essays.* London, UK: Monthly Review Press, 170–186.

Butler, J., 1997. *The psychic life of power: theories in subjection.* Standford, CA: Stanford University Press.

Butler, J., 2010. Performative agency. *Journal of cultural economy*, 3 (2), 147–161.

Cameron, M., 1998. *On the edge of the auspicious: gender and caste in Nepal.* Urbana, IL: University of Illinois Press.

Central Bureau of Statistics. 2014. *Population monograph of Nepal* Vol. II *(social demography).* Kathmandu, Nepal: Central Bureau of Statistics.

Chopra, P., 2011. (Un) veiling desire: re-defining relationships between gendered adult education subjects and adult education programmes. *International journal of educational development*, 31 (6), 634–642.

Davies, B., 2006. Subjectification: the relevance of Butler's analysis for education. *British journal of sociology of education*, 27 (4), 425–438.

Duckworth, V. and Brzeski, A., 2015. Literacy, learning and identity: challenging the neoliberal agenda through literacies, everyday practices and empowerment. *Research in post-compulsory education*, 20 (1), 1–16.

Foucault, M., 1982. The subject and power. *Critical inquiry*, 8 (4), 777–795.

Foucault, M., 1977. *Discipline and punish: the birth of the prison. In*: A. Sheridan (Trans). New York, NY: Pantheon

Freire, P. and Macedo, D., 1987. *Literacy: reading the word and the world.* South Hadley, MA: Bergin & Garvey.

Government of Nepal (GoN). 2016. *Non-formal education in Nepal: status report 2015–2016.* Bhaktapur, Nepal: Non-formal Education Centre.

Kelly, P., 2001. Youth at risk: processes of individualisation and responsibilisation in the risk society. *Discourse: studies in the cultural politics of education*, 22 (1), 23–33.

Nepal National Education Planning Commission (NNEPC). 1956. *Education in Nepal: report of the Nepal national education planning commission.* Kathmandu, Nepal: College of Education.

National Foundation for Development of Indigenous Nationalities (NFDIN). 2003. *National foundation for development of indigenous nationalities (NFDIN): an introduction.* Kathmandu, Nepal: NFDIN.

Prins, E., 2008. Adult literacy education, gender equity and empowerment: insights from a Freirean-inspired literacy programme. *Studies in the education of adults*, 40 (1), 24–39.

Robinson-Pant, A., ed., 2004. *Women, literacy, and development: alternative perspectives.* London, UK: Routledge.

Robinson-Pant, A., 2001. Women's literacy and health: can an ethnographic researcher find the links?' *In*: B.V. Street, ed. *Literacy and development: ethnographic perspectives.* London, UK: Routledge, 150–170.

Regmi, K.D., 2015. Can lifelong learning be the post-2015 agenda for the least developed countries? *International journal of lifelong education*, 34 (5), 551–568.

Sherchan, D., 2014. Personal narratives of thakali women: an anthropological inquiry into their life experiences and aspirations. Unpublished MA dissertation. Tribhuvan University.

Skinner, D. and Holland, D., 2009. Schools and the cultural production of the educated person in a Nepalese hill community. *In*: P. Bhatta, ed. *Education in Nepal problems, reforms and social change.* Kathmandu, Nepal: Martin Chautari, 295–332.

Street, B.V., 2003. What's "new" in new literacy studies? Critical approaches to literacy in theory and practice. *Current Issues in Comparative Education*, 5 (2), 77–91.

Street, B. V., 1984. *Literacy in theory and practice.* Cambridge, UK: Cambridge University Press.

Tamang, S., 2010. The politics of 'Developing Nepali Women. *In:* K.M. Dixit, and S. Ramachandaran, eds. *State of Nepal.* Kathmandu, Nepal: Himal Books, 161–175.

Tong, R., 2009. Multicultural, global and postcolonial feminism. *Feminist thought: a more comprehensive introduction.* Boulder, San Francisco, CA: Westview Press, 212–245

UNESCO. 2017. *Reading the past, writing the future: a report on national literacy campaign and literate Nepal mission.* Kathmandu, Nepal: UNESCO.

Turin, M., 1997. Too many stars and not enough sky: language and ethnicity among the Thakali of Nepal. *Contributions to nepalese studies*, 24 (2), 187–199.

Rao, N. and Robinson-Pant, A., 2006. Adult education and indigenous people: addressing gender in policy and practice. *International journal of educational development*, 26 (2), 209–223.

Indigenous knowledge, skills and action: Indigenous women's learning in the Peruvian Amazon

Sheila Aikman

ABSTRACT
Drawing on long term ethnographic research in the SE Peruvian Amazon this article asks what kinds and forms of learning do indigenous women value, how are the knowledge and skills they value changing over time and what is the nature of their agency in the face of the discrimination and prejudice that permeate their lives. Harakmbut women's lives have been transformed over the past 40 years in the wake of neoliberal globalisation, rapacious exploitative economic practices and unregulated illegal gold mining. Within this context, three types of learning emerge as important: learning about indigenous cosmology and way of life; experiential learning through engagement with an expanding capitalist society; and learning through training and capacity building for participation, voice and rights-based advocacy. The article argues that all three types of learning give meaning to Harakmbut women's lives, their relationship to their history and their views of the world.

Introduction

As the introduction to this special issue discusses, indigenous women have suffered and continue to suffer from discriminatory stereotypes. Generic social indicators of health, wealth and education show indigenous women as lagging behind in relation to global and Latin American regional norms, while formal assessments of learning suggest that indigenous peoples consistently obtain the lowest results in learning achievement over the past ten years (UNESCO/OREALC 2017). Literacy rates in Latin America for indigenous women are less than half of those of non-indigenous women (Vinding and Kampbel 2012) while in terms of schooling and formal education indigenous people are counted among the most marginalised and discriminated against groups (UNESCO 2014). Such indicators feed into dominant discourses of indigenous women as under-educated, as victims of poverty and as vulnerable and disempowered. These discourses promote homogenising stereotypes about who indigenous women are, their educational performance and expectations for what education can do for them.

Taking a historical approach, this article looks at the lives of indigenous Harakmbut women living in the SE Peruvian Amazon to question this recognition of indigenous women as under-educated, poor, vulnerable and disempowered. It asks, on the contrary, what kinds and forms of learning do indigenous women themselves value, how are the knowledge and skills they value changing over time and what is the nature of their agency in the face of the discrimination and prejudice that permeate their lives. Harakmbut women's lives have been transformed over the past 40 years in the wake of neoliberal globalisation, rapacious exploitative economic practices and unregulated and illegal gold mining that have led to the loss of their indigenous territory and its biodiversity.

Drawing on my research with the Harakmbut people of the community of San Jose de Karene over a period of 40 years, the article looks at the life of one woman, Tambet[1], and her daughters, investigating the learning she values and has valued at different periods over her adult life and through periods of radical social, economic and environmental change. It focuses on three types of learning: (a) learning and developing knowledge, skills and understandings of Harakmbut way of life, relationships to territory, spirituality and view of the world (cosmovision); (b) knowledge, skills and understandings acquired through experiential learning in an expanding capitalist society; and (c) learning through training and capacity building for indigenous participation, voice and rights-based advocacy. For each type I ask, what aims do Harambut women have for their learning, what recognition do they seek, what new knowledge and skills do they value, and what kind of action are they taking with the knowledge and skills they have developed?

These questions and the interpretative approach I take emerge from ongoing ethnographic research with the Harakmbut people and broad concerns with questions of social justice, indigenous rights and gender equality (see for example May and Sleeter 2010, Tikly and Barrett 2013). It asks about indigenous women's own values and agency, drawing on human development theory and education (see Unterhalter 2007) and is influenced by post-colonial and post-structural analysis in relation to understanding the nature of inequalities and recognition which indigenous peoples experience (see Blaser 2004, de la Cadena 2010). As Radcliffe (2015) notes there are not some definable or essentialised qualities of being an indigenous woman but 'their uniqueness arises from the interplay in interlocking hierarchies' (p.29) and historical marginalisation. In this way, the article provides insights into indigenous Harakmbut women's learning in relation to the unique positions they occupy culturally, socially and historically as indigenous Harakmbut women, not as a generalised category of 'indigenous woman' (Fennell and Arnot 2008).[2] There is an extensive and diverse literature on indigenous education and the education of and by indigenous peoples, (see for example: Battiste 2008, Minde 2008, Bellier and Hays 2016, Lopez and Sichra 2016) which discusses indigenous knowledge and indigenous education in relation to formal, non-formal and informal education. In this article the focus is on learning, where learning is 'an activity of obtaining knowledge' (https://dictionary.cambridge.org/dictionary/english/education [Accessed 20 December 2018]) rather than formalised education and the process of teaching and learning.

Based on ethnographic research carried out between 1980 and the present day in the community of San Jose de Karene, the article explores the changes in Harakmbut women's lives over this period, viewing culture and indigeneity as dynamic concepts, rather than static and descriptive (Postero 2013). Specifically, I draw on fieldwork experiences and relationships developed as a participant observer over two periods of 20 months living in the community of San Jose in the 1980s and 1990s and annual and biannual periods of fieldwork of shorter duration over twenty years. The narrative of Tambet and her daughters has developed from ongoing analysis over this period, drawing on field note books kept while living and gardening, fishing, gathering in the forest and gold panning with Tambet, her daughters and sisters. It also draws on previously published and more detailed and expansive writing on the lives of the Harakmbut of San Jose de Karene (see Aikman 1999a, 1999b, 1999c, 2001, 2012, 2017). Research was carried out in both Harakmbut and Spanish languages.

Fieldwork in the Harakmbut community was complemented by participation in meetings, conversations and congresses of the Federation of Natives of Madre de Dios. (FENAMAD), semi-structured interviews and conversations with representatives of the Interethnic Association for the Development of the Peruvian Amazon (AIDESEP), through the collection of minutes, reports and other unpublished material and through my attendance at meetings of the UN Working Group on the drafting of the Declaration of the Rights of Indigenous Peoples in Geneva. Sections discussing Harakmbut cosmology, kinship and politics draw on three volumes by Gray (1996, 1997a, 1997b). Since the early 1980s, I have been an active supporter of indigenous rights and the development of FENAMAD as a critically engaged anthropologist (Low and Merry 2010).

When I first met Tambet in late 1979 she had experienced the decimation of her kin and clan from disease, flight and relocation, marriage and childbirth. Since then she has lived through dramatic rapid socio-cultural change and destructive environmental change from gold mining, timber extraction, and a plethora of exploitative economic relations, engendering a shift from the hunting/fishing small scale agricultural livelihood she pursued with her husband, children and extended family, to living today on the margins of an environmental wasteland created by massive in-migration of impoverished, landless and marginalised Peruvians turned gold panners[3].

As a broad context within which to locate the discussion of indigenous Harakmbut women, the first section briefly considers Latin America and Peruvian attitudes, policies and practices towards indigenous peoples and education. Three subsequent sections investigate the specific experiences of Tambet and the Harakmbut with the three types of learning. The first follows Tambet's early life to investigate Harkambut learning, knowledge and the importance of territory and the invisible spirit world. The second considers the changes taking place in the community of San Jose de Karene and examines new knowledge, skills and understandings acquired by Tambet and her daughters through their experiences as part of an expanding capitalist and intercultural society, dominated by gold mining. The third looks at the ways in which Harakmbut women's activism has emerged and the value attached to training and capacity building for furthering their goals of recognition, participation and self-determination as indigenous women. The final discussion section considers the ways these types of learning interrelate, their interdependence and their meaningfulness in the context of social and environmental change and generational shift.

The recognition of indigenous women and education for indigenous peoples in Latin America

While the experiences of Tambet and her daughters are unique to them, they emerge in the wider context of conditions shared with other indigenous peoples. In Latin America and the Caribbean region the indigenous population, that is the population which traces its ancestry before the arrival of Europeans, is estimated to be around 36.6 million, some 7% of the total population, amounting to 600 indigenous peoples living in diverse social and economic situations. Bolivia, Guatemala, Mexico and Peru have the largest indigenous populations, comprising around 80% of the regional total (World Bank cited in World Bank 2015, UNESCO/OREALC 2017). However, as Morrison and Vaioleti (2011) highlight, definitions of indigeneity for statistical census purposes tend to rely on whether or not individuals speak an indigenous language ignoring socio-cultural-political aspects of being indigenous and self-definitions of indigeneity, which may or may not include language.

The ILO Convention 169, of which 15 Latin America and Caribbean countries are signatories, states that indigenous peoples are

'peoples in independent countries who are regarded as indigenous on account of their descent from the populations which inhabited the country, or a geographical region to which the country belongs, at the time of conquest of colonization or the establishment of the present state boundaries and who irrespective of their legal status, retain some or all of their own social, economic, cultural or political institutions' (ILO convention 169, Article 1.1b).

With the European conquest of the Americas, the concept of race emerged for the first time as the term 'European' no longer identified a population in a continent (Europe), but was used to discriminate between coloniser and colonised. While the terms by which the non-European populations have been labelled may have changed over time (e.g. savage, Indian, *campesino,* native), they all denote 'otherness'. Similarly, the term indigenous has come to be used to identify those peoples perceived as being different from the dominant population of European descent and from subsequent migrant groups (Quijano in Del Aguila 2016, p.5).

The indigenous population of Peru is estimated to be around 4 million, which represents 14.76% of the population of which 94% are Andean and 6% Amazonian (Defensoria del Pueblo 2011). The indigenous population of the Andes have a different history of recognition to that of the Amazon where many indigenous peoples have remained in relative autonomy well into the 20th century (Del Aguila 2016). In the 1940 Peruvian census, the Amazonian Departments of Peru only gave a rough estimate of the 'jungle' population, meaning that for the most part, the diverse socio-cultural-linguistic indigenous population was invisible in the statistics. The Harakmbut are numerically small, with a population that decreased from around 10,000 at the beginning of the 20th century to some 1000 individuals (Gray 1996). Until the beginning of the boom in gold mining in the 1980s, the Harakmbut in the socially and economically marginalised Madre de Dios region of the South Eastern Amazon had been invisible to the state.

A uniformity of approach towards the indigenous populations of many Latin American countries continues to be a persistent feature of social and educational policy and to replicate social, cultural, political and economic divides through what Quijano (2000) calls the coloniality of power. It obscures their diversity as peoples and denies their distinct histories and cosmologies as well as the diversity of their age- and gender-related relationships with their ancestral territories. Stereotypes about modernity's impact on indigenous women mean that they are often seen as more 'traditional' than men in contexts where the gradual erosion of subsistence hunting and gathering gives men a more dominant role in economic activities and commerce. Changing gender hierarchies can mean that women often have less experience of urban types of work and less dominant economic positions within the community (Wade 2010). IWGIA (1999) notes that relationships between indigenous men and women have often been viewed from the outside as embedded in customary ways of living and as pertaining to their culture, leaving issues of violence and gendered abuse unchallenged. While many of these dynamics are part of indigenous women's experiences, to treat them as universal or inevitable is to deny indigenous women's own perspectives, as well as their aspirations, agency and struggle.

The representation of all indigenous women as similarly poor, under- or un-educated and/or illiterate ignores, for example, the diversity of their economic situations be these urban or rural. Many indigenous women have incomplete or no formal education, while others, albeit a minority, have university degrees and diverse professional qualifications and careers. Missionary and government education policies through much of the 20th century were oriented to educating indigenous populations out of their 'backwardness' and integrate or otherwise assimilate them into modern society through formal schooling. Today there is recognition that indigenous peoples have been historically underserved by education systems in terms of access to formal education and that current persistent educational gaps and inequalities are related to broader economic, cultural, social and political inequalities. There are calls for more effective strategies and programmes in order to meet the needs of disadvantaged young people and adults in today's fast-changing world (UNESCO/OREALC 2014, 2017). The solution to high drop-out rates for the poorest young people and those living in rural areas has been to expand primary and secondary schooling in indigenous areas but there has also been a questioning of the nature of curricula and pedagogies which bear little relationship with the kinds of lives and challenges that indigenous students face (Cueto *et al.* 2009, Trapnell 2003). Critique of the content and orientation of schooling led to the emergence of intercultural bilingual education, which has been actively pursued in the region for over 20 years by indigenous organisations, UNESCO agencies and international and national NGOs. Today most governments have intercultural bilingual departments or offices within their Ministries of Education and have been enacting laws recognising their societies as intercultural and multilingual (see e.g. Lopez 2008). However, expectations for intercultural bilingual education are often very ambitious, including extolling its potential for 'overcoming poverty, social inequalities, exclusion and the lack of social integration' (Defensoria del Pueblo 2011, p.9). What happens in the name of 'intercultural bilingual education' is diverse and often contested (Lopez and Sichra 2016).

Beyond the focus on primary and secondary schooling for indigenous children, Schmelkes (2011) notes that campaigns and plans for intercultural education for adults seem to have evaporated and there has been little progress in developing intercultural adult education. The 2005 Peruvian Intercultural Bilingual Education Law (No. 27818) legislates for intercultural bilingual education for adults and literacy but there is little evidence of this happening. So, while the educational practice lags behind and is extremely challenging, the global and regional policy discourses for adult education call for new kinds of recognition. The CONFINTEA V and CONFINTEA VI [4] reports refer to 'respecting different cultural groups' beliefs, practices and ways of knowing and learning as a condition for relevant and quality education' (Schmelkes 2011, p.93). The UNESCO/OREALC (2017) document entitled 'Indigenous Knowledge and Practices in Education in Latin America' calls for 'the recognition and legitimation of indigenous culture and knowledge, and their inclusion in public policy' (2017, p.5). Indeed, it goes further and demands 'cognitive and epistemic justice' (p.5), that is the transformation of relations of power in the construction of knowledge and the acceptance of marginalised and excluded knowledge (Rodriguez *et al.* 2016).

In the absence of education programmes of any orientation for indigenous women in the SE Peruvian Amazon, how do Harakmbut women value their marginalised and excluded knowledge, how and what are they learning through their intercultural lives in an exploitative gold mining environment, and what learning do they want in order to support their movement for recognition and rights as women, as indigenous women and an indigenous people? The next three sections consider types of learning that are meaningful for Harakmbut women in their changing lives.

Harakmbut ways of learning and knowing: life, territory and the spirit world

Tambet is an indigenous Harakmbut-speaking woman, today in her late 70s. In her early years, she lived with her family and kin in their communal longhouse in their ancestral forest territory in the headwaters of the Madre de Dios river. Their way of life centered around fishing, hunting and small-scale swidden agriculture. But as a young girl in the early 1960s, her people were forced to flee to a Dominican mission to seek relief from infections and fevers contracted through incursions into their territory by explorers, lumberers and game hunters. Illnesses that were new to the Harakmbut, such as yellow fever, measles and influenza, were decimating the population. At school in the mission, she learned that her way of life, beliefs and values were 'uncivilised' and should be cast aside to make way for Christian beliefs and an Iberian missionary concept of what a good and dutiful woman should be and do (Junquera 1978). Tije (1995) writes that this schooling devalued their culture, changed their ways of eating and dressing, their economic activities and also their language. 'In all this process they showed us that learning Spanish was more important than our own language' (Tije 1995, p4). Being confined within the mission led to continuing deaths, and sickness and tensions between different Harakmbut clans and kin groups. As the game became scarcer for hunting and accusations of witchcraft abounded, Tambet and her kin group decided to leave. They left at night, silently and travelled upriver by canoe to where they established the community of San Jose de Karene and regained their autonomy. By the 1970s, the Peruvian government had officially recognised the community and provided collective legal title to a defined and delimited territory, situated within the much wider rainforest lands of their ancestors.

Tambet arrived in San Jose de Karene as a young mother positioned within a strong extended family. There she was able to build on her knowledge and learning through practical experience, through listening and watching her elders, both men and women, through learning about the significance and meaning of myths and stories, and also though communicating with the spirits through dreaming and chants. She continued to expand her knowledge of the forest and river and her skills in agriculture. To be the successful gardener that she became and to provide for her growing family meant learning about the forest and the creatures that inhabit it and learning how to develop relationships with the spirits of the forest and river so that they would guide her gardening and keep her and her family safe (Aikman 1999a).

For the Harakmbut, the world is unpredictable and inhabited by invisible spirits which influence health and wellbeing. Women and men learn to communicate with the spirits to help maintain the health of the family members and the community. This learning is lifelong and knowledge accumulates with experience, allowing men and women to develop distinct and specialised vocabularies to communicate with the spirits of the forest (Aikman 1999a, Gray 1997a, 1997b). Over the decades I have known Tambet she has developed the knowledge and skills to cultivate several gardens with a diversity of crops and use her knowledge to ensure her family's physical and spiritual health as well as forge strong reciprocal relationships with her kin and clan. She is recognised within her community as a woman of status and wisdom. Tambet is also a teacher, encouraging her daughters as they learn through their joint activities and expand their knowledge, understanding and wisdom through its application. Learning and gaining knowledge that is constituted in the setting of everyday life – 'knowledge-in-practice' (Lave 1988) – is based on values of trust and respect for the teacher, the meaningfulness of the skill and knowledge itself and through the patience of the learners as active seekers and users of knowledge (McCarthy et al. 1991, see also Aikman 1999a).

Through Tambet's early life and adulthood, she grew in stature, learning from and through her participation and experience in activities of cultivating her own gardens, becoming skilled in biodiversity-management, acquiring an extensive knowledge of different varieties of crops, their properties and optimum conditions for their cultivation and accumulating extensive ethnobotanical wisdom. While her daughters could list seven different types of pineapple grown in her mother's garden, Tambet herself could name 17 randomly intermixed varieties growing in one of her gardens which was situated on high ground suited to pineapple cultivation. Her knowledge of how to garden, how to fish in the rivers and gather in the forest, had developed through dreaming and forming relationships with the spirits of the invisible world. From the myth and storytelling of the elders, she learned about Harakmbut relations with the spirits of the forest and the gardens, and learned about the behaviour of animals, birds and fish.

For Tambet using her learning for the benefit of her family and community gained her recognition as an able gardener with great knowledge of the forest and river, as a woman of wisdom and understanding of the interplay between the visible world of the Harakmbut and the invisible world of the spirits and as someone who uses this knowledge to try to keep her family safe. She is respected for these qualities and over her adult life gained status, recognition and influence within her family and community.

Learning through experience in an encroaching and expanding capitalist society

The 1980s and 1990s were a time when the Harakmbut experienced a gradual but profound change in their lives. Alongside their gardening, fishing and gathering women also took part with the men in panning for gold during the dry season in the sediment of the rivers. As the price of gold soared nationally and internationally, the number of seasonal migrant gold panners arriving in the Karene river multiplied and tensions increased over their incursions onto San Jose titled land. Game became scarcer as squalid settler gold camps lined the river banks and penetrated deep inland where over time semi-permanent settlements transformed into sprawling informal townships[5]. Well-organised and powerful gold bosses and gang masters expanded their enterprises using increasingly larger and more highly mechanised machinery to extract the gold-bearing soil and sediment, dredging the river beds and excavating the forest all year round.

The impact of the burgeoning migrant population's ecologically destructive economic practices had subtle but pervasive effects on Harakmbut women's ability to use their learning in their daily lives. It also restricted their freedom to move through their territory and access the forest resources. The Harakmbut men began to spend more time on gold work, as their ability to sustain their families through hunting and fishing were compromised by the destruction of the forest cover, pollution of rivers and scarcity of wild pig, tapir, deer and birds. From being one of several different economic family-oriented activities within their subsistence economy, gold mining became a crucial income generating activity dominated by the men who for the most part controlled the money. This, in turn, had an impact on internal social and gendered relations. Senior women such as Tambet gradually stopped growing surpluses of manioc for beer making as men could directly purchase bottled beer available in the shanty gold mining settlements along the rivers (Aikman 1999b, 1999c). Men no longer had time to help the women clear the forest for new gardens to plant manioc and plantains, while migrant labourers working together with the Harakmbut in gold mining would not eat Tambet's garden produce demanding instead bought foodstuffs, such as potatoes, rice and pasta.

So Tambet learned that wider changes were influencing her ability to use her knowledge and complex understandings of the physical and spiritual environment for the good of her family. Gold mining and the ability to obtain a fair rate for gold at the trading post had taken on a new importance. On trips to the trading post to sell gold and buy foodstuffs, she experienced discrimination and humiliation and learned that her way of speaking Spanish marked her out as a 'nativo'. She and her family were viewed with suspicion and in some instances with fear by migrants with ingrained prejudices about the indigenous peoples of the rainforest. She learned through repeated invasions of the community's legal territory by miners, the plunder of hardwoods and forest fruits and other infringements of their freedoms that their rights went unheeded by the Departmental authorities, the police and the judiciary. On the contrary, she was discriminated against on the basis of her race, ethnicity and gender. After some years she rarely went to the trading post with the men and kept to the community.

As Tambet's daughters grew, they too learned through gardening, collecting and fishing together with their mother and aunts. Harakmbut knowledge is oral and belongs to an individual as the culmination of a lifetime of learning. While Tambet's daughters learned much about their cosmology, the spirit world, how to provide for a family and live a rich and valued life in the forest environment, the forest environment itself was changing through the activities of gold mining. Tambet passed on her learning as well as she could to her daughters who were also learning through schooling and close interaction with migrant gold miners now living in and around the community. Travelling salesmen and saleswomen brought their wares – beer, clothes, mobile video screenings of Tarzan and other adventure films which caused much mirth in San Jose – laboriously upriver by canoe to the community. Meanwhile, Puerto Maldonado, the Departmental capital, was slowly transformed from frontier outpost to regional hub, thanks to the burgeoning gold economy, commercial agriculture and forestry. State institutions became established, the banking sector expanded and communications with Lima were regularised.

Since her brief attendance in the mission school in the 1960s, Tambet had no access to any educational opportunities offered by the state or the missionaries. This is not to say that she did not value schooling for her children. As mining took a hold over the subsistence activities and hunting and fishing no longer provided the basis of the economy, she hoped that school certificates would provide her daughters with alternatives to heavy work involved in gold mining, cooking in gold camps or, worse still, prostitution. Tambet's daughters attended the Dominican mission-run primary school in San Jose. The school, first set up in the early 1980s, is staffed by Spanish speaking lay-missionaries and follows the national curriculum. The demands of schooling five days a week meant that they had less time to accompany their mother and to learn from and with her about the intimate spiritual links between crops, how they grow and the nutritional and wellbeing of the family and community. At the same time, they had less inclination and motivation to do so as they saw their mother toil in their gardens, struggling to bring home enough fish from the contaminated rivers to feed the family once the forest game – wild pig, tapir, birds and monkeys – had become scarce. Schooling for Tambet's children was focussed on learning to be Peruvian citizens through a curriculum and educational practice that was ignorant of Harakmbut knowledge, learning and teaching (Aikman 1999b). Schooling was, as Corbett (2007) writing about Canada aptly puts it, about learning to leave, to leave behind Harambut values and knowledge and to look for new kinds of lives elsewhere. On completing primary schooling, Tambet's daughters boarded in a nunnery in the regional capital in order to attend secondary school.

In their daily lives, Tambet and her children learned that social institutions and individual Peruvians of diverse backgrounds held deep-seated prejudices against them. They learned this in multiple contexts and reinforcing ways: from their struggle to mine for gold legally according to ever-changing laws and regulations; their attempts to eke out a subsistence through fishing, agriculture or hunting in their territory that had been illegally invaded and occupied; their interactions with miners, commercial travellers, bureaucrats, representatives of the police, judiciary and the law; the proselytising strategies of the Dominican missionaries and through the education system and its national curriculum. In this environment, Tambet learned the importance of finding ways to continue to keep her family safe through her skills of gardening, fishing and gathering, her knowledge of Harakmbut ancestral territory and her relationship with the spirits of the invisible world.

For her daughters growing up in a changing environment, being schooled in Spanish, mobile, smart at business negotiations, able to engage with and use the diverse discourses of miners, officials and non-indigenous people were important aims and valued for alternatives to the potential penury that gold mining and the destruction of the physical environment presaged (Aikman 2001). They used their learning, their knowledge and skills to seek out new ways to lead their lives and assert themselves as indigenous women and as Peruvians in the midst of rapid social change and an abrasive intercultural environment. They valued the opportunities that schooling afforded them in terms of encounters and relationships with individuals from diverse indigenous and non-indigenous backgrounds, learning a good level of Spanish from the lay-missionary teachers and acquiring academic qualifications on a par with other Peruvians. While some young women of this generation have taken up opportunities to train as health workers, teachers or forestry technicians, others have become involved in the emerging movement for the recognition of indigenous rights, finding new ways to challenge stereotypes and assert themselves as indigenous peoples and as indigenous women.

Learning through training and capacity building for indigenous participation, voice and rights-based advocacy

In 1982, the Harakmbut, together with 46 indigenous communities from the 17 indigenous peoples of SE Peruvian Amazon, established the Federation of Native of Madre de Dios (FENAMAD) (www.FEMAMAD.org). It was set up to defend indigenous territories from invasion and destruction and to sustain the ways of life embedded in these territories. Its mandate included a search for alternatives to gold mining in order to secure the futures of the indigenous communities. As with other indigenous organisations emerging in the 1980s and 1990s (Deten 1999), men were most active and held leadership positions. Over time, however, the women began to engage more actively within FENAMAD and pushed for the establishment of a Secretary for Women's Issues where they could be represented and their voices heard. In 1990, women representatives from the Harakmbut and other neighbouring indigenous communities held the First Meeting of Native Women of Madre de Dios, organised with the express aim of uniting as indigenous women. Travelling for several days by canoe and lorry, they congregated in one community to discuss their status and representation in the organisational structures of their communities and how they felt their positions as women in these structures were being devalued. They gave voice to their anxieties about changes emanating from beyond their communities, stating that

In recent decades we have suffered from alienation because of contact with western society and the introduction of ideas, values, which have brought with them an alteration in our ways of being and thinking as well as that of all our cultures of origin (FENAMAD 1990, p.1).

Using Spanish as their common language, the Harakmbut women learned that they could work together with other Amazonian indigenous women, could voice their opinions, develop their analyses and shape their own development. They felt they had been 'poorly advised by the colonists and because of this we have come to view our traditions as something outdated and of little importance today' (FENAMAD 1990, p.1). They felt marginalised because: 'we know little about the importance of revaluing and recognising the worth of our culture, customs and values' (FENAMAD 1990). They also voiced concern for their low level of inclusion in community decision-making and voiced their desire to be more active in the welfare of their communities.

With a growing determination, they discussed the importance of the family as a locus for children's learning and looked for new ways to reassert their indigenous knowledge and practices. They began with sharing their own knowledge of medicinal plants and crops and also looked to indigenous health promoters from other regions of the Peruvian Amazon to expand their skills and knowledge in areas of childbirth, hygiene and nutrition. They agreed that schooling had not equipped them with the resources needed to negotiate their futures in the harsh and brutal environment of gold panning, timber extraction and oil exploration. And there was an absence of adult basic education or non-formal programmes in their communities. They wanted learning that would help them secure their rights vis-à-vis the burgeoning migrant population, the state and international businesses and organisations (FENAMAD 1995).

The women voiced concern that the schooling provided in indigenous communities was irrelevant not only for indigenous children's functioning in wider Peruvian society but also for their relationship with their own society. A study carried out for indigenous organisations in Peruvian Amazon at this time concluded that schooling was contributing to the loss of indigenous cultural knowledge and languages and that indigenous children's performance in locally administered tests was 'disastrous' (Chirif 1991, p.61). As schooled women themselves they valued bilingual education but noted that even when bilingual teachers were posted to indigenous schools, they were not necessarily bilingual in the children's indigenous language. The lay-missionary school teacher in the Dominican-run school in San Jose in the 1990s, claimed to be a bilingual teacher because he spoke Quechua and Spanish, but he had no knowledge of Harakmbut. They used their insights to demand better coordination with the Departmental Office of Education and for appropriately qualified indigenous teachers who were alert and sensitive to young peoples' learning and knowledge of their indigenous heritage, experienced in the way of life in this gold mining frontier environment and also knowledgeable about their country as citizens.

By sharing their experiences of the changes that were taking places in their lives and the lives of their families and community the Harakmbut women found common cause with other indigenous women. Together they learned from each other, shared, taught and organised themselves. On the one hand, they learned how to revalue the ways of learning and knowing about Harakmbut land, life and the spirit world they had acquired from their mothers' generation, Tambet's generation. On the other hand, like other indigenous women in Peru they 'learned that it is not a natural condition to be discriminated, mistreated or disadvantaged' (Tarcila Rivera, Quechua indigenous leader, Rivera 2000, p.36). They learned a language of critique and rights and identified abilities and skills they required for effective collective action through training work-shops, capacity building and regular meetings to search together for solutions to their collective problems and challenges as indigenous women (FENAMAD 1995).

While Harakambut women were strengthening their presence within FENAMAD and raising pressing issues related to the condition of indigenous women, access to land and resources, violence and marginalisation in their daily lives, they also forged alliances with indigenous women from across the Peruvian Amazon region. FENAMAD is an affiliate of AIDESEP (the Interethnic Association for the Development of the Peruvian Amazon) an indigenous organisation influential on the national and international stage lobbying for indigenous rights, legal titling on indigen-ous lands, health and education. In the run-up to the 1995 Fourth World Conference on the Status of Women held in Beijing indigenous women established an AIDESEP Office of Women's Affairs to provide them with a platform within the women's move-ment and enable them to take their demands to global policy arenas (Oliart 2008). The Office of Women's Affairs initiated a national workshop to support indigenous women from regional organisations such as FENAMAD to articulate their priorities within their communities and to deliver leadership training to develop their capacity to organ-ise and actively take part in developing a political agenda (AIDESEP 2007). So, while engaging in the wider women's movement for recognition and rights, they sought to highlight the inequalities and discriminations they experienced as *indigenous* women. In 2000, Rivera noted:

> There has been progress for women in Peru, seeking spaces for participation, influencing policy formulation, laws, and seeking alternatives with which to improve the conditions of Peruvian women in general but that, in this context indigenous women have still not managed to gain recognition or respect with regard to gender, ethnicity or culture (Rivera 2000, p.36).

Slowly Harakmbut women and the women of FENAMAD strengthened linkages and expanded their networks with indigenous women around the globe. In 2013, the World Conference of Indigenous Women, took place in Lima Peru, and the Conference Statement 'Indigenous Women Towards Visibility and Inclusion' notes: 'we recognise ourselves as rights holders and, also at the collective level, we identify specific problems because of our condition as women and as members of indigenous peoples' (WCIC 2013, Section 7). This statement calling for the 'development of leader-ship and continuous training and capacity building processes based on principles, val-ues and methodologies that are in accordance with our cultural worldview' (ibid) echoes FENAMAD women's demands and has grown out of their grounded experien-ces. Indigenous women's learning through training and capacity building has shaped their action as women, as indigenous and as indigenous women. The International Indigenous Women's Forum at the UN Permanent Forum on Indigenous Issues has a programme for training in rights and other issues identified by indigenous women to enable a 'breaking with paradigms of victimisation and vulnerability' (p.12). This is training to build their capacity as self-determining actors within their dynamic societies today and 'building on indigenous cosmovisions, spirituality and intergenerational dialogue' (IIWF 2009, p.22).

Learning through training and capacity building for indigenous participation, leadership, voice and rights-based advocacy is part of a clear and explicit demand of indigenous women engaged in action for recognition as self-determining actors. It has been identified by indigenous women from FENAMAD to the UN Permanent Forum on Indigenous Issues as vital for achieving the kind of recognition they desire in order to shape for themselves the kinds of change they value.

Concluding discussion

The previous sections have investigated three different types of learning that Harakmbut women value in different ways. The first – developing knowledge, skills and understandings of Harakmbut society, relationships to their territory and spirit world – is discussed through the example of Tambet. A glimpse into her young and adult life has offered some insights into the value and meaningfulness of this kind of learning for Harakmbut women of her generation. Learning emerges from and through the relationships Tambet develops with the visible world around her as well as the invisible world of the spirits and links her with her predecessors and their collective territory. How she uses her learning and teaches her daughters and subsequent generations contributes to her recognition as a strong and respected Harakmbut woman. Non-Harakmbut are not interested in this learning and its language and are ignorant of the view of the world (the cosmovision) and understandings it encompasses. Hence Tambet's knowledge and wisdom go unrecognised and unvalued in the turbulent and often violent gold mining society on the fringes of the Peruvian state.

The second type of learning for Harakmbut women is experienced through daily encounters in what was and continues to be an increasingly intercultural environment through the relentless increase in migrants trying to eke out a livelihood in the gold economy. Tambet and her daughters' experiences offer insights into the complex and abusive relationships that Harakmbut women experience in their encounters with migrants and representatives of state institutions. Their learning happens through unplanned and unanticipated interactions, the cut and thrust of life in the gold economy and through experiences of humiliation and discrimination. But the language skills, social skills, and different bodies of knowledge that Harakmbut women learn are important for their navigation and survival in this changing social and physical environment. Schooling became a regular feature of Tambet's daughters' childhood and youth and there they gained schooled knowledge, albeit disconnected from the lives they were living. They also gained certificates and qualifications which brought a certain status as 'educated' Peruvians, despite its potential to alienate them from the values and knowledge they learn from their mother.

The third type of learning emerged in context of expansion of the gold economy, the lack of regulation and the need to act in the face of marginalisation and structurally embedded inequalities. The first steps taken by Harakmbut women to organise themselves through FENAMAD illustrates two aspects to this learning. One the one hand,

Tambet's daughters' generation began to question their internalisation of their supposed inferiority and their prejudicial stereotyping as ignorant, vulnerable and powerless. They began to reassess and revalue the knowledge and skills which they learn from their mothers and came together as women to challenge the dominance of men in decision-making in their own families and communities. Drawing strength from the growing women's movements in Peru and Latin America they joined in the call for women's equality but defining and engaging on their own terms to dismantle homogenising and discriminatory conceptions of who indigenous women are (Duarte 2012). In her 2008 article, Oliart traces the nature and trajectory of indigenous women's resistance in Andean Peru. She refers to the diversity of indigenous women's agency and actions and their positionality and histories throughout Latin America to note that indigenous women respond to the challenges they face and the opportunities they have on their own terms and in their own ways.

Looking back over the past 40 years, as this article has done, it is clear that not all Harakmbut women have had the same challenges and opportunities in their lives. Harakmbut women have tread different paths at different times and made different decisions about their learning and the knowledge and skills they value. Tambet has not been active in formal campaigning for indigenous rights and indigenous women's rights – and nor have all her daughters or those of her daughters' generation – but she supports the aims and work of FENAMAD and supports the younger women who do. She has continued to live and work in San Jose, while the gold mining economy has expanded around her, destroying huge tracts of forest cover and polluting the rivers. Her three daughters left the community to attend missionary secondary schooling. While one returned, two continued on to further education and were posted to positions as a health worker and teacher respectively far from San Jose. Nevertheless, they are engaged in different ways with the work and campaigning of FENAMAD. The daughter who returned has worked in the gold economy, cooking for groups of miners and working with her mother in their gardens. Her children are growing up alongside children of mixed Harakmbut-non-indigenous marriages and non-indigenous children of the contract miners. Tambet's grandchildren have only a rudimentary ability in the Harakmbut language and their knowledge of Harakmbut territory, rivers and forest are dominated by the destructive effects of gold mining. They attend the community school which is still run by Dominican lay-missionaries and still offers only a monolingual Spanish national curriculum. The dominant language heard in the community today is the language of the gold economy.

Tambet has learned how to fish and garden and sustain her family in a changed physical and social environment. She has learned how to interact with miners living in her community and her house and how to maintain her distance and dignity. Her knowledge and relationship with the forest and river, despite their erosion, has continued to give meaning to her life as an Harakambut woman. She maintains her self-respect through relationships with the spirits of the forest and rivers of her ancestral territory inhabiting remote areas still untouched by gold mining. While her daughters' lives are being played out in a different social and physical environment the knowledge passed on from their mother and her generation grounds them as Harkambut. The women who began to speak out in FENAMAD have developed a new awareness of the worth of their culture, language and way of life. It is this knowledge of their indigenous cosmologies, histories and their Harakmbut ways of learning that gives meaning to their struggle and their search for new skills in leadership, negotiation and advocacy. Indigenous women are bound together at national and international levels by the knowledge, skills and understandings of their indigenous world views, relationships to their respective territories and spirituality.

Harakmbut society and culture has changed since Tambet was a young woman and mother, a society and culture that has always been dynamic and changing. But the shifts over recent decades have been swift and profound. A younger generation now uses the skills and knowledge they have gained of contemporary Peruvian society to set out demands and strategies for the recognition and benefit of their families, communities and people. And they are doing this having re-valued the learning and knowledge they acquired from their mothers and grandmothers and by shaping it for the lives they lead today. All three types of learning are interdependent and integral to achieving individual and collective recognition as Harakmbut women. It is their ongoing learning that helps them continue to reshape their indigenous ways of life, their relationship to their history and their Harakmbut view of the world in ways that are meaningful. From the outside and at a quick glance, it would be easy to categorise Tambet and her daughters as poor, disempowered and vulnerable. But that would be to deny their agency, dignity and recognition.

Disclosure statement

No potential conflict of interest was reported by the author.

Notes

1. Tambet is a pseudonym. I have changed some of the details of 'Tambet's life and situation to ensure her anonymity.
2. I write as a non-indigenous academic – I am not writing on behalf of Tambet or Harakmbut women – but offer my analysis from the privileged insights I have gained through sharing in the lives of these women (see for example the work of Smith (1999) on decolonising methodologies).
3. The miners who have settled in Madre de Dios are diverse ethnically, economically, in terms of their provenance, the kind and scale of the mining they carry out, their relationship to the environment, and their aims and their relationships with the Harakmbut. For more details see for example Aikman (1999c, 2012).
4. CONFINTEA, the UNESCO International Conference on Adult Education is held every 12 years. CONFINTEA V was held in 1997 and CONFINTEA VI was held in 2009 in Belem, Brazil (see Morrison and Vaioleti (2011) for more detail about the discussions of indigenous peoples at these conferences).
5. The growth of gold mining over this period is documented in Gray (1986).

ORCID

Sheila Aikman   http://orcid.org/0000-0001-5404-5982

References

AIDESEP., 2007. Encuentro de Mujeres Indigenas Amazonicas, lineamentos de Plan de Accion/Agenda Politica. Accessed 10.5.2018. Available from: www.AIDESEP.org

Aikman, S., 1999a. *Intercultural education and literacy: an ethnographic study of indigenous knowledge and learning in the Peruvian Amazon.* Amsterdam: John Benjamins.

Aikman, S., 1999b. Schooling and development: eroding amazon women's knowledge. *In*: C. Heward and S. Bunwaree, eds. *Gender, education and development: beyond access to empowerment.* London: Zed Books. 65–82.

Aikman, S., 1999c. Alternative development and education: economic interests and cultural practices in the Amazon. *In*: F. Leach and A. Little, eds. *Education, cultures, and economics.* London: Falmer Press, 95–110.

Aikman, S., 2001. Literacies, languages and developments in Peruvian Amazonia. *In*: B. Street, ed. *Literacy and development: ethnographic perspectives.* London: Routledge, 103–120.

Aikman, S., 2012. Interrogating discourses of intercultural education: from indigenous Amazon community to global policy forum. *Compare*, 42 (2), 235–258.

Aikman, S., 2017. Changing livelihoods and language repertoires: hunting, fishing and gold mining in the southeast Peruvian Amazon. *International journal of the sociology of language*, 246, 85–108.

Battiste, M., 2008. The struggle and renaissance of indigenous knowledge in eurocentric education. *In*: M. Villegas, S. Neugebauer and K. Venegas, eds. *Indigenous knowledge and education: sites of struggle, strength and survivance.* Cambridge, MA: Harvard Educational Review, 85–92.

Bellier, I. and Hays, J., eds., 2016. *Quelle Education pour les Peuples Autochtones?* Paris: SOGIP/L'Harmattan.

Blaser, M., Feit H., and McRae G., eds., 2004. *In the way of development: indigenous peoples, life projects and globalization.* London: IDRC/Zed.

Chirif, A., 1991. Contexto y Características de Educación Oficial en Sociedades Indígenas. *In*: M. Zúñiga, I. Pozzi-Escot and L. E. Lopez, eds. *Educación Bilingüe Intercultural: reflexiones y desafíos.* Lima: Fomciencias, 29–69.

Corbett, M., 2007. *Learning to leave: the irony of schooling in a coastal community.* Canada: Fernwood Publishing.

Cueto, S., *et al.*, 2009. Explaining and overcoming marginalisation in education: A focus on ethnic/language minorities in Peru. Background paper for the EFA Global Monitoring Report 2010. 2010/ED/EFA/MRT/P1/11.

Defensoria del Pueblo., 2011. *Aportes para una Politica Nacional de Educacion Intercultural Bilingue a favour de los pueblos indigenas. Serie Informes Defensoriales – Informe no. 152.* Lima: Republica Del Peru.

Del Aguila, A., 2016. *The labour situation of indigenous women in Peru - a study. ILO Office for the Andean Countries.* Geneva: International Labour Organization.

De la Cadena, M., 2010. Indigenous cosmopolitics in the Andes: conceptual reflections beyond 'politics. *Cultural anthropology*, 25 (2), 334–370.

Deten, R., 1999. Peru: Experiencias de las Mujeres Nativas en la Amazonia Peruana. *In*: IWGIA, ed. *Mujeres Indigenas en Movimiento.* Documento 11. Copenhagen: International Work Group for Indigenous Affairs, 15–20.

Duarte, B., 2012. From the margins of Latin American feminism: indigenous and lesbian feminisms. Signs. *Journal of women in culture and society*, 38 (1), 153–178.

FENAMAD., 1990. Informe del Primer Encuentro de Mujeres Nativas de Madre de Dios. Federation of Native of Madre de Dios, Unpublished Report.

FENAMAD., 1995. Proyecto: Promocion de la Mujer Indigena en la Cuenca del Rio Madre de Dios. Federation of Natives of Madre de Dios, Unpublished Project Document, March.

Fennell, S., and Arnot, M., 2008. Decentring hegemonic gender theory: the implications for educational research. *Compare*, 38 (5), 525–538.

Gray, A., 1986. *And after the gold rush...? Human rights and self-development among the Amarakaeri of Southeastern Peru. IWGIA Document 55.* IWGIA: Copenhagen.

Gray, A., 1996. *Mythology, spirituality and history in an Amazonian community.* Oxford: Berghahn Books.

Gray, A., 1997a. *The Last Shaman: change in an Amazonian community.* Oxford: Berghahn Books.

Gray, A., 1997b. *Indigenous rights and development: self-determination in an Amazonian Community.* Oxford: Berghahn Books.

[IIWF] International Indigenous Women's Forum., 2009. *Analysis and follow up of the UN Permanent Forum on Indigenous Issues.* UN Permanent Forum on Indigenous Issues, New York, Eight Session, May. Item 3(B). Available from: www.un.org/esa/socdev/unpfii/documents/E_C_19_2009_8_en.pdf [Accessed 6 February 2018].

IWGIA., 1999. *Gender and indigenous women. Position paper and strategy, unpublished document.* Copenhagen: IWGIA.

Junquera, C., 1978. Los Amarakaeri Frente a la Cultura Occidental [The Amarakaeri in the Face of Western Culture]. *Antisuyo*, 1, 77–79.

Lave, J., 1988. *Cognition in practice: mind, mathematics and culture in everyday life.* Cambridge: Cambridge University Press.

Lopez, L. E., 2008. Top-down and bottom-up: counterposed visions of intercultural bilingual education in Latin America. *In*: N. Hornberger, ed. *Can schools save indigenous languages: policy and practice on four continents.* Basingstoke: Palgrave Macmillan, 42–65.

Lopez, L. E., and Sichra, I., 2016. Indigenous bilingual education in Latin America. In O. Garcia, eds. *Bilingual and multilingual education, encyclopaedia of language and education.* 3rd ed. Switzerland: Springer, 1–12.

Low, E.M. and Merry, S.E., 2010. Engaged anthropology: diversity and dilemmas. *Current anthropology*, 51 Supplement (2), 203–225.

May, S. and Sleeter, C., 2010. Introduction. Critical multiculturalism: theory and practice. *In* S. May and C. Sleeter, eds. *Critical multiculturalism: theory and practice.* London: Routledge, 1–18.

McCarthy, T., Lynch, R.H., Wallace, S., and Benally, A., 1991. Classroom enquiry and Navajo learning styles: a call for reassessment. *Anthropology & education quarterly*, 22, 42–59.

Minde, H., ed. 2008. *Indigenous peoples: self-determination, knowledge, indigeneity.* Delft: Eburon.

Morrison, S. and Vaioleti, T., 2011. Inclusion of indigenous peoples in CONFINTEA VI and follow-up process. *International review of education*, 57 (1–2), 69–87.

Oliart, P., 2008. Indigenous women's organizations and the political discourses of indigenous rights and gender equity in Peru. *Latin American and Caribbean ethnic studies*, 3, 291–308.

Quijano, A., 2000. Coloniality of power, eurocentrism and Latin America. Neplanta, views from the South, 1.3 Copyright, Duke University Press, 533–580.

Postero, N., 2013. Introduction: negotiating indigeneity. *Latin American and Caribbean studies*, 8 (2), 107–121.

Radcliffe, S., 2015. *Dilemmas of difference: indigenous women and the limits of postcolonial development policy.* London: Duke University Press.

Rivera, T., 2000. Peruvian women; indigenous women: different faces, same problems, same expectations. *Indigenous affairs*, 3, 34–37.

Rodriguez, I., *et al.*, 2016. A Proposito del Fuego: dialogo de Saberes y Justicia Cognitiva en Territorios Indigenas Culturalmente Fragiles [Dialogue of knowledge and cognitive justice in culturally weak indigenous territories]. *Trilogia, Ciencia, Tecnologia y Sociedad*, 8 (15), 97–118.

Schmelkes, S., 2011. Adult education and indigenous peoples in Latin America. *International review of education*, 57 (1–2), 89–105.

Smith, L. T., 1999. *Decolonizing methodologies: research and indigenous peoples.* London: Zed Books.

Tije, M.E., 1995. Identidad Cultural de la Mujer Indigena de la Cuenca Del Rio Madre de Dios. Jornada Sur, Mujeres e Identidad Cultural [Indigenous women's cultural identity in the Made de Dios River Basin], Cusco, January.

Trapnell, L., 2003. Some key issues in intercultural bilingual education teacher training progammes. *Comparative education*, 39 (2), 165–184.

UNESCO. 2014. *Education for All (EFA) in Latin America and the Caribbean: Assessment of progress and post-2015 challenges.* Lima Statement, Geneva: UNESCO.

UNESCO/OREALC., 2014. *UNESCO Latin America and the Caribbean Education for all 2015 Regional Review.* OREALC/2014/PI/H/1. Available from: https://unesdoc.unesco.org/search/3a765fa0-d004-43c0-a7eb-78294685fae8 [Accessed 10 September 2018].

UNESCO/OREALC., 2017. *Indigenous Knowledge and Practices in Education in Latin America.* Education 2030. Latin America Bureau of Education for Latin America and the Caribbean. Available from: https://unesdoc.unesco.org/ark:/48223/pf0000247754_eng [Accessed 20 August 2017].

Unterhalter, E., 2007. *Gender, schooling and global social justice.* London: Routledge.

Vinding, D., and Kampbel, E., 2012. *Indigenous women workers: with case studies from Bangladesh, Nepal and the Americas.* Geneva: International Labour Office, Bureau for Gender Equality.

Wade, P., 2010. *Race and ethnicity in Latin America.* 2nd ed. London: Pluto Press.

World Bank., 2015. *Indigenous Latin America in the twenty-first century: the first decade.* Washington: The World Bank Group.

[WCIC] World Conference of Indigenous Women., 2013. *Political Position Document and Plan of Action of the World's Indigenous Women.* Lima, Peru. 28–30 October. [Accessed 20 July 2018].

Adult learning for nutrition security: Challenging dominant values through participatory action research in Eastern India

Rama Narayanan and Nitya Rao

ABSTRACT

National statistics point to the severe problem of hunger and undernutrition within indigenous communities in India. Several state interventions exist, in terms of both supplementary feeding and nutritional literacy, yet not much progress is visible. This paper explores the experiences of a participatory, educational, action research programme on nutrition for indigenous women and men in Eastern India. Spanning a period of three years, it examines the adult learning approaches involved in the process and their implications for gender relations as well as improved nutritional outcomes. It became clear, that to bring change, the facilitators needed to listen to women's voices and question their own assumptions about ethnicity/caste, class and gender, as well as nutrition. Based mainly on their field reports, this paper seeks to highlight the emergent insights in terms of indigenous women's priorities, their focus on the 'collective', and emphasis on recognition and reciprocity, vis-a-vis institutions of both state and society, articulated during the process of dialogue, reflection, action and learning.

1. Introduction

Given the persistent problem of hunger, food insecurity and undernutrition in the world, as acknowledged by Goal 2 of the Sustainable Development Goals, there is today global recognition that 'nutrition literacy' can play a key role in changing outcomes. The UN Standing Committee on Nutrition notes that 'for all populations, nutrition education and social marketing are crucial components of national, municipal and community efforts for sustained improvements in food and nutrition security' (UNSCN 2010). The UN's Food and Agriculture Organization also emphasizes the need to educate people about eating the right food, besides facilitating a supportive environment for healthy balanced diet and lifestyles (FAO 2011, Ecker *et al.* 2012). Despite this acknowledgement of the importance of nutrition literacy, and a body of evidence that establishes the need for collaborative, flexible and rights-based approaches to literacy, especially when working with indigenous people (Rao and Robinson-Pant 2006), there are few programmes that specifically adopt participatory, adult learning approaches to attain this goal; a majority focus on transmission of information and knowledge on the subject.

In this paper, we focus on a three-year adult learning intervention with indigenous groups in Eastern India, launched in 2012, by an Indian NGO, the M.S Swaminathan Research Foundation (MSSRF). The main objective of the nutrition literacy programme was to create learning spaces for the community to reflect on their nutrition and health practices, specifically the status of women and children, in the context of their groups' histories and identities. The project, using participatory action research (PAR) methods, sought to facilitate a process of action and reflection by community representatives, both women and men, identified as Community Hunger Fighters (CHFs). Through this process, it hoped to help them identify, prioritize and take action, at least in areas under their control, to augment food and nutrition security at the household level. Simultaneously, it was hoped that engagement with the project facilitators would help them gain insights into other knowledge and skills, which could contribute to identifying alternate, collective pathways for claiming their entitlements. Finally, the project hoped to observe and document the transformative process at the individual and community levels as a toolkit for future interventions.

India, lauded as one of the fastest growing economies in the world, performs poorly in the field of hunger and malnutrition. The Global Hunger Index, 2017, ranked India 100 out of 119 countries, with close to 15% of the total population undernourished; 38% of under-5 children stunted and 21% wasted, placing the country is the 'serious' category (IFPRI 2017). A disaggregated poverty analysis in India, reveals that districts with higher proportions of Scheduled Tribe populations, referred to locally and in this paper as *Adivasis* ('original inhabitants' or indigenous people), are likely to have higher levels of undernutrition as well (Dubey 2009). In fact, according to the Rapid Survey on Children, 2013–2014, Scheduled Tribe children do worse than all other social groups across nutrition indicators (GOI 2014).

The Indian State, which launched a National Nutrition Mission on International Women's Day 2018, has historically provided a range of services to address the problem of hunger and malnutrition. These include social protection measures such as subsidized food grains to the poorest through the Public Distribution System, child nutrition and immunization through the Integrated Child Development Services, nutrition and health literacy through the Accredited Social Health Activists (ASHAs), amongst others. Many of these measures were converted into entitlements under the National Food Security Act, 2013 (http://dfpd.nic.in/nfsa-act.htm). Yet, the nutritional indicators for the Scheduled Tribes in India have worsened over the past three decades (NNMB 2009). Rather than addressing the institutional drivers for this situation, whether a loss of access to common property and forests, changes in cropping patterns involving a shift from millets (a nutritious grain) to eucalyptus plantations, inadequate access to resources and technology for agriculture, low productivity or male out-migration for casual wage work in urban centres (Rao and Mitra 2017), state agencies attribute this to 'Adivasi backwardness', and link it to their non-literate status.

This paper, based on an analysis of MSSRF's adult learning intervention, investigates its impacts on both gender relations and nutritional outcomes. It identifies elements of indigenous women's perspectives and knowledge that challenge researcher and elite assumptions and point to a more holistic understanding of nutrition and food security as an element of their life and lifestyle, and of social and gender equality more broadly. The next section sets out our conceptual starting points for the analysis. Section 3 discusses the methodology of the study, while Section 4 sets out the research context and implementation process. Section 5 provides insights into Adivasi women's perspectives and reflections on some of the outcomes in practice. Section 6 concludes.

2. Conceptual starting points: adult learning for nutrition security

Adult learning approaches, drawing on the work of the Brazilian educator, Paulo Freire, have for long seen adult education as a process of 'learning to question' (Freire and Macedo 1998:186); a critical understanding of reality; an understanding that emerges from dialogue, and is based on values of equity and justice. Embedded in both a critical process of action and reflection, and in everyday social practice (Lave and Wenger 1991, Street 1984), the very idea of literacy, or adult learning, becomes to change the world, to challenge unjust power relations and transform one's sense of worth (Freire and Macedo 1998: 88, Campbell and Burnaby 2001: 1). The process of working together to unpack the structural features of the experiences narrated is important since it is a way of building relationships and enhancing support, the first step towards collective decisions and action against oppression (Oakley and Marsden 1984).

In the field of nutrition, two broad approaches to adult learning are visible, namely, 'nutrition education' and 'behaviour change communication'. Both seek to transform behaviour but vary in their theoretical underpinnings. The understanding of the first, nutrition education, ranges from helping individuals, families and communities to make informed choices about food (USDA 2012), to planned, educational activities aimed at certain population groups, perceived to be practising suboptimal behaviour from a health and nutrition perspective. In fact, Mcnulty's (2013) observations on nutrition education – that the definitions range from a narrow perception of knowledge dissemination to complex descriptions of a multi-faceted discipline – seem to apply to most nutrition literacy programmes too, which focus on delivering nutrition knowledge rather than creating spaces for a broader discussion of food, health, the body, and the power relations embedded therein.

Behaviour change communication has gained popularity as a research-based consultative process for addressing knowledge, attitudes and practices (UNICEF 2012). It makes strategic use of communication to provide messages and inspiration and uses both interpersonal and mass media channels to help people adopt desired behavioural outcomes (FHI 360 2018). According to UNICEF (2012), individual behaviour change must be accompanied by social change, a process of transformation in the way society is organized and power is distributed within various social and political institutions. For this, focusing on individuals is not enough, rather institutional changes that support and promote such behaviour change are required, including the formulation of suitable policies, provision of services or infrastructure, and mechanisms and spaces that allow for questioning of social norms.

Whatever be the definition or terminology used, the key question to consider is how far such interventions enable the creation of 'learning spaces' (Kral and Schwab 2016), where people can critically reflect on their own priorities and knowledge as well as the information and messages they receive through development interventions. How far do they provide fora for questioning hierarchical power relations, reflected in the unequal access to and alienation from their natural resource base, and for women, in particular, invisibility from decision-making processes? For us, nutrition literacy was an entry point for discussions around these broader sets of issues and challenges confronting indigenous women and men in their daily lives and livelihoods. The project, therefore, was not planned to impart information, or even reading and writing skills, but rather understanding local knowledge and practices, the reasons for their disruption, the consequences for health, and possible strategies for addressing the impasse. It was not meant to transfer knowledge but rather facilitate the co-production of socially situated knowledge (Lave and Wenger 1991) through 'access to a range of social, cultural, material, textual, and technological resources and learning spaces' (Kral and Schwab 2016: 474). In striving for individual and socio-economic transformation through creating a democratic organisation (Campbell and Burnaby 2001), the structure of the programme was flexible, based on participatory and critical pedagogy, that allowed for the emergence and discussion of a range of issues.

Based on a review of fifteen interventions, Shi and Zhang (2011) confirm that successful interventions are those that are 'culturally sensitive, accessible and integrate local resources.' Yet, learner-centred approaches, involving adult learning principles, which acknowledge that the participants bring their own lifetime experiences into the learning processes, are either inadequate or missing in most nutrition education programmes (Vella 2002). People's participation is central to such approaches, however, today the term has lost some of its critical edges and been appropriated by development agencies to meet their programmatic goals (Kothari 2001, Cornwall and Jewkes 1995). Several writers have nevertheless sought to re-appropriate the concept by disaggregating its meanings from nominal and instrumental participation to processes of substantive representation and transformation (White 1996, Cleaver 2001, Mosse 2005). Participation that is transformative has empowerment as its aim; creates an enabling environment for the participants to make their own decisions and set their goals (Kesby 2005). Peoples' participation here becomes a dynamic process, moving beyond participation in development interventions to citizen engagement in local associations, campaigns, formal governance spaces, and so on, in order to make their voices heard and secure their legitimate rights (Gaventa and Barrett 2012).

Perhaps the one criticism of a participatory approach is the lack of adequate attention to gender and other power inequalities, the key to enabling reversals of knowledge and practice (Mosse 1994). Characterised by intersecting power relations of

gender, race, class, ethnicity, sexuality and age, amongst others (Collins 2009: 8), people experience social inequalities differently, they also organise and respond differently. In fact, gender equality does not imply that women and men do the same
things or engage in similar activities, but rather it seeks to ensure that they have
equal opportunities to make choices in their lives, to achieve the 'beings and doings'
they value (Sen 1999). Given that experiences are shaped by social location and position, and these relationships change over time and space; aspirations, choices and
needs are also likely to be fluid (Rao 2017). Further, cooperation is an element of
gender relations that is often overlooked (Sen 1990), yet for indigenous women in
particular, in a general context of marginality and exclusion, their survival depends
on cooperation within the household and the social group to which they belong.

With this conceptualization of adult learning, participation, and gender relations,
we turn next to a discussion of the methodology and implementation of the nutrition
literacy intervention and draw out key lessons for research, policy and practice.

3. Methodology and process

As a research methodology, participatory action research (PAR), draws on concepts
of participation and critical action-reflection, to break from the top-down, researcher-
led model of conventional research. It seeks to bring in local knowledge on equal
terms, and contribute to social transformation by challenging power hierarchies
(Chambers *et al.* 1989, Cornwall and Jewkes 1995, Campbell and Burnaby 2001). In
line with Freire's approach, the researchers/practitioners focus explicitly on
'empowering marginalized groups to take action to transform their lives' (Cornwall
and Jewkes 1995: 1671).

The specific problem we were dealing with was high levels of undernutrition
amongst the Adivasis, in particular women and children, in Koraput district, one of
the poorest and most under-developed districts in the country. While endowed with
rich biodiversity and recognized as the home of several indigenous rice varieties, sur-
veys have shown that it is one of the most food insecure districts in Odisha, with a
per-capita calorie intake of 1559 Kcal/day, and the lowest per-capita protein intake of
36 gms/day (IHP and WFP 2008). Fifty-five per cent of children below five years of
age were underweight, and 70 per cent stunted, indicating prolonged periods of inadequate food intake (Naandi Foundation 2011).

The action intervention envisaged, therefore, was to work with a group of women
and men selected by the community, who would be empowered to critically analyse
their own situation of poverty, food and nutrition inadequacy, share their reflections
with others in their community, and build strategies to achieve individual and collective wellbeing goals. A three-year process (April 2012–May 2015) of continuous action
and reflection was planned with 90 community representatives from 18 villages,
referred to as 'Community Hunger Fighters' (CHF). Communities are not homogenous but internally divided by ethnicity, class, and gender, each with their own dynamics and cultures (Table 1). Hence, to represent the heterogeneity, each village was
asked to select five persons, whom it trusted, representing different ethnicities or
caste groups present in the locality. Further, it was hypothesized that since women's

Table 1. Programme implementation sites in Koraput district, Odisha State, India.

S. No	Villages	Block	ST	SC	OBC	Others	Total
			\multicolumn{5}{c}{Households}				
1	Baiguda	Kundra	54	13	24	7	98
2	Bhatiguda	Kundra	35	51	16	8	110
3	Disguda	Kundra	9	125	120	18	272
4	Simguda	Kundra	11	28	65	4	108
5	Lachnaguda	Kundra	37	8	37	6	88
6	Maiguda	Kundra	34	22	22	0	78
7	Atariguda	Boipariguda	2	0	89	0	91
8	Baiguda	Boipariguda	107	0	29	0	136
9	Bheemaguda	Boipariguda	60	14	4	0	78
10	Bolguda	Boipariguda	42	13	31	0	86
11	Dumaria	Boipariguda	44	2	3	0	49
12	Khara	Boipariguda	0	7	58	0	65
13	Palli	Boipariguda	126	0	2	0	128
14	Cheput	Kundra	41	15	47	2	105
15	Pipri	Kundra	20	20	49	1	90
16	Gunguda	Kundra	71	5	4	0	80
17	Namguda	Kundra	39	0	0	0	39
18	Dhartiguda	Kundra	44	0	3	0	47
Total			776 (44%)	323 (18%)	603 (35%)	46 (3%)	1748

powerlessness was a key determinant of their undernourished status, sensitization of men along with women, was necessary to help communities in transforming behaviour. Nevertheless, at least two of the representatives from each village were to be women.

The process was triggered initially by a series of residential, training workshops. A range of methods was used to initiate and facilitate discussion from pictorial cards and games to case studies and role plays. These enabled participants to engage in meaningful dialogue, deliberate on personal and social values, norms and relationships, and share their experiences on the conflicts they had faced and how they handled them. The entire training was activity-based, with participants working in pairs, small groups, larger groups, interacting with people from their own and other villages, other genders, castes and ethnic groups, in order to stimulate critical thinking, dialogue and analysis (Freire 1994), while also understanding each other's perspectives. Together with the group of CHFs, the village community could then identify roles and responsibilities and jointly plan the next steps, including, if needed, engagement with wider economic, political and administrative structures, helping bridge the gap between service providers and users. So for instance, while the village development committee was seen to be responsible for the maintenance of check-dams near the village, the supervisors appointed by the Integrated Child Development Services (ICDS) were perceived as responsible for ensuring good quality and reliable service delivery.

The programme was open-ended, on the assumption that one action will flow from the other, responding to needs as they arise, and the sequence will unfold as it went along. A key element of the process was building and nurturing relationships with the CHFs and the community, based on warmth, integrity, trust and empathy. In situations of change, ambiguity and uncertainty, in particular, trust in the person who is facilitating such change is fundamental. Ethical standards in terms of honesty,

Table 2. Qualitative indicators for programme assessment.

Parameters	Evidence of outcomes
Building a community resource base for nutrition security	• critical reflection by participants • changes in attitudes and perceptions • behavioural changes towards food and nutrition security at household level • sharing of information and networking with community • effective and responsible utilization of opportunities
Community action	• networking by people to discuss issues pertaining to food and nutrition security • collective planning and action for attaining nutritional goals • challenges/changes to stereotyped gender roles and relationships • assertive action by marginalized groups such as SC/ST • forming new or utilizing existing structures for action • utilization of new opportunities with mutual cooperation & accountability • Emergence of new/collective leadership
Government entitlements	• monitoring/effective utilization of existing government programmes • demand for accountability in Govt programmes • willingness to transact with government officials • individual and collective demand for entitlements and getting them sanctioned • cooperative implementation of collective entitlements

confidentiality and openness of the project personnel were vital to breaking barriers and creating trust.

As part of the action research process, we sought to assess how far our approach to adult learning had contributed to changing everyday social practices at the household level, or empowered individuals and communities to claim state entitlements for strengthening household nutrition security. Qualitative process indicators were developed, based on participant observation – listening, seeing, questioning and analysis – to develop a sense of how power relations were being challenged or not through the process (Ellen 1984). The set of indicators are presented in Table 2. The objective was to use observation to describe the intangible, the relationships between parts, and the underlying connections and meanings (CDRA 1999).

Despite attempts to recruit women investigators, we could not find anyone with a development background, able to work independently, and more importantly, live and work locally. The lone woman candidate who applied, wanted an office rather than a field-based job, hence ultimately two male investigators were recruited, alongside the project coordinator. Each investigator worked with nine villages. They lived close to the village and visited every day, interacting, observing, facilitating and documenting the initiatives of the community. They developed good rapport in the communities, yet issues like menstrual hygiene, pregnancy or lactation, could not be explored in-depth.

The primary source of information was the monthly descriptive reports of the field staff, which were read collectively and subjected to detailed discussion. During this process, if new questions emerged, or there were gaps in understanding, these were clarified through field visits and discussions with the CHFs. Over time, the observations in these reports got sharper. For instance, if reporting a village meeting, the records included not just who and how many were present at the meeting, but nuances on the quality of participation, who spoke, what issues they raised, were views conflicting, and if so, how were they resolved. The investigators also recorded verbatim statements during their field interactions. The process of analysis started with free thinking around their observations. These were then grouped into themes such as food security, government entitlements, cropping patterns, coping with disasters, child health etc. The themes were not predetermined, so reflected the local context and changing priorities, especially with season (for example, procuring seeds was the priority before planting, raising money for festivals post-harvest). The quotes presented in this paper were selected to illustrate the nature of discussions on particular themes and the learnings they reveal. Names of villages and individuals have been changed to ensure anonymity.

4. Research context and implementation

Adivasis, belonging to the Bhumia, Paroja, Gadaba and Saura communities, considered the most 'marginal' group in Indian society, constitute over 50% of the total population of the district. The other socially downtrodden group, the Scheduled Castes or Dalits, constitute 14% of the local population (GOI, 2011). Literacy levels are generally low amongst the Adivasis in the district, more so amongst women (60% for men and 38% for women). Adult literacy levels were very low in our study villages, ranging from one per cent in two hamlets to a maximum of 41% in one. Most were small and marginal farmers, practising subsistence agriculture, growing rice, millets and some vegetables, primarily for household consumption.

The early period of relationship building and selection of the community hunger fighters was critical since much depended on the community's understanding of the programme. Initial contact with the community was primarily made by the field staff visiting each village several times and holding discussions with different stakeholders including traditional, political and caste leaders, women's groups, and other local institutions. The challenge lay in explaining the programme, as while hunger is widespread in the locality, and well understood; undernutrition is not recognisable or visible. It was therefore not easy to speak about tangible outcomes in terms of nutrition security, or indeed empowerment and transformation in their lives. It was also difficult for people to imagine that years of deprivation could be addressed through a few capacity building exercises.

In order to make the intangible tangible, the project implementers decided to undertake anthropometric assessments of children below three years of age and adolescent girls in all the villages. The results were presented in village meetings. This opened the space for discussion on the causal factors for undernutrition and the potential role the programme could play in facilitating and enriching dialogue and analysis, while also helping people take action at different levels. Following this, it was agreed that five persons would be selected from each village to participate in the programme. While the selection of men was done in a village meeting, with women attending as silent observers, selection of women took place in separate women's meetings. In terms of criteria for selection, for men, the selected person was often an acknowledged leader if possible, socially active, an effective communicator, helpful and smart. In the case of women, the person additionally was someone with older children, relatively 'free' of care burdens, and hence the family willing to allow her to participate.

The selection was not always easy as gendered perceptions of the programme came into play. Health and nutrition are generally perceived as women's issues, while production or technology are seen as relevant to men. In several villages, such as Cheput and Namguda, initially only women were selected, the argument being that men were already part of other interventions, such as use of the power tiller, promoted by the same NGO. Only after considerable debate did some men agree to join. There was also a class issue, with hunger and nutrition seen as problems of the poor; better off women were more interested in joining groups that could help them access government loans. However, finally, of the 90 selected, 39 (44%) were women and the rest men. Forty-seven participants (52%) were Adivasis, though there were variations across villages. For instance, while Cheput had an equal number of Adivasis and other communities in its population, only one of the selected persons was an Adivasi. In Simguda and Pipri, on the other hand, though dominated by other communities, most of those selected were Adivasis. Ultimately, the selection depended on perceptions of who was acceptable to the community, but also on the individual's life-stage and family obligations. In fact, class and gender biases had to be discussed and addressed throughout the process.

Following selection, a residential training programme was the initial 'trigger' activity in the reflection process followed by subsequent, demand-driven capacity building exercises. The residential training provided an opportunity for the participants to stay together, share common facilities, discuss issues pertaining to their villages and critically reflect on ways of improving the quality of life for themselves and their communities. While in real life, social spaces as well as interaction between people are defined by considerations of ethnicity, caste and gender, the residential programme created space for equal participation and learning, encouraging people to speak up freely on the existing social scenario and its impacts on their everyday lives, including their health and nutritional status.

The residential programme, completed between February and April 2013, was designed in three modules, each lasting two and a half days. A gap of 15–20 days was provided between modules, to enable participants to try and relate the learning experiences to their daily lives. The principal trainers were women while the male project personnel also participated in the discussions. The first module dealt with the concept of diets and the nutrients therein and exposed participants to various techniques used in nutritional assessment such as anthropometry, clinical and biochemical analysis. Demystification of technologies was considered essential for people to gain confidence and effectively utilize health programmes. The second module presented 21 Government entitlements, including direct food-based schemes such as the School Midday Meal and the ICDS, giving an insight into possibilities for claims-making. It also enabled discussions on peoples' participation in local self-governance mechanisms and class, caste and gender perceptions (c.f. Campbell and Burnaby 2001). The third module was envisaged to help participants identify individual as well as community goals for achieving nutrition security. Prioritization of tasks and identification of further capacity building needs were built into the programme. While most sessions were common for all participants, the theme on menstrual hygiene had to be discussed separately with the women for reasons of cultural appropriateness.

4.1. Critical reflection during residential training

Four themes were explored in-depth by the participants during the residential workshops: the relationship between nutrition and their social conditions, value systems pertaining to class, caste and gender, participation in village development and demystification of technology. In one exercise, the participants used pictures of food groups to analyse their daily diets, what they ate once in a fortnight and what they ate occasionally. During the discussion, the women realised that they were only consuming two-three food groups regularly. This also varied by caste, hence they started relating aspects of their life and the values they held to their food habits. For instance, under the influence of a Hindu priest, the Bhumia Adivasis, especially women, had taken to regular fasting, while at the same time giving up non-vegetarian food (Mitra and Rao 2018). They reflected on the fact that they hardly ate on time, especially during the peak agricultural seasons, when they were immersed in work. Lack of time for cooking meant that they managed with rice and tamarind paste (Rao and Raju, forthcoming). While they produced food, they usually sold the good quality grains in the market and ate only those of a lower grade. This exercise helped them realize how little priority they gave their health; the motivation for eating was to fill their stomachs. Poverty was not a real constraint, as there were a number of small things they could do to eat and live better, even within their own contexts and constraints. The programme personnel too, who had this far considered local availability of food to be the major determinant of food intake, learnt that people's everyday lives, their priorities, beliefs and value systems played a key role in influencing food consumption.

The nutritional assessment revealed that most of the women were undernourished. This led to a discussion of existing inequalities and how they affected women's health. Participants identified some of the common causes including working without taking rest, especially during pregnancy, getting back to work within a few days of delivery and lack of health care during pregnancy. Further, women identified poor quality drinking water and lack of sanitation as important determinants of poor health and nutrition. As one woman participant remarked 'All our problems will go away if we have good water. Either we or the girl children are always doing the job. It is high time our authorities gave us water'. The issue that touched them the most was of young child undernutrition. Several participants said, 'while we know children have to be cared for, we never knew that undernutrition during this period can cause so much damage throughout life;' 'We never knew birthweight was so important'; 'Children are our greatest wealth. We cannot let anything happen to them'; or 'Both male and female babies are affected if women are weak. The welfare of the entire society rests on the welfare of women'.

The subject of toilets generated the most heat between women and men participants. While everyone agreed that open defecation posed a public health hazard, men initially argued that the lack of toilets was a problem only at night. However, women argued that they faced several hardships, such as loss of modesty, hygiene issues during menstruation and difficulty during pregnancy and lactation. During the course of the discussion men agreed that 'we never thought of it this way till now'.

Since nutritional status assessment of all participants was carried out during the residential training it helped to understand the science behind the technologies. For some, it proved an opportunity to overcome fears. The child growth chart generated a lot of interest among women and the interpretation of its plotting and marking were eagerly sought. The State Coordinator of the ICDS gave an overview of the programme, leading to a lively discussion. The participants raised questions on provisioning, implementation and grievance redressal mechanisms. In the final module, the participants developed several messages and action points relating to sanitation, complementary feeding, empowerment of women and the need for unity for village development.

4.2. Further capacity building

As an offshoot of the residential training, participants identified further training needs, and capacity building exercises continued throughout the project period. These ranged from exposure visits to community models for nutrition security and technical training in agriculture to interfaces with the Collector and other Government officials to better understand how entitlements could be secured. A total of 12 sessions were organized, the purpose ultimately was to expand the range of possibilities and strategies open to them, both individual and collective.

These sessions had a further aim, namely, to provide learning spaces to additional people from the community, as the originally selected CHFs could not always attend all the training programmes for a host of reasons. Apart from events such as marriages and deaths, many women in particular encountered personal problems such as illness of a family member, or non-cooperation by families. Given the precarity of their lives, sudden changes in economic status were also common. Paro Majhi, a woman CHF, had borrowed money, and as she was unable to repay it on time, she had to serve as a 'bonded labour' for a year at the home of the moneylender. She lost all control over her own labour and time and could not participate as a result. There was also an issue of interests and preferences. Trainings on seed treatment were of particular interest to women since seed conservation was considered a woman's job, while the *Mali* community, traditional vegetable cultivators, took a lot of interest in discussions around vegetable cultivation. Similarly, women's participation fell in exposure visits, as they could not stay away from their homes for more than three days at a stretch. Yet the CHFs soon became quite strategic, so when a visit was organized to a water and sanitation programme, they wanted the elected local government representatives to accompany them, as they could then follow up on such public works.

In short, the entire training programme, whether residential or follow-up, was organized in consultation with the selected CHFs. While 90 CHFs were selected as participants at the start, due to replacements and additions, a total of 155 persons participated over the course of the programme. Women's participation increased from an initial 39 to 69, with the ratio of women and men becoming almost equal in most villages.

5. Indigenous women's perspectives on food and nutrition security

Through the process of dialogue, discussion and critical reflection, the participants enhanced the scope of nutrition security, to move beyond food availability, access and absorption (FAO 1996), to include concepts of consumption and a healthy lifestyle. As some of the women participants said, 'what is the point in growing food if we do not eat ourselves.' Reminiscing about eating stale and leftover food instead of fresh food, one male participant remarked, 'We thought satisfying our hunger was enough. Now we are conscious of bringing in dietary diversity and eating all seasonal foods'. While analyzing food habits, it emerged that Adivasi women, as compared to other caste groups, had greater knowledge about 'wild' or uncultivated foods and the potential these offered for enhancing dietary diversity. However, they rued the decline in forest cover, and the gradual take-over of forest lands, and also their own uplands, where they earlier grew millets and vegetables, by eucalyptus plantations. Eucalyptus brought in cash incomes, but this was used for bulk expenses like repairing their house or paying school fees. They lost a source of food and nutrition (Rao and Mitra 2017). Interestingly, and surprisingly for us, in the discussions around consumption, Adivasi women suggested activating their village forest protection committees, as access to forests and common property resources they felt was central to their nutrition security.

Women further opined that lifestyle patterns such as chewing of tobacco and alcoholism posed potential health hazards. A critical discussion took place on this issue between the women and men participants. Men challenged women on the consumption of alcohol, claiming that women too drank. The women replied that they drank neither on a daily basis nor spent an entire day's wages or the household grains on liquor and never to such an extent that they were dysfunctional. What was clearly beginning to emerge during the dialogue and reflection was that nutrition security was not just a technical issue, nor was it an individual one. It needed attention at both relational and collective levels, in values, practices and 'interfaces' with the state and economy. Women realised that they could not bring change on their own, so strategically sought to bring in male leaders, staff and CHFs, hoping to 'enrol' their support for their own projects (Long and Long 1992). They invited those men whom they could trust in their meetings, and in one village secured their support for raising the issue of childcare with the local administration. They also sought their support where larger issues such as forest conservation or claiming accountability from state services were involved.

From the recorded observations, we analysed the changes visible at the individual level of the CHFs and their households, but also the community, especially the steps taken towards challenging the existing 'doxa' and transforming norms around gendered responsibilities and voice (c.f. Bourdieu 1977). We focus next on women's strategies for building bridges with their own men, as well as women of other groups.

5.1. Changing practices: individual and collective

At the individual level, 23 observations were recorded under three dimensions of nutrition identified during the workshops, namely, actions for improving dietary diversity, personal hygiene practices, and child health and nutrition. Within each of these dimensions, the specific activities varied, in line with the resources available and the possibilities the CHFs saw for making changes in their lives. Thirteen observations pertained to efforts to consume a diverse diet, but each of them was different. While several changed their agricultural practices and started growing more vegetables and fruits, one woman had to get her land back from lease for this purpose, one landless CHF had to lease in some land, and another landless woman started growing vegetables in the foundation of the house she was constructing. She said 'now it is going to be monsoon. No construction will take place for a few more months. I might as well use the space for growing vegetables for my consumption.' One CHF brought in crop rotation in her field and also started tending to the kitchen garden, while a fifth, who was selling mangoes and papayas, started to keep some for her own consumption.

With assured security of land, men tended to focus on improving the productivity of their agriculture. Two of them had taken steps to ensure irrigation facilities to enable cultivation throughout the year. Women's strategies were different, as not only did they not have independent land titles, but their customary rights to uplands too were being rapidly eroded (by eucalyptus plantations). Women were additionally burdened with the responsibility for domestic and care work. Yet the CHFs, women and men, were keen to compare notes and support each other's practices in whatever way possible.

In the second area concerning personal and environmental hygiene, handwashing and keeping the house clean were identified by several of the CHFs as central to improving nutrition. They began using terms such as 'insist on hand washing', 'very strict about hand washing with the family,' and so on. One of the male CHFs from Simguda took a lot of pride in his action, noting that 'I brought the childcare (Anganwadi) worker and showed her how clean the house was'. Mangal Paroja of Baiguda got his child weighed at the Anganwadi centre, and when the child was found to be severely underweight, started looking for solutions. Here the traditional image of the child being 'women's business' was deconstructed, with men beginning to play active roles in child health and nutrition, albeit through their engagement with external institutions, be it the Anganwadi or the health centre. While men perhaps had not yet started contributing, at least equally, to the performance of the daily chores of cooking, cleaning, bathing children and washing, they were beginning to acknowledge that these were important tasks for nutrition security and needed to be recognized and supported. Giving visibility to the unequal gender division of labour and initiating critical discussions around care work as central to nutrition security, was a first step in redistributing work and responsibilities more equitably within households and communities (c.f. Razavi 2007, Rao 2018).

The uniqueness of these actions and the manner in which they were done reiterate the limitless possibilities of reflective action that is not likely to be facilitated in a formal education programme. While men's growing engagement in child nutrition and health was a positive development, it also brought out the structural constraints confronting women. First, while each village had several women's groups that were supposed to facilitate women's participation in social and developmental activities, they were only perceived as loan servicing institutions and not as platforms for empowerment. Secondly, women were unable to participate meaningfully in village meetings, as they were relegated to the back and their voices remained unheard. Finally, nutrition interventions by development agencies generally stereotype gender roles, providing men with technological training, and women cooking demonstrations. The curriculum and pedagogy is generally inflexible, and fails to seriously engage with indigenous women's knowledge, or indeed priorities and practices.

After the residential training, the women CHFs started discussing issues of health and nutritional status of children and adolescent girls in the women's group meetings. Visualizing child health (using the growth chart) as central to community welfare, they collectively identified village development issues such as safe drinking water, sanitation, clean environment, functioning schools and child care centres, basic infrastructure including good roads, improved agricultural production, addressing the problems of alcoholism and unemployment, in this order of priority, as key inputs towards nutrition security. Some women's group leaders, CHFs and women ward members started mobilizing women in large numbers to attend village level meetings.

The CHFs of Cheput wanted to revive the defunct village development committee (VDC). With the support of the women's groups and the male CHF, they mobilised both the women and men to attend a meeting in July 2013. Of the 37 who attended, 29 were women. In the meeting, new office bearers were elected, with a mandate to collect monthly subscriptions for village development work. They decided to demand better facilities for the local childcare centre, revive activities undertaken by the Forest Protection Committee, and start a seed and grain bank for collecting, storing and lending seeds and grains to needy households. In this entire process, two distinct shifts could be identified. First, through a conscious process of dialogue, organising and decision making, a male-dominated peoples' institution saw the control of resources shifting from men to women.

The second shift related to the meaningful, and not just equal, participation of women in changing the social reality of their lives, addressing areas of concern they had identified. On April 1st 2014, SHG (self-help group) members met and decided to ask nine families in Dhaniguda village, preparing and selling country liquor, to close down their shops, given the nuisance created by their clients. The women of Khara village took the initiative to organize other women in their own and neighbouring villages. On the 3rd morning, 35 women from these villages asked the concerned families to stop commercial sale of liquor, however, the families refused. On 5th April, a large number of women again met the families, who now asked for a week's time to wind up their operations. After waiting 10 days, when there was no sign of closure, about 100 women marched to the premises where liquor was being brewed and broke the pots. While four families stopped all operations, one continued defiantly. In May 2014, a large number of women along with some male villagers proceeded to the Sub-collector's office to lodge a complaint. On his advice, they filed a police complaint and waited for further action. Not just did the Adivasi women, led by the CHFs, take a lead, but were also able to gain male support in order to take their action beyond the boundaries of their village.

Great priority was given to improving the delivery of childcare services at the Government-run Anganwadi centres through regular monitoring, conflict resolution through dialogue and by providing material and physical support to the personnel. Parvathy Majhi, the woman CHF of Palli, moved to a house close to the Anganwadi and started monitoring the services, ensuring that the worker, who used to come once a week, came regularly. In fact, some of the male CHFs, conscious of their own privileged position, and recognising the constraints faced by women, actively pursued the implementation of the ICDS, recognizing its significance for child care, health and nutrition, while their women were working.

All eighteen villages prepared 'action plans' for ensuring nutrition security wherein they gave voice to both individual and collective entitlements. This required mobilization of traditional leaders, elected representatives, members of village committees as well as women and men from individual households. Women used the SHG space to discuss their priorities and agendas and attended village meetings in large numbers. Male CHFs, such as Arjun, who owned a teashop in Dumaria, not only started discussing nutrition issues with his clients but also prevailed upon the community members to accommodate women's needs in the village development plan. They convened village meetings at times convenient for women and invited the women CHFs to address the gathering. As one male CHF put it, 'it served two purposes, one in helping women to get a leadership role and the other to avoid ridicule from fellow villagers that 'men' chose to speak about issues of childcare and sanitation'.

Several male CHFs took an active role in involving women in village development issues including when applying for Government entitlements such as toilets. While very few households had toilet facilities at the start of the project, 64% across the 18 villages had applied for Government subsidy to build toilets by the end. During the project period, seven villages secured the sanction and in three the constructions were completed. One finds here growing cooperation and indeed relations of respect between women and men in dealing with common problems that affect their wellbeing.

Women also started creating their own spaces, supporting each other in their personal lives. Samari and Ghasma in Baiguda actively reached out to other women, resolving conflicts between husband and wife, and in the process gained considerable respect. Clearly here learning in one sector was being internalised and applied to all aspects of women's lives. Encouraged to air their views and engage in dialogue, they also sought respect and dignity in their everyday lives. The learning was not just about improving indicators but embraced issues of power and inequality more broadly.

6. Some tentative conclusions

This paper has presented some insights into adult learning programmes for indigenous women (and men) that facilitate processes of action and reflection through examining a nutrition literacy project. Technical fixes have clearly not worked, as evident in the case of India, where food and nutrition interventions have existed for several decades. For change to occur, it is important to understand and give voice to indigenous women's perspectives and knowledge through flexible and responsive learning approaches, as nutrition security entails a complex interwoven web of technical, social, ethical and political considerations.

The participatory action research project, involving indigenous women and men as 'Community Hunger Fighters' highlighted the links between adult learning, gendered power relations, and action for nutrition security, be it with respect to control over common property resources, addressing women's time and work burdens, or giving them an equal say in decision-making at the community level. Women resented the fact that state institutions responded to men's complaints on the poor functioning of the *Anganwadis*, for instance, rather than their own, yet in the short-term, they sought male support for attaining these goals. While 'critically conscious' of the issues they confronted (Freire 1994), they were able to effectively strategise to ensure the outcomes they desired. Empowerment here was central to their learning processes.

While the discourses on nutrition education and behaviour change do speak of social transformation, this vision needs to be put into practice as a bottom-up, collective process, contextually and spatially embedded, addressing local power dynamics by first 'naming (it) within educational settings' (Campbell and Burnaby 2001:3). Since communities are not homogenous, the project underscored the need for representative participation based on class, caste and gender, consciously maximizing opportunities for the 'marginalized', while at the same time, 'enrolling' those with more power to help fulfil these 'projects' (Long and Long 1992). While 'participation' may be critiqued, it continues to provide spaces for learning, collective action, and resisting structures of oppression (Kesby 2005) and was central to the success of the intervention.

Initiating collective community action needed a trigger and this was provided by the CHFs sharing the ideas generated and discussed in the residential training in formal group and village meetings, informally in tea shops, agricultural fields and in places where people converged, as well as with individual households. Their efforts were manifest in different planes, namely, in revitalizing existing social institutions to move towards a broader development agenda sensitive to nutrition security, in demanding and utilizing legal entitlements to food and nutrition, and in challenging existing social norms with regard to caste, class, gender and leadership. A key adult learning principle is the relevance of the issue to the lives of the community, women and men, and hence their desire to put their learning into practice.

Learning here incorporated both formal and informal acquisition; it developed a meaning and purpose in their everyday lives through the visible link to health and wellbeing, especially of their children. Multimodal forms of communication were used from anthropometric measurements and growth charts to more open-ended discussions of social problems, labour arrangements and resource access. While the structural power of the state and markets are not easy to confront, we hope that the creation of learning spaces facilitated by the CHFs, will help forge partnerships to enable empowered action for a better life, including meeting their goals of nutrition security.

Acknowledgements

This paper is derived from the report entitled 'Towards Nutrition Security – Community Hunger Fighters Programme' authored by Rama Narayanan, Tusar Ranjan Nayak, Sanjay Kumar Swain and Ramachandra Tosh that outlines an adult nutrition literacy project implemented in Odisha by the M S Swaminathan Research Foundation with financial support from Global Alliance for Improved Nutrition (GAIN). Insights from subsequent work on women in agriculture and nutrition in the same area under the research programme on Leveraging Agriculture for Nutrition in South Asia has been drawn on to set the context. Apart from the CHFs and other community members who shared with us their views and insights, we would like to thank the two anonymous reviewers and the editors of the special issue for their comments.

Disclosure statement

No potential conflict of interest was reported by the authors.

Funding

This study was implemented in Odisha by the M S Swaminathan Research Foundation with financial support from Global Alliance for Improved Nutrition (GAIN). The contextual analysis for this paper was also supported by Leveraging Agriculture for Nutrition in South Asia (LANSA), an international research consortium funded by UK aid from the UK Government (Department for International Development).

ORCID

Nitya Rao http://orcid.org/0000-0002-6318-0147

References

Bourdieu, P., 1977. *Outline of a theory of practice*. Cambridge: Cambridge University Press.
Campbell, P., and Burnaby, B., 2001. *Participatory practices in adult education*. New York and London: Routledge.
Chambers, R., Pacey, A., and Thrupp, L. A., 1989. *Farmer first: farmer innovation and agricultural research*. London: Intermediate Technology Publications.
Cleaver, F., 2001. Institutions, agency and the limitations of participatory approaches to development. *In:* B. Cooke and U. Kothari, eds. *Participation: the new tyranny*. London: Zed Books, 36–55.
Collins, P.H., 2009. The new politics of community. *American sociological review*, 75 (1), 7–30.
Community Development Research Association (CDRA). 1998–1999. Development Practitioners - Artists of the Invisible, Annual Report.
Cornwall, A., and Jewkes, R., 1995. What is participatory research? *Social science and medicine (1982)*, 41 (12), 1667–1676.

Dubey, A., 2009. Poverty and under-nutrition among scheduled tribes in India: a disaggregated analysis IGIDR proceedings/project reports series PP-062-13. Mumbai: IGIDR. Available from: http://www.igidr.ac.in/pdf/publication/PP-062-13.pdf

Ecker, O., Bresinger, C., and Pauw, K., 2012. Growth is good, but is not enough to improve Nutrition. *In:* S. Fan and R. Pandya-Lorch, eds. *Reshaping agriculture for nutrition and health.* Washington D C: International Food Policy Research Institute. Available from: www.ifpri.org/sites/default/files/publications/oc69.pdf

Ellen, R. F., 1984. *Ethnographic research.* London: Academic Press.

Food and Agricultural Organization of the United Nations (FAO), 1996. *Declaration on world food security.* Rome: FAO.

FAO, 2011. The state of food and agriculture, 2010-11. Women in agriculture: closing the gender gap for development. Rome: Food and Agriculture Organisation.

FHI 360, 2018. A 360 degree approach to social and behaviour change. Available from: https://www.fhi360.org/resource/360-degree-approach-social-and-behavior-change

Freire, A. M., and D. Macedo, eds, 1998. *The Paolo Freire reader.* New York: Continuum.

Freire, P., 1994. *Pedagogy of hope: reliving pedagogy of the oppressed.* New York: Continuum.

Gaventa, J., and Barrett, G., 2012. Mapping the outcomes of citizen engagement. *World development,* 40 (12), 2399–2410.

GOI (Government of India), 2011. Census of India Population of Koraput District of Odisha, Census office. Available from: https://www.census2011.co.in/census/district/422-koraput.html [Accessed 20 Nov 2018].

GOI (Government of India), 2014. Rapid Survey on Children 2013-2014 Fact Sheets. Ministry of Women and Child Development. New Delhi. Available from: http://wcd.nic.in/acts/rapid-survey-children-rsoc-2013-14 [Accessed 20 Nov 2018].

IFPRI, 2017. Global hunger index: the inequalities of hunger. International Food Policy Research Institute. Washington D.C. Available from: http://www.ifpri.org/publication/2017-global-hunger-index-inequalities-hunger [Accessed 10 Dec 2018].

IHP (Institute for Human Development) and WFP (World Food Programme) 2008. Food Insecurity Atlas of Rural Orissa. WFP, New Delhi. Available from: https://www.wfp.org/content/india-food-security-atlas-rural-odisha-2008 [Accessed 20 Nov 2018].

Kesby, M., 2005. Retheorizing empowerment-through-participation as a performance in space: beyond tyranny to transformation. *Signs,* 30 (4), 2037–2065.

Kothari, U., 2001. Power, knowledge and social control in participatory development. *In:* B., Cooke and U. Kothari, eds. *Participation: the new tyranny.* London: Zed Books, 139–152.

Kral, I., and Schwab, R.G., 2016. A space to learn: a community-based approach to meaningful adult learning and literacy in remote indigenous Australia. *Prospects,* 46 (3–4), 465–477,

Lave, J., and Wenger, E., 1991. *Situated learning: legitimate peripheral participation.* Cambridge: Cambridge University Press.

Long, N., and Long, A., 1992. *Battlefields of knowledge: the interlocking of theory and practice in social research and development.* London: Routledge.

Mcnulty, J., 2013. Challenges and issues in nutrition education. Rome. Nutrition education and consumer awareness group. Food and Agricultural Organization of the United Nations. Available from: www.fao.org/ag/human nutrition/nutrition education/en/ [Accessed 20 Nov 2018].

Mitra, A., and Rao, N., 2018. Gender, food-cultures, nutrition and religious nationalism. *Lansa Draft Paper.* MSSRF. Chennai. (under review).

Mosse, D., 1994. Authority, gender and knowledge: theoretical reflections on the practice of participatory rural appraisal. *Development and change,* 25 (3), 497–526.

Mosse, D., 2005. *Cultivating development: an ethnography of aid policy and practice.* London: Pluto Press.

Naandi Foundation 2011. HUNGama: Fighting hunger and malnutrition. The HUNGama Survey Report, Hyderabad.

National Nutrition Monitoring Bureau (NNMB). 2009. Diet and nutritional status of tribal population and prevalence of hypertension amongst adults: Report on second repeat survey. NNMB Technical Report No. 25. Hyderabad: National Institute of Nutrition.

Oakley, P., and Marsden, D., 1984. *Approaches to participation in rural development.* Geneva: ACC Task Force on Rural Development, ILO.

Rao, N., and Robinson-Pant, A., 2006. Adult education and indigenous people: addressing gender in policy and practice. *International journal of educational development*, 26 (2), 209–223.

Rao, N., and Mitra, A., 2017. Understanding transitions in gendered work and care in a fragile ecosystem of Eastern India. Paper presented at workshop on 'Sustainability, Ecology and Care,' Friedrich Ebert Stiftung, Berlin. Jan 19–20, 2017.

Rao, N., and Raju, S., forthcoming. Gendered time, seasonality and nutrition: Insights from two Indian districts. Feminist Economics (accepted for publication)

Rao, N., 2017. Assets, agency and legitimacy: towards a relational understanding of gender equality policy and practice. *World development*, 95, 43-54. http://dx.doi.org/10.1016/j.worlddev.2017.02.018.

Rao, N., 2018. Global agendas, local norms: mobilizing around unpaid care and domestic work in Asia. *Development and change*, 49 (3), 735–758.

Razavi, S., 2007. 'The Political and Social Economy of Care in a Development Context'. UNRISD Gender and Development Programme Paper 3. Geneva: United Nations Research Institute for Social Development.

Sen, A., 1990. Gender and cooperative conflicts. *In:* Irene Tinker, ed. *Persistent inequalities: women and world development.* New York: Oxford University Press, 123–149.

Sen, A., 1999. *Development as freedom.* Oxford, UK: Oxford University Press.

Shi, L., and Zhang, J., 2011. Recent evidence of the effectivenesss of educational interventions for improving complementary feeding practices in developing countries. *Journal of tropical paediatrics*, 57 (2), 91–98.

Street, B. V., 1984. *Literacy in theory and practice.* Cambridge: Cambridge University Press.

UNICEF (United Nations International Children's Emergency Fund) 2012. Communication for Development, Behaviour and Social Change. Available from: www.unicef.org/cbsc/index_42352.html [Accessed 15 Nov 2018].

UNSCN (United Nations Standing Committee on Nutrition). 2010. Progress in Nutrition. 6th Report on the World Nutrition Situation, Geneva.

USDA 2012. Nutrition website, National Institute of Food and Agriculture. Available from www.nifa.usda.gov/nutrition.cfm [Accessed 15 Nov 2018].

Vella, J., 2002. *Learning to listen, learning to teach: the power of dialogue in educating adults.* San Francisco, CA: Jossey-Bass. (Cited in Mcnulty J 2013. Challenges and issues in nutrition education. Rome. Nutrition education and consumer awareness group. Food and Agricultural Organization of the United Nations).

White, S.C., 1996. Depoliticising development - the uses and abuses of participation. *Development in practice*, 6 (1), 6–15.

Indigenous women's perceptions of the Mexican bilingual and intercultural education model

Ulrike Hanemann (iD)

ABSTRACT

This article examines perceptions of indigenous women of the *Bilingual Indigenous Education Model for Life and Work* (MIB) programme which the Mexican Government initiated a decade ago as an alternative route for indigenous youth and adults into basic education. Programme objectives include the promotion of equal access to quality basic education by reducing gender and ethnic disparities and the empowerment of indigenous peoples. A particular focus on the gender dimension of the MIB programme is not only mandatory because of the existing gender disparities in education – two-thirds of indigenous adults without literacy skills are women, – but also because the vast majority of its participants are women (92%). Therefore, this article intends to explore the empowering potential of the programme. The analysis is drawing from a diagnostic study conducted in 2012 considering enabling and constraining factors of the MIB programme by using four analytical dimensions – acceptance, appropriation, relevance and usefulness. The analysis of the findings, resulting from discussions with indigenous women, which includes an additional gender dimension, reveal a range of issues that need to be addressed in order to better exploit the empowering potential of the MIB programme for indigenous women.

Introduction

While language is considered a key element of indigenous people's cultural identity, when it comes to education, language rights of indigenous peoples are far from being realised. This undervaluing of minority languages and cultures in education, in turn, reflects the broader context where rapid changes in the economy, the nature of work, the role of media and digitisation, as well as migration and incessantly advancing urbanisation, put strong pressures on indigenous populations to linguistically and culturally assimilate and integrate (UNDP 2004). For organisations such as UNESCO (2003, 2006), bilingual or multilingual approaches to teaching and learning are considered central to intercultural education and a means of furthering social and gender equality. In recognition of the important role that languages play in the achievement of indigenous peoples' rights, the United Nations have declared 2019 the International Year of Indigenous Languages.

Latin America is home to approximately 50 million indigenous peoples, about 10% of the total population. At about 11 million people Mexico has the largest indigenous population in the region. Indigenous women living in rural areas are often the most marginalised, are denied education and other public services at much higher rates than non-indigenous women, and suffer from higher incidences of poverty (UNDP 2004). Access to education and proficiency in the dominant language play a crucial role for indigenous women's empowerment and participation in the society (UNDP 2013), yet educational data for adult literacy and basic education – where disaggregated by sex, ethnicity and geographic location – shows the greatest disparities for rural indigenous women. While the gender parity index in Latin America indicates that some 56% of adults reported as non-literate in the region are women, those countries with large indigenous populations (i.e. Bolivia, Ecuador, Guatemala, Mexico, Paraguay and Peru) show a marked relative difference in favour of men (UNESCO/OREALC 2004).

Women's literacy is usually bound up with issues of equity, violence, health, girls' and family education, and community involvement (Eldred 2013, Robinson-Pant 2014, Hanemann 2015). This also applies to indigenous women who face discrimination compounded by gender, economic status, and ethnicity. Although indigenous women face particular challenges, they are also active change agents with essential roles in passing on indigenous cultures, languages and traditional knowledge to future generations (Commission on the Status of Women of the UN Economic and Social Council 2017).

This paper will analyse the perceptions of indigenous women participating in the *Bilingual Indigenous Education Model for Life and Work* (MIB)[1] programme initiated by the Mexican Government's National Institute for Adult Education (INEA) a decade ago as an alternative route for indigenous youth and adults to gain access to basic education. The programme's objectives include the promotion of equal access to quality basic education by reducing gender and ethnic disparities and the empowerment of indigenous peoples to (1) be self-reliant and improve their living standards; (2) facilitate their integration into mainstream Mexican society; and (3) value and preserve their culture and cultural identity. This article focuses on the gender dimension of the MIB programme because of the existing gender disparities in education – two-thirds of indigenous adults without literacy skills in Mexico are women, – but also because 92 per cent of its participants are women (SEP/INEA 2012).

As a staff of the UNESCO Institute for Lifelong Learning (UIL), I provided technical assistance to the development of a diagnostic study of the MIB programme commissioned by the Mexican National Institute for Adult Education (INEA)[2] to UNESCO Mexico in 2012. I participated in the analysis of the findings from field work conducted by the national non-governmental organisation Tanesque and was involved in meetings with INEA, UNESCO Mexico, Tanesque and national experts. The study identified the perceptions of the main actors on different aspects of the programme. This was done using four key dimensions namely: acceptance, appropriation, relevance and usefulness.[3] Tanesque combined quantitative methods – with 951 MIB personnel participating in a standardised questionnaire – and qualitative methods – in-depth interviews and group discussions with indigenous technical personnel and learners. This article focuses on the qualitative data collected and compiled by Tanesque (UNESCO Mexico 2012) on perceptions of indigenous women on the MIB programme. Drawing from this data and other background documents on the MIB programme, this article applies a gender lens, in addition to the four key dimensions of analysis in the study (acceptance, appropriation, relevance and usefulness), in order to explore the empowering potential of the programme. The gender dimension was not an explicit aim at the design and field work stages of the diagnostic study.

With the overall aim to explore the empowering potential of the MIB programme for indigenous women, this article asks: how were levels of acceptance, appropriation, relevance and usefulness of the programme reflected in the perceptions of the indigenous women; what challenges does the implementation of the MIB programme pose; and what indications are given by the participants to suggest ways of improving the programme in the future to better contribute to their empowerment?

Bilingual and intercultural approaches to gender equality in adult literacy and education

Indigenous cultures and languages continue to be marginalised in Mexican society where there is a strong drive towards assimilation of indigenous identities. While an analysis of policy documents demonstrate a commitment of the government to enabling educational access through the languages spoken by the indigenous groups, the current education sector plan (2013–2018) does not include specific actions for indigenous groups nor does it raise the question of the language of literacy[4] (Robinson 2015).

While the academic research and debate on the 'intercultural bilingual education model' in Mexico remains generally restricted to formal primary education for children (e.g. Hamel 2016), in recent years the indigenous sociolinguistic settings have become increasingly diverse (López and Sichra 2007). This requires flexible educational responses that are adaptable to the needs in both rural and urban contexts with indigenous learners who are monolingual and bilingual (at different levels). Some scholars suggest the articulation of inclusive education with interculturality into a new model that subsumes indigenous learners under the category of vulnerable groups to be integrated into the mainstream education system (Mendoza Zuany 2017, 2018). However, in adult literacy and basic education, issues of motivation, persistence and relevance of learning play a greater role, and this requires tailoring the programmes to the expressed needs and interests of specific groups of indigenous learners.

Before examining the Mexican bilingual and intercultural education model, this section looks at some of the key concepts framing approaches to bilingual and intercultural programmes and meanings of indigenous literacy and women's empowerment. Furthermore, this section demonstrates the interrelationships between literacy, language, interculturality and indigenous women's empowerment which are crucial for the subsequent analysis and discussion.

A study of indigenous[5] adult literacy and education policies and programmes in seven Latin American countries with indigenous populations (López and Hanemann 2009) showed that despite the existence of culturally and linguistically sensitive legislations, policies and educational reforms, the majority of these programmes did not transcend the discourse and symbolic spheres to make their way into application. Measures to improve educational quality rather focussed on effectiveness and efficiency at the expense of cultural, linguistic and social relevance, equity, integral personal development and empowerment of learners. Youth and adult education was neglected in most countries and the lack of adequate investment contributed to the poor quality that related services frequently suffer from.

The different ways indigenous children and adults learn has been well-researched in the case of the Tseltales, one of the two Mexican indigenous groups in the diagnostic study analysed in this article. Their learning and knowledge creation takes place 'through the soul' (King 1999), engaging 'souls and body' (Pitarch 2000), and with 'the joy of the heart' (Urdapilleta Carrasco and Parra Vázquez 2016). Learning is described to happen even without teaching: it is necessary that everybody becomes 'wise by him- or herself' (Maurer Ávalos 2011). 'Wisdom of the heart' is acquired in a lifelong process of experiential learning by each person. This is an interactive process where people help each other through questions, discussions and collective reflections to better observe, interpret and understand the reality (Maurer Ávalos 2011).

Analysis of existing research evidence further shows that language, ethnicity, gender and poverty can combine to produce complex patterns of compounded disadvantage and extremely high risk of exclusion (GEMR 2016). The use of a learner's mother tongue, their first or home language, as the language of instruction has been found to have a positive impact on learning across the board (GEMR 2016 and The World Bank 2018). To systematically relegate indigenous languages to performing simple bridging functions to the dominant language is seen by critics as a step towards killing those languages and with them an important dimension of indigenous identities (Skutnabb-Kangas 2001). This subtractive approach to language learning contrasts with an additive approach, whereby learning a new language complements and is not detrimental to the first or mother language(s).

Other researchers highlight the importance of oral practices in indigenous communication, knowledge, learning and teaching and that indigenous learners, who are often oral bilinguals, should acquire bilingual literacy through a 'simultaneous or concurrent process' whereby they may 'develop their interpretative and productive capacities, as well as their creativity in general, in their two languages' (López 2001:220). However, orality should not be seen in opposition to literacy. They rather complement and enrich each other.

There is evidence that in multilingual and multi-ethnic contexts particularly women benefit from mother-tongue instruction in non-formal settings However, often, existing gender hierarchies determine who has access to which languages, and which languages are used in domains of social, economic and political power. Evidence (Hanemann and Scarpino 2016) indicates that language policy and, specifically, the language of instruction appropriate for literacy and adult education programmes, should, therefore, be based both on cultural and ethnic factors and on gender relationships and perspectives.

Interculturality is a paradigm that has emerged in multicultural societies as an alternative to assimilation and integration in multicultural societies. The UNDP understands 'interculturality' as a process of building a horizon of living together between cultures or peoples. This horizon is rather a mutual enrichment while conserving ones' own identity rather than a common culture (UNDP 2013).

It is based on the recognition of diversity and multiple identities. Intercultural education is seen as 'indispensable to deconstruct the prevalent racism in our societies' and genuine intercultural dialogue can only work if conducted in condition of equality between parties (Schmelkes 2005). Schmelkes (2006) argues that interculturality should be applied as a guiding principle in all education including adult education, not only for indigenous learners but for the whole population. While there is some research on the integration of intercultural education in national legislation and education reforms (Aikman 1997, López and Hanemann 2009, Schmelkes *et al.* 2009), as well as on intercultural education as a discourse (Dietz and Mateos Cortés 2011), there is less evidence on which methodological approaches have worked best in adult literacy and education and what has been the impact of such educational measures in Latin America.

In general terms, empowerment can be seen as a multi-dimensional social process that helps people gain control over their own lives. In the context of literacy, empowerment has been related to 'the set of feelings, knowledge, and skills that produce the ability to participate in one's social environment and affect the political system' (Stromquist 2009:2). This ability comprises cognitive, economic, political and psychological dimensions. The latter dimension, reflecting personal feelings of being 'competent, worthy of better conditions, and capable of taking action on their own behalf', often acts as a prerequisite for the other dimensions (Stromquist 2009:2). The analytical categories used to analyse the Mexican MIB programme in the diagnostic study, – acceptance, appropriation, relevance and usefulness, – can be framed within this concept of empowerment.

Empowerment has been studied indirectly, by documenting feelings and perceptions to determine levels of self-esteem, self-confidence, and self-efficacy, and data is typically based on self-report (Stromquist 2009:2). Research evidence (e.g. Infante 2000, Prins 2008) supports a correlation between literacy and empowerment. However, according to Stromquist, literacy most commonly leads to psychological empowerment, while the cognitive, political and economic dimensions of empowerment are less likely to emerge. In order to realise the full empowering potential of a literacy programme leading to an 'empowered identity', adult literacy needs to be reconceptualised in its entirety 'from programme design to instructional approaches, from objectives to criteria for successful impact, from instructor/facilitator training to provision of graduated reading materials' (Stromquist 2009:10).

Recent research studies make a clear case for the provision of literacy learning opportunities for women, based on evidence of how literacy and learning can lead to empowerment. However, there are many challenges that must be addressed before women can access and make better use of such opportunities including socio-economic barriers to education, social norms, traditional beliefs and cultural expectations as well as distance and insecurity (UNESCO 2012, Eldred 2013, Robinson-Pant 2014). Feminist scholars have defined empowerment of women 'as a process through which structures of power can be identified, negotiated and transformed', and have recognised that 'literacy and education are critical means through which such processes can be unleashed' (Ghose and Mullick 2015: 350). This requires the facilitation of learning processes that lead to awareness and organised action to transform those uneven power relationships and structures. By taking conscious, self-determined and active roles in this process, learners are helped to increasingly become effective change agents. Adult literacy and education programmes that are sensitive to culture, language and gender hold the potential to reinforce the importance of the transmission of indigenous knowledge and wisdom, and to increase indigenous women's visibility (Cunningham 2010, Eldred 2013, Robinson-Pant 2014, Hanemann 2015, Hanemann and Scarpino 2016).

This brief review of evidence on bilingual and intercultural approaches to indigenous literacy provides a sense of the complexity of related processes, the many challenges, and the potential for contributing to gender equality. Against this background, the next section will analyse the Mexican experience.

The Mexican indigenous bilingual education model

Since 1992, the Mexican government has been trying to establish new and improved relationships with indigenous populations through the implementation of specific educational programmes that incorporate indigenous languages and cultures and, in particular, foster the ideal of interculturality for all (López and Hanemann 2006). The most recent and notable effort of the Mexican government in this field is the Bilingual Indigenous Education Model for Life and Work (MIB).

According to the 2010 General Population and Housing Census in Mexico, there are 31.9 million adults over 15 years of age (40.7%) without having completed basic education or being in the situation of 'rezago educativo', that is not knowing how to read or write and/or has not started or completed primary or secondary education[6]. Of the 5.4 million adults who cannot read or write at all (6.9%), 61% are women and 39% are men; 73% are Spanish-speaking, while 27% speak an indigenous language. Fifty percent live in urban areas and the rest in 97,000 rural communities. This means that one out of every four indigenous adults aged over 15 years cannot read or write. For women this proportion further rises to one in three. Today, the indigenous population is affected by illiteracy in the same proportion as the Spanish-speaking population was four decades ago. Seven out of every ten indigenous adults without literacy skills reside in six states in the south of Mexico. Sixty eight percent of them live in rural areas, while the rest has moved to urban areas (Gobierno de México 2014).

Since 2000 the Education Model for Life and Work (MEVyT) is the main adult education programme in Mexico leading to recognised certificates equivalent to formal primary and secondary education (basic education). It was developed and is implemented by the National Institute for Adult Education (INEA), which was established in 1981 as the federal governmental agency in charge of non-formal education. The process of creating the Indigenous Bilingual (MIB) proposal[7], in the framework of the MEVyT, started in 2002. But the programme was only launched in 2007 gradually involving those 17 federal states that have significant indigenous populations. The MIB programme aims to empower indigenous peoples through bilingual educational opportunities that value and respect the indigenous cultures and identities and promote intercultural dialogue. The use of learners' respective mother tongues in teaching literacy skills is expected to particularly benefit rural indigenous women who have less exposure and opportunity to learn the mainstream language (Spanish).

The long development and piloting process reflects the complexities and challenges facing the MIB model. The creation of the 'Maya Project' started with three state-level adult education institutes in Yucatán and comprised (1) state teams in charge of research, material development, field-testing of the materials and inter-state coordination among the three teams; (2) Maya (indigenous) language specialists in charge of sorting out issues with existing language variations in the three states by finding consensus, language revision of the learning materials, and preparation of workshops to reflect on language issues identified during the revision of the learning materials; and (3) pedagogical coordination and support with the task to train the teams in the educational approach, design the learning activities, assist with the material development, promote reflection about the feasibility of writing texts in indigenous languages for different every day uses, and coordinate the material development of the three state teams to ensure a common perspective and approach (Schmelkes *et al.* 2009). Only one-third of the team members at state level including the language specialists were women.

The challenges included the need to overcome the predominant perception in the teams that the Maya language was limited and that it was only possible to express everything in Spanish language writing. Many team members were not sufficiently proficient in (written) Maya language and there was no budget available to pay for linguistic assistance. In addition, the teams were also challenged by a lack of experience with the development of learning materials and the educational approach proposed by the federal INEA. Furthermore, a number of team members, in particular indigenous teachers who were invited to participate in the process, did not seem to agree to the proposed approach (Schmelkes *et al.* 2009).

The overall goal of the MIB is to create sustainable learning opportunities for indigenous communities in order to address the challenges that limit their ability to access formal basic education as well as to facilitate their interaction within mainstream society through Spanish. It also aims at their empowerment and the promotion of sustainable development within indigenous communities. While there is mention of the reduction of regional, gender and ethnic disparities with regard to access to education, the objectives do not include any mention of gender equality or women's empowerment. The programme is based on an integrated, diversified and modular curriculum covering three levels: initial, intermediate (equivalent to primary education) and advanced level (equivalent to secondary education). The initial level of the MIB route consists of five modules out of which two are to learn to read and to write in the indigenous language (MIBES 1 and 3), two are dedicated to learn Spanish (orally MIBES 2 and in writing MIBES 4), and one is bilingual (MIBES 5) (SEP/INEA 2012).

The MIB approach to written language, a 'functional communicative' approach, is based on the assumption that written language is a form of communication that is practiced through its social use. Further it is supported by the view that this communication takes place in concrete contexts, real situations and with specific intentions, and that there are specific texts for each context, situation and intention. The learning modules and methodologies were developed on the basis of a diagnostic study previously conducted in two of the three pilot states in order to (1) map communication situations and levels of bilingualism of the Maya-speaking population; (2) identify and collect texts of social use in the community and through municipal services that adults use (irrespective of the language); and (3) recognise and rebuild the situations in which the texts are or could be used for reading and writing activities in the learning materials (Schmelkes *et al.* 2009).

Over the years, the outreach of the MIB was extended and is currently being implemented in over 50 of the largest indigenous languages. Over 90 percent of the programme participants have been women. According to experience, it takes learners an average of 18 to 21 months to complete the initial level, and 6 to 10 months to complete the intermediate level (SEP/INEA 2012).

As the learning materials have to take into account the particular cultural and linguistic situations and interests of each indigenous group, the MIB modules were developed at state level and are different from each other. The themes covered in each module reflect the specific worldviews, cultures, existential realities, linguistic characteristics as well as the needs and aspirations of each group. The institutional approach to provide the courses is flexible and open to adapt to learners' situations. Since each indigenous language has its own structure and characteristics, no unique method of literacy and language learning is prescribed by INEA. However, facilitators are encouraged to organise a variety of learner-centered activities and use meaningful discussion-generating approaches inspired by Paulo Freire. In 2010, INEA initiated a training model for bilingual trainers and pedagogical personnel of the MIB called 'Indigenous Prototype of Training' model (UNESCO Mexico 2012).

To date, several studies, articles and reports (e.g. INEA 2007, Mendoza 2008, Schmelkes *et al.* 2009, UNESCO Mexico 2012, Sánchez 2017) suggest lessons that can be drawn from the first years of implementing the MIB. According to Schmelkes *et al.* (2009) the main success of this experience consists in the existence of a high quality bilingual literacy proposal which was developed by a team that was neither specialised in language nor in learning material development. This indicates that this can be also done for other languages and in other contexts (Schmelkes *et al.* 2009). However, the implementation of the MIB is facing major challenges mainly due to weak political support and consequently severe underfunding. This has a negative impact on the programme quality. One of the principle obstacles hampering the quality of the programme implementation is the reliance on non-professional teaching personnel (volunteers) with high turn-over rates and little training or direct pedagogical support.

The diagnostic study of the indigenous bilingual education for youth and adults in Mexico

As noted, this article examines the diagnostic study commissioned by INEA to UNESCO Mexico in 2012 (UNESCO Mexico 2012) to look at the perceptions of key stakeholders involved in the implementation of the MIB programme. It draws primarily on group discussions to analyse the perceptions of indigenous technical personnel and learners in six selected tsotsiles and tseltales communities in three municipalities of the state of Chiapas. Altogether 12 'community of inquiry' discussions with 101 indigenous women (learners) were conducted. The 'community of inquiry' approach – in Spanish '*Comunidades de Indagación*' – is described as a rigorous, democratic and reflective form of discussion built up over time with the same group of learners (Lipman 2003). In Mexico this reflective educational model has been adapted linguistically and culturally to work with marginalised groups since 1979 (UNESCO Mexico 2012). The selection criteria included the representativeness of the communities with regard to their context aspects, presence of MIB learning groups with a minimum number of learners, in particular at module 4 and 5 levels, accessibility of communities and other logistical aspects as well as available time and resources for the field work. Most (87%) of the 101 women participating in the group discussions from the three Tsotsil and three Tseltal communities in Chiapas were aged between 20 and 50 years and studying at MIBES 4 and 5 levels (80%). In order to complement and triangulate the information collected in these group discussions, 13 in-depth interviews were conducted with facilitators, technicians, coordinators and beneficiaries of the programme active in those communities. Eight of the interviewees were educational personnel (five facilitators, two technicians, and one coordinator) while five of them were beneficiaries (learners).

INEA, UNESCO Mexico and the NGO Tanesque had several inter-institutional meetings before the field work started (UNESCO Mexico 2012) to agree on three questions for the analysis (using the four key dimensions of acceptance, appropriation, relevance and usefulness). These were (1) what factors affect favourably and unfavourably the acceptance and appropriation of the MIB by the learners and educational, managerial and operational personnel; (2) what are the factors or indicators of the relevance of the contents, educational materials and processes of the MIB with regard to the needs and interests expressed by the beneficiaries of the programme, its socio-linguistic and cultural context, and the intentions of literacy; and (3) what elements on the usefulness of literacy and written culture are provided by learners and the educational, operative and directive personnel of the MIB?

The findings are presented according to the four dimensions of analysis: acceptance, appropriation, relevance and usefulness. I add a fifth gender dimension in order to examine the testimonies of the interviewed indigenous women with a particular 'gender-lens' along the research questions of this article. All quotations are from the final report of the diagnostic study (UNESCO Mexico 2012), translated from Tsotsil and Tseltal into Spanish by local facilitators, and from Spanish into English by myself.

Acceptance

With regard to the acceptance of the MIB programme, learners gave testimony of their different motivations to enrol in the study circles. These were related to family subsistence, community participation and movement in urban areas. For them it was important to '*understand*' in different situations of their daily lives (e.g. go to see the doctor, shopping, etc.), '*so that we do not walk blindly*'. The women expressed that they experience enjoyment when they meet and learn together: '*It is not the same as we are alone sitting at home, there is no one to cheer up our hearts, we have no one to talk to, but when we are all together, we talk and we encourage ourselves to do things, so we are happy.'* This indicates that the learning circle represents a space of great value for socialisation and communication. Intrinsic motivation developed to do something for their personal development: *'Now I liked it and I will study as far as I can'.* The women reported a range of achievements including that they have learnt to speak up with confidence: *'We lose our fear, the shame of speaking, we can speak in our communities'.*

The women interviewed also referred to the need to learn to write in their indigenous language to reconnect with their ancestors and to avoid *'losing the language'* in their communities. In this regard no significant differences between the two ethnic groups (Tseltal and Tsotsil) were identified. They saw themselves as important links and role models to ensure the transmission of their cultural and linguistic knowledge to the next generation(s): *'I think both languages are useful for us, because if you lose the Tsotsil, you lose your way of being'.* The women value and wish to learn to speak and write in both languages. This reflects the combination of a pragmatic and utilitarian logic with the community tradition of keeping the indigenous language alive. The women saw themselves in the duty to take action against current trends of assimilation to the mainstream culture and language: *'I am of the opinion that we begin with ourselves, as mothers of families, let us teach our children Tseltal and Spanish...'*

However, the testimonies also reflect challenges with learning: *'There we go, little by little, it's difficult!'* These difficulties were related to different reasons including their socio-economic living conditions and lack of study habits, but also to challenges with writing in the indigenous language: *'I find it easier to write Spanish, I think that because I know how to speak a bit.'* This suggests that prior learning experiences of these persons were shaped by teachers who taught literacy only in Spanish, while 'writing in Spanish' was often limited to copying words and sentences without fully understanding their meaning.

In the in-depth interviews, facilitators and other educational personnel confirmed that they find it harder to learn to read and to write in their indigenous language because they themselves became literate in Spanish at school. The research team also observed low levels of proficiency in Spanish among facilitators, even in the case of those who had completed secondary school. In addition to the language challenges, the educational personnel identified a number of other obstacles including the difficulties to find suitable facilitators, to recruit learners and to ensure regular attendance (of both learners and facilitators) due to migration to the urban areas.

Appropriation

The women participating in the 'community of inquiry' sessions provided evidence of high levels of appropriation of the MIB. They expressed that the programme *'makes them happy'* because *'it is teaching them a lot'.* According to research on the Tseltal learning culture, 'happiness of the heart'[8] and 'practicing' play important roles in significant learning, and learning has to be done 'from the heart' (Urdapilleta Carrasco and Parra Vázquez 2016). However, it seems that there were challenges with frequently practicing newly acquired knowledge and skills, also beyond the classroom sessions: *'Our heart rejoices because it [the programme] is teaching us a lot, but it does not stay in our hearts because it is not the same as a child who goes to school every day, that is why we forget, little by little, because our heart encourages us to acquire more knowledge'.* Short-term memory, visual attention and phonological awareness play an important role in successful written language acquisition (Landgraf *et al.* 2012). However, it seems that these are not systematically developed in classes. Both learners and educational personnel criticised the lack of opportunities and stimulations to apply their reading and writing skills in indigenous language in their everyday context. In other words, the lack of literate environments was identified as a major obstacle to the full appropriation of the MIB.

The women clearly perceived the importance of literacy and language for preserving their culture and strengthening their identity: *'Our language is very important and if we could write a single page because we don't want to lose the culture, the language, the food, the way of walking of our grandparents, so that there is a memory of what those will leave behind who are already old…'.* Also the educational personnel revealed strong appropriation of the significance of written culture in indigenous language. At the same time they stressed the requirement of publishing indigenous knowledge in writing: *'We tell the señoras that writing serves to capture our roots, usages and customs. Because of what use is it for us to know everything about usages and customs, if it is not reflected in a book? The new generations will not recognise it [the knowledge], if we do not recognise it'.* This illustrates that both learners and facilitators are aware that there is much more at stake than learning to read and write.

Relevance

The dimension of relevance was mainly analysed in relation to the MIB curriculum and learning materials. With reference to the bilingual approach the women explained that their literacy process started in their mother tongue and that this supported their comprehension ability: *'The first book comes in Tseltal only! If it is in Tseltal, the letters open our eyes'.* Furthermore, one of the participants suggested that all learning modules should be made available bilingually: *'I would like the books to always be in both languages, in Tsotsil and in Spanish because that would allow us to understand them'.* While the women provided an array of examples how the contents of the learning materials were relevant for the improvement of their life quality, there were expressions of frustration with regard to their slow progress in reading and writing.

Related comments indicate problems with the methods of decoding letters and words in disconnection from meaning: *'We can name the letters already, we put the letters together but sometimes it's useless if we cannot understand what we write. I feel like we're just stuck'.* That progress with literacy development is also hampered by a lack of language skills becomes clearer with the following comment: *'I can write the letters, but I do not understand the meaning because I can't speak Spanish, I can make the letters come together, that's not so difficult, I even make them speak, the problem begins when I do not understand what I read and what I write'.* Those who skipped the first step of learning to read and to write in their indigenous language experienced major difficulties to achieve reading comprehension in Spanish.

To make things even more complex, learners and facilitators also mentioned issues with existing linguistic variations of the indigenous language: '*A bit difficult, because it is not the same variant that we speak which comes in the book*'. This seems to reflect a lack of understanding of how these local variations relate to an agreed upon standard version of the indigenous language in their learning modules. Although facilitators report that they have benefitted from some training activities organised by INEA, in the interviews they also recognise their limitations with regard to teaching methods and Spanish skills: '*We as facilitators also [struggle], well, sometimes we can't, that means we try to find a [methodological] strategy[...]*'. There were indications that the majority of them used the same way of literacy teaching and learning that they had experienced at school.

Usefulness

The usefulness of literacy in both languages was a recurrent topic in the 'community of inquiry' discussions. The testimonies reflect experiences of discrimination, shame and fear because they were not able to communicate in the dominant language: '*I speak to people in Tsotsil, because here I am not afraid to walk, but when they speak to me in Spanish, then I get scared*'. Often dwellers of urban areas deny their indigenous roots and even if they are bilingual they refuse to speak anything else than Spanish: '*As we are Tseltals we should not lose our language, but we must also learn Spanish, since many times you are going to ask something, and they do not answer you if you do not know how to speak Castila [Spanish], they pretend they do not understand you*'. Something similar was reported by another learner: '*When I went to Ocosingo to the clinic, I came to ask for my medication, but since at that time I was not yet in class [MIB], the nurses ignored me, they did not want to give me anything ...*'

The women provided a number of examples where the acquisition of literacy, numeracy and language skills has proven to be useful in their everyday lives including helping their children with schoolwork, writing messages to relatives who live distant, reading the bible and official documents, sending messages to be communicated through local radio stations, reading and signing contracts, writing minutes and reports, applying for a credit or birth certificate, making accounts, calculating prices for their products, among others. Their testimonies indicate that they understood the usefulness of what they learnt through the MIB and that this would increase access to their rights: '*I think we should continue learning to write in Tseltal and in Spanish ... so that when a paper arrives, if there is fabrication of crime, that we are not cheated by the caxlanes [mestizos], so we have to be very attentive.*'

Gender

Even though the gender dimension was not in focus of the diagnostic study, the findings reveal pattern of cultural ('*machista*') behaviours that impinge on participants' self-confidence with regard to their learning capabilities. The testimonies reflect awareness of the reasons for the existing gender disparities in education: '*Because in the past men were allowed to study and women were not allowed*'. However, when it comes to explain their learning difficulties, they tend to have internalised the traditional belief that (elderly) women are unable to learn. *'I do not keep in mind what I learn, I only know a few letters nothing more… but it [new knowledge] does not stay, maybe because our heads are already sick …* '

Not much research has been done on simultaneous processes of literacy and second language acquisition, but there is evidence that the ability to discriminate and process phonemes – a crucial factor for the acquisition of written language - develops much slower in literacy learning in a second language than literacy in the first language (Landgraf *et al.* 2012).

Other testimonies reflect feelings of dependence, fear and insecurity when they move into mestizo or urban spaces due to their lack of education: *'If I had knowledge then I would go wherever I want because one already knows, but since I am stupid I need company [of a man] for when I leave. When I take the taxi, I start to think: will it be somebody from my community? And if I were intelligent it would not matter which taxi… If I were a bit smart, I would go where I want to go, but as I do not know, I walk in the streets with a companion [a man], because I'm afraid, that's why I want to continue learning so that my head is stimulated …* '.

Indication of low self-esteem and underestimation of their abilities to learn at times seem to be reinforced by husbands: *'That's what my husband says: Why is it that you do not learn, why do you not learn to speak in Castila [Spanish]? … I receive my scolding'*. These perceptions of seeking the reasons for assumed failure in learning with themselves were found frequently in the interviews.

Discussion

The findings of the diagnostic study confirm still high levels of acceptance, appropriation, relevance and usefulness of the programme as identified in the survey and interviews among the different actors involved in the programme. However, the results also reflect a range of challenges that programme implementation faces. Indeed, these are largely the same as those discussed earlier and identified during the initial implementation phase of the MIB by Schmelkes *et al.* (2009).

While the perceptions of the interviewed indigenous women indicate that the MIB seems to be particularly attractive to women who enjoy making use of this meeting and learning space, there is room for a stronger gender focus of the programme with the aim to work towards gender equality and empowerment of the indigenous women. This involves taking into account the processes, outcomes and impacts of the whole programme cycle and engage the whole community, not only women. As in many countries (UNESCO Mexico 2012, Eldred 2013, Robinson-Pant 2014), women are significantly under-represented in decision-making, management and leading functions in the MIB structure.

Although the interviewed women express themselves in favour of the bilingual approach of MIB, a certain tension resonates between valuing their local language and culture, and the desire to benefit from socio-economic services and opportunities available through the dominant language. There is indication of various difficulties around the language approach and slow learning progress is felt as a problem. While there is little support for a subtractive dominant Spanish language approach to learning, it was clear that the additive bilingual or multilingual approach to language and literacy learning as well as the interrelationship and difference between spoken and written language forms are not necessarily well understood by everyone. However, this is a prerequisite to make flexible and effective use of this approach. Furthermore the classroom practices do not seem to mirror the pedagogical and linguistic intentions of the MIB 'prescribed curriculum'. This divergence points to the need for an enhanced understanding of the complexities of the bilingual literacy programme to develop strategies that work for both learners and facilitators.

Although the MIB promotes 'intercultural dialogue', there does not seem to be much emphasis on interculturality. However, if we assume that knowing one's own culture is a prerequisite for learning about other cultures (Maurer Ávalos 2011), then the MIB is offering good opportunities to lay such foundations. The findings reveal that the interviewed women are well aware about the importance of indigenous (written) language for the strengthening of their identity and culture, as well as of their responsibility to pass this on to the next generation(s). As awareness can be seen as a first and necessary step towards empowerment, the programme appears to have been successful in this regard.

The MIB has made commendable efforts to produce good quality learning materials in indigenous languages with the involvement of local language experts and pedagogical staff. Indeed, according to Castro (2011), the production of contextualised educational materials, reflecting cultural and linguistic diversity, made up the highest programme costs. The findings indicate that learners consider the contents of the programme to be relevant and useful and the learning modules motivating. However, demand for learning resulting in higher proficiency levels and thereby strengthening the cognitive dimension of empowerment can be further raised by providing learners additional reasons and opportunities for practicing reading, writing and numeracy, particularly outside of the class context (Kalman 2005, Hanemann and Krolak 2017).

Most of the findings suggest that efforts to strengthen the quality aspects of the programme require a clearer focus on facilitators, trainers, supervisors and other pedagogical personnel at the local level. Improvement of recruitment, training and retention of facilitators as well as the professionalisation of all MIB personnel requires a long-term planning horizon and adequate financial resources. While there is awareness among the interviewed women about the existence of gender disparities, wider transformative processes seem to be hampered by slow learning progress and language challenges. There is indication of low self-esteem and underestimation of their abilities to learn. More in-depth analysis of learning materials and class observation could improve understanding of the difficulties and determine which specific learning activities strengthen the self-esteem and independence of learners. On the whole, the transformative potential of the MIB in terms of women's empowerment appears to be largely untapped.

Conclusions

In general terms, the perceptions of the indigenous women interviewed reflect a positive balance with regard to their acceptance, appropriation, relevance and usefulness of the MIB programme. However, the findings also show the challenges the programme approach faces in the application of the bilingual and intercultural approach to literacy and learning. Better trained educational personnel would allow for more flexibility in tailoring the educational model to specific learners' needs and interests as well as in making creative use of local knowledge. Linking this professionalisation of the MIB personnel to participatory action research would greatly benefit the further development of the pedagogical, linguistic and intercultural approaches of the programme.

Even though the gender dimension was not a main focus of the original diagnostic study, the analysis of the findings reveal a range of issues that could be addressed in the future in order to make better use of the empowering potential of the MIB programme for indigenous women. The identified issues range from uneven representation of women in the hierarchies of the programme operation structure to pattern of cultural ('*machista*') behaviours that limit or affect women's self-confidence with regard to learning. The interviews with indigenous women also provide clues to the kind of learning they value and what they need. In contrast to assimilation-promoting strategies, they favour the MIB's intercultural bilingual approach to learning. They are aware of the importance of literacy and language for the maintenance of their cultural identity and their role of passing this on to the next generations.

Further, the testimonies of the indigenous women provide insights into the kind of changes that could be implemented, in order to better meet their needs. These include ensuring that (1) the indigenous women have equal voices and representations in the decision-making processes and operation structure of the programme; (2) gender equality and women's empowerment is prioritised as a transversal task; (3) that interculturality and bi-/multilingualism are well understood and promoted by all as key principles of the programme; (4) that dynamic literate environments motivate, support and nurture a culture of learning in indigenous families and communities; and (5) adequate financial resources allow for high quality services with a longer-term planning horizon. In this way the Mexican intercultural bilingual MIB programme could become a more effective means of indigenous women's empowerment and also contribute to social transformation and gender equality. This is the real potential of the MIB programme. The Mexican authorities would be well advised to further strengthen and roll it out as it can achieve model function at the regional and global levels.

Notes

1. The MIB is a specific programme for indigenous learners which is run under the Education Model for Life and Work (MEVyT), the main governmental adult education programme in Mexico.
2. INEA is the federal governmental agency in charge of the implementation of the MIB programme.
3. These dimensions were agreed upon by INEA, UNESCO Mexico and the NGO Tanesque before my involvement at the analysis stage.
4. Even more concerning is that adult literacy does not appear in the plan: 'Indeed, no strategies for adult literacy are proposed in the plan [...] and the MEVyT initiative is omitted' (Robinson 2015:14).
5. There does not exist any single accepted definition of 'indigenous peoples' that captures their diversity. See the Introduction to this Special Issue and Hanemann 2005.

6. http://www.inea.gob.mx/index.php/serviciosbc/ineanumeros/rezago.html
7. Mexico is the only country in Latin America that introduced a model of intercultural bilingual education without financial and technical support from international cooperation (Oviedo and Wildemeersch 2008).
8. In Tseltal emotions are defined as different conditions of the heart (Urdapilleta Carrasco and Parra Vázquez 2016).

Disclosure statement

No potential conflict of interest was reported by the author.

ORCID

Ulrike Hanemann (iD) http://orcid.org/0000-0001-6235-9607

References

Aikman, S., 1997. Interculturality and intercultural education: a challenge for democracy. *International Review of Education (IRE)*, 43 (5–6), 463–479.

Castro, J. de D., 2011. A review of Mexico's lifelong learning model. In: Yang, J. & Valdés-Cotera, R. eds. (2011) Conceptual evolution and policy developments in lifelong learning. Hamburg, Germany: UNESCO Institute for Lifelong Learning, pp. 145–153.

Commission on the Status of Women of the UN of Economic and Social Council 2017. Interactive dialogue on the focus area: empowerment of indigenous women. Sixty-first session 13-24 March 2017 http://www.un.org/ga/search/view_doc.asp?symbol=E/CN.6/2017/12 (Accessed 14 November 2017)

Cunningham, M., 2010. Laman laka: our indigenous path to self-determined development. In: Tauli-Corpuz, V., Enkiwe-Abayao, L. &, de Chavez, R. (Eds.) Towards an alternative development paradigm: indigenous peoples' self-determined development. Philippines: Tebtebba Foundation.

Dietz, G. and Mateos Cortés, L. S., 2011. Interculturalidad y educación intercultural en México: Un análisis de los discursos nacionales e internacionales en su impacto en los modelos educativos mexicanos. México: SEP-CGEIB.

Eldred, J., 2013. Literacy and women's empowerment: stories of success and inspiration. Hamburg: UNESCO Institute for Lifelong Learning (UIL).

Ghose, M., and Mullick, D., 2015. A tangled weave: tracing outcomes of education in rural women's lives in North India. *International Review of Education*, 61, 343–364.

GEMR 2016. If you don't understand, how can you learn? (UNESCO Policy Paper 24, February 2016) http://unesdoc.unesco.org/images/0024/002437/243713E.pdf (Accessed 12 November 2017).

Gobierno de México 2014. Programa de Alfabetización y Abatimiento del Rezago Educativo 2014-2018. Programa Institucional. Secretaría de Gobernación. Diario Oficial de la Federación. México D.F. DOF: 08/05/2014. http://dof.gob.mx/nota_detalle.php?codigo=5343876&fecha=08/05/2014 (Accessed 17 November 2017)

Hamel, R. E., 2016. Bilingual education for indigenous peoples in Mexico. In: García, O. *et al.* (eds). Bilingual and multilingual education. Encyclopedia of language and education. Springer Publishing International Switzerland. DOI: 10.1007/978-3-319-02324-3_30-2.

Hanemann, U. ,2015. Narrowing the Gender Gap: Empowering Women through Literacy Programmes. Hamburg. UIL (online accessible http://unesdoc.unesco.org/images/0024/002432/243299E.pdf).

Hanemann, U., 2005. Literacy for special target groups: indigenous peoples. Background paper prepared for the UNESCO Education for All Global Monitoring Report 2006 Literacy for Life. http://unesdoc.unesco.org/images/0014/001460/146004e.pdf (Accessed 14 November 2017).

Hanemann, U., and Krolak, L., 2017. Fostering a culture of reading and writing: examples of dynamic literate environments. Hamburg, Germany: UNESCO Institute for Lifelong Learning. http://unesdoc.unesco.org/images/0025/002579/257933e.pdf (Accessed 30 November 2017).

Hanemann, U. and Scarpino, C., 2016. Literacy in multilingual and multicultural contexts: effective approaches to adult learning and education. Hamburg, Germany: UIL. (online accessible http://unesdoc.unesco.org/images/0024/002455/245513e.pdf)

INEA 2007. Programa de Educación para la Vida y el Trabajo (PEVyT). Subcomponente 1.4.: Educación Intercultural Bilingüe. Plan de Desarrollo para la Atención al Rezago Educativo en la Educación Indígena. http://documents.worldbank.org/curated/en/439951468774643998/pdf/IPP96.pdf (Accessed 17 November 2017).

Infante, M. I. (ed.), 2000. Alfabetismo funcional en siete países de América Latina. Santiago: UNESCO Oficina Regional para America Latina y el Caribe.

Kalman, J., 2005. Discovering literacy: access routes to written culture for a group of women in Mexico. Hamburg, Germany: UNESCO Institute for Education.

King, L., 1999. Learning through the soul: concepts relating to learning and knowledge in the Mayan cultures of Mexico. *International Review of Education (IRE)*, 45 (3–4), 367–370.

Landgraf, S., *et al.*, 2012. Impact of phonological processing skills on written language acquisition in illiterate adults. *Developmental Cognitive Neuroscience*, 25 (2012), 129–138.

Lipman, M., 2003. Thinking in education. (2nd ed.). Cambridge: Cambridge University Press.

López, L. E., 2001. Literacy and intercultural bilingual education in the Andes. In: Olson, David R./Torrance, Nancy (eds.) The making of literate societies. UK: Blackwell Publishers, 201–223.

López, L.E. and Hanemann, U. (eds.) 2006. Adult education for indigenous peoples and minorities: a thematic review. Report on the workshop held at the CONFINTEA V Mid-Term Review Conference, Bangkok, Thailand, September 2003. Hamburg: UNESCO Institute for Lifelong Learning.

López, L. E. and Hanemann, U. (eds.) 2009. Alfabetización y Multiculturalidad: Miradas desde América Latina. Guatemala: UIL/PACE-GTZ. http://unesdoc.unesco.org/images/0018/001889/188921s.pdf (Accessed 12 November 2017).

López, L. E., and Sichra, I., 2007. Intercultural bilingual education among indigenous peoples in Latin America. PROEIB Andes, Universidad Mayor de San Simón, Cochabamba, Bolivia. http://bvirtual.proeibandes.org/bvirtual/docs/Indigenous_bilingual_education.pdf (Accessed 23 November 2018).

Maurer Ávalos, E., 2011. ¡Los tseltales aprenden sin enseñanza! *Revista Latinoamericana de Estudios Educativos*, XLI (3–4).

Mendoza, S. E., 2008. Un quehacer para aprender: la alfabetización con personas jóvenes y adultas indígenas. In: Decisio. Pátzcuaro, México: CREFAL, pp. 31–36.

Mendoza Zuany, R.G., 2017. Inclusión educativa por interculturalidad: implicaciones para la educación de la niñez indígena. *Perfiles Educativos*, 39 (158), 52–69. http://www.scielo.org.mx/pdf/peredu/v39n158/0185-2698-peredu-39-158-00052.pdf (Accessed 23 November 2018).

Mendoza Zuany, R.G. (2018) Inclusión como política educativa: Hacia un sistema educativo único en un México cultural y lingüísticamente diverso. https://sinectica.iteso.mx/index.php/SINECTICA/article/view/780/1002 (Accessed 23 November 2018).

Oviedo, A., and Wildemeersch, D., 2008. Intercultural education and curricular diversification: the case of the Ecuadorian Intercultural Bilingual Education Model (MOSEIB). *Compare*, 38 (4), 455–470.

Pitarch, P., 2000. Almas y cuerpo en una tradición indígena tzeltal. *Archives de Sciences Sociales et Des Religions* (112), 31–48. https://assr.revues.org/20245 (Accessed 20 November 2017).

Prins, E., 2008. Adult literacy education, gender equity and empowerment: Insights from a Freirean-inspired literacy programme. *Studies in the Education of Adults*, 40 (1), 24–39.

Robinson, C., 2015. Languages in adult literacy: policies and practices during the 15 years of EFA (2000-2015). Background paper prepared for the UNESCO Education for All Global Monitoring Report 2015. Paris.

Robinson-Pant, A., 2014. Literacy and education for sustainable development and women's empowerment. Hamburg: UNESCO Institute for Lifelong Learning (UIL).

Sánchez, L., 2017. 'I Read and Write in My Own Language': A Case Study of a Non-Formal Indigenous Language Literacy Programme in Mexico. Dissertation European Master's in Lifelong Learning: Policy & Management 2015-2017. UCL, Institute of Education, London (unpublished)

Schmelkes, S., 2005. Educar en y para la diversidad. *Pensamiento educativo*, 37, 38–51.

Schmelkes, S., 2006. La interculturalidad en la educación básica. Ponencia presentada en el contexto de la Segunda Reunión del Comité Intergubernamental del Proyecto Regional de Educación para América Latina y el Caribe (PRELAC), Santiago de Chile, 11 al 13 de Mayo de 2006,

Schmelkes, S., *et al.*, 2009. Alfabetización de jóvenes y adultos indígenas en México. In: López, L. E. and Hanemann, U, (eds). Alfabetización y Multiculturalidad: Miradas desde América Latina. UIL/PACE-GTZ, Guatemala.

SEP/INEA 2012. Bilingual Indigenous Educative Model for Life and Work (MIB) Mexico. Unpublished paper on the basis of UNESCO Institute for Lifelong Learning: Bilingual Literacy for Life. In: Effective Literacy and Numeracy Practices Database:uil.unesco.org/literacy/effective-practices-database.

Skutnabb-Kangas, T., 2001. The globalisation of (educational) language rights. *International Review of Education*, 47 (3–4), 201–219.

Stromquist, N. P., 2009. Literacy and empowerment: a contribution to the debate. Background study commissioned in the framework of the United Nations Literacy Decade. Paris, France: UNESCO.

The World Bank. 2018. World development report 2018. Learning to realize education's promise. Washington, D.C: The World Bank.

UNDP. 2004. Human Development Report 2004. Cultural liberty in today's world. Published for the United Nations Development Programme, New York, USA

UNDP. 2013. *Ciudadanía intercultural. Aportes desde la participación política de los pueblos indígenas en Latinoamérica.* Programa de las Naciones Unidas para el Desarrollo (PNUD), 2013, Nueva York.

UNESCO Mexico. 2012. *Diagnóstico de la Educación Indígena Bilingüe para Jóvenes y Adultos. Documento Final en su Versión Preliminar del Diagnóstico* (28 de Septiembre 2012 - unpublished).

UNESCO 2003. Education in a multilingual world. UNESCO Education Position Paper 2003, Paris, UNESCO. http://unesdoc.unesco.org/images/0012/001297/129728e.pdf (Accessed 12 November 2017).

UNESCO/OREALC 2004. EFA (Education for All) in Latin America: a goal within our reach. Regional EFA Monitoring Report 2003. Santiago de Chile: UNESCO/OREALC.

UNESCO 2006. UNESCO Guidelines on intercultural education. Paris. France.

Urdapilleta Carrasco, J., and Parra Vázquez, M.R., 2016. Aprendizaje Tseltal: construir conocimientos con la alegría del corazón. *LiminaR*, 14 (2), http://www.scielo.org.mx/scielo.php?pid=S1665-80272016000200085&script=sci_arttext (Accessed 20 November 2017).

Exploring the informal learning experiences of women in a pastoral community in Ethiopia: The case of pastoral women in *Karrayyu*

Turuwark Zalalam Warkineh (iD) and Abiy Menkir Gizaw (iD)

ABSTRACT

In Ethiopia, there has been increasing recognition of the differing educational needs and experiences of pastoralists as compared to 'settled' agricultural communities. Although the starting point has usually been how to integrate such marginalised groups into mainstream schooling, research has revealed important insights into learning outside educational institutions and the ways in which people in pastoral communities learn informally from a young age how to lead a pastoralist life. Building on a qualitative study conducted in the *Karrayyu* (also spelled as *Kereyu, Karayu, Karrayu, Karrayyuu*) pastoral community of Ethiopia, this article explores how Karrayyu women are engaged in intergenerational and informal learning. It considers a range of knowledge and skills learned through informal means and examines traditional midwifery in depth through a 'community of practice' lens. While the Karrayyu value their knowledge and skills they are ignored and denigrated outside of their community. Karrayyu pastoralist society is facing huge change but literacy, health and agriculture training and extension work are not based on the indigenous knowledge and ways of knowing. Nevertheless, the Karrayyu are learning the non-indigenous skills and knowledge necessary for survival through informal methods.

Introduction

A number of international declarations that comprise a framework for the provision of quality education for indigenous people and the recognition of their educational rights are in place (King and Schielmann 2004, Rao and Robinson-Pant 2006, Schmelkes 2011). However, no matter how the provision and right to learn is underscored in these frameworks, many indigenous groups, especially indigenous women, remain excluded from learning opportunities and are lagging behind other population in all goals (Morrison and Vaioleti 2011). Rao and Robinson-Pant (2006), also clearly indicate that most of these policy frameworks and programmes do not address gender issues. These policy frameworks, including the *Belem Framework for Action* (UIL 2010) portray indigenous people as homogenous. Contrary to dominant assumptions of most of the policy declarations, indigenous knowledge is not only heterogeneous but also gendered. King and Schielmann (2004) summarize this:

> Indigenous knowledge is not homogenous, and not all knowledge is necessarily shared by everyone in the indigenous community, but rather depends on age, gender and specific roles. The context of education, who holds or 'owns' what knowledge is crucial, as well as to whom and by whom this knowledge is transmitted (P.33).

Indigenous people's right to education goes beyond having access to non-indigenous educational opportunities; it involves provision of linguistically and culturally appropriate education that draws from indigenous culture and knowledge and that empowers people (King 2000, King and Schielmann 2004). Regarding this, Rao and Robinson-Pant (2006, pp. 210, 217) distinguished between 'Adult Education for Indigenous people' and 'Indigenous Adult Education' in terms of being based on 'instrumental approach' as opposed to 'right-based approach' to adult education. Indigenous Adult Education advocates that adult education, beyond improving economic and health situation, should be linked to indigenous people's political struggle for resources control, self-identify and recognition of their culture. However, Aikman's (2011) study revealed that available education opportunities for many indigenous communities in Africa are inadequate to extend their capabilities and to empower them to realize all their rights. The task of providing Indigenous adult education, thus, requires understanding of 'where they are now' (Rao and Robinson-Pant 2006, p. 218) and respecting their beliefs, practices, and ways of knowing and learning (Schmelkes 2011). Nevertheless, establishing links between indigenous knowledge and mainstream education is a challenging process (King and Schielmann 2004), as it requires deeper understanding of indigenous knowledge, skills and values of indigenous people.

Indigenous people such as nomadic pastoralists have been perceived to lead an outdated, 'backward and peripheral way of life best integrated as soon as possible' (Aikman 2011, p. 16). In Ethiopia pastoralists are considered 'uncivilised and even barbaric'; for instance, the Amharic word *Zelan*, meaning nomad, is literally an insult implying an uncultured, mannerless, lawless and aimless wanderer (Engidasew 2012). Even in the Ethiopian Pastoral Education Strategy (MoE 2008), pastoralists are described as having 'deep-rooted backward mind-set and harmful traditional practices' (p.4). Although they are often regarded as 'illiterate' and 'uncivilized', research conducted in pastoral areas has shown that they are also engaged in learning non-indigenous knowledge and skills including literacy and using mobile phone to be able to respond to the rapid socio-economic transformation they are facing (Robinson-Pant 2016). Most of such learning takes place informally. Unfortunately, informed by a deficit approach to development and learning, many programmes, developmental or educational, targeting pastoralists often start from what they lack rather than what they have (Robinson-Pant 2016). Engidasew (2012) noted how the Ethiopian adult literacy curriculum ignores pastoralists' values and traditions. This has resulted in lack of motivation to learn and high rate of withdrawal among women.

Overall, in order to provide quality indigenous adult education and respond to the needs of indigenous people, particularly women, empirical research is needed to inform policy and practice. We adopt the starting point that diverse indigenous knowledge and informal learning practices should be identified and recognized to build on what is already there. From the above statements, it can be noted that, the key to quality indigenous adult education is a clear understanding of what knowledge and skills indigenous people already have; how they learn them and why. Though there are several studies conducted in the areas of indigenous people, only a few (Usman 2010, Robinson-Pant 2016, Takayanagi 2016, 2017) have addressed indigenous and informal learning practices of pastoral women. The current study, taking the case of pastoral women of *Karrayyu* community in Ethiopia – semi-nomadic pastoralists who belong to the Oromo, the largest linguistic group of East Africa – aims to contribute to this gap.

Who is indigenous in Africa and in the Ethiopian context?

The word 'indigenous' comes from the Latin word – 'indigena' referring to 'something that comes from the country in which it is found', 'native of', or 'aborigine', (Barume, 2014, p. 24). However, in Africa, the concept of 'indigenousness' is understood differently from this definition. Barume (2014, p. 24) and Aikman (2011, p. 17) partly associate the different understanding of the term with the recognition 'that all Africans are indigenous to Africa in the sense that they were there before the European colonialists arrived and been subject to subordination during colonialism.' Although this notion of 'indigenous' might be acceptable in the context of the existence of European colonisers, the issue of 'indigenousness' is much deeper and debatable that needs to be looked at again in the African context.

Due to this, the use of the term 'indigenous' in Africa has shifted from its etymological meaning to one that is 'a human rights construct' (Barume 2014, p. 37). In its human rights sense, the term 'indigenous' represents African communities, such as hunter-gatherers and nomadic-pastoralists, whose social, economic and cultural identities face alienation, dispossession, different forms of discrimination and marginalisation compared to other people in their country (Aikman 2011, Barume 2014).

Defining 'indigenous' in Ethiopia is difficult and more complex as it is not a term widely used due to the absence of colonization. Nevertheless, there are several groups of people who fit the definition of 'indigenous' provided above (Barume 2014). 'The groups meeting the criteria for identification of indigenous peoples in Ethiopia include the pastoralists and the hunter/gatherers … that make up a significant proportion of the country's estimated 95 million population' (IWGIA 2016, p.394). Pastoralists reside in different parts of Ethiopia and their situation is very difficult as 'there is no national legislation that protects them (indigenous people), and Ethiopia has neither ratified ILO Convention No. 169, nor was present during the voting on the UN Declaration on the Rights of Indigenous Peoples (UNDRIP)' (IWGIA 2016, p.394).

Introduction to the context: the Karrayyu and social change

The Karrayyu are semi-nomadic pastoralists who belong to the Oromo ethnic group – the largest ethnic group in Ethiopia, speaking Afan Oromo. The Karrayyu are the indigenous inhabitants of the Metehara Plain and Mount Fentale area, which belong to the current administrative district of Fentale, Oromia Regional State. According to the Ethiopian Central Statistics Agency (2008), Fentale district (home of Karrayyus) has a total population of 82,225, of which 47% are female. The large majority (75%) of Fentale's population lives in rural areas of the district. Fentale district covers an area of 150,000 hectar and is made up of 18 *Kebeles*. Fentale is two hundred kilometres from the capital, Addis Ababa. Originally, predominantly followers of *Waqefannaa* – an indigenous monotheist Oromo belief system, in the past few decades, the Karrayyu have also adopted Islam and Christianity. The major source of Karrayyu livelihood comes from animal husbandry.

The Karrayyus are undergoing rapid and multifaceted changes. To mention a few, since the 1950s, they have been deprived of their dry and wet season grazing sites, which constitutes around 60% of their traditional land holdings (Gebre 2001) and watering resources. The land was used for commercial investments such as *Wonji Shoa* and *Metehara* Sugar Plantation and The Awash National Park (Gebre, 2001, Malifu 2006). Due to these schemes, the Karrayyu pastoralists were deprived not only of their grazing sites and watering resources such as Awash River, but also sacred ritual places and funeral sites… and they were forced to leave the plains to inhabit the marginal lands around the hills that are less suited to pastoral production (Elias and Abdi 2010).

The ever expanding salty Lake Beseka and the invasive thorny tree species – *Prosopis juliflora* have also contributed to the shrinking of grazing resources. These have challenged their traditional pastoralist way of life and forced them to start cultivation and other livelihood options like charcoal making, petty trading, etc. However, they remain divided on the issue of cultivation – some have accepted it while many kept their allegiance to pure pastoralism by saying '… making us stop pastoralism is carrying out genocide on us…'. Parallel to the declining pastoralist practice, they are facing changes in the food they are consuming. Their dominantly dairy-based diet is giving way to an increasingly cereal-based one. While some of the younger Karrayyu welcomed this change, many of the young and older people are critical of the 'modern' diet: '… it is dry… useless… it resulted in proliferation of new diseases'. Reflecting the Karrayyu's continuous sedentarisation, their housing style is also being changed from the traditional 'birds' nest' made of thin wood by women to a stronger, mud-plastered one made mostly by the neighbouring *Tullama* Oromo men. Apart from these, the present day Karrayyu have witnessed and expressed concern about the continuous erosion of the traditional value system, partly due to the influence of formal school curriculum and constant flow of neighbouring people. According to many of the respondents, a declining culture of mutual respect, establishing sexual relationship with young Karrayyu women/girls and with non-Karrayyus, chewing khat, drinking alcohol, divorce and marital conflict, etc. among Karrayyu men are illustrative of the changes.

Changes in Karrayyu life style affect women in markedly and significantly different ways. As their traditional knowledge and skills accumulated over the years are being devalued, they have had to learn new roles, new skills, new values, and new ways of managing and organizing life as well as hand down these to the new generation.

Methodology

We chose *Karrayyu* people because few studies have addressed *Karrayyu* women's issues and none have looked into their indigenous knowledge and the informal learning practices they engage within their everyday life. We designed a short qualitative study which we carried out ourselves, and were alert to the ethical issues of working with these particular pastoralist women. We received ethical clearance from Bahir Dar University's Research Office and permission from the zone and district level Culture and Tourism Bureaus in Fentale District. We were aware of the power inequalities between ourselves (university instructors, urban dwellers and with a different culture, dressing style, language, dialect and beliefs) and the Karrayyu women. We were also well informed of the distinct values and norms of the community by the Culture and Tourism Bureau. An expert from the Culture and Tourism Bureau accompanied and guided us in the field to get to the villages. To respect the culture and values of the people, we were dressed culture-appropriately. We talked to them politely and with the respect forms of pronouns. We explained the purpose of the research, showed our identification cards and letter of support (written by Bahir Dar University) to each interviewee and we requested their willingness to provide information for the study. We collected the data with the informed consent of participants by using the native language of the community – Afan Oromo as one of us speaks the language. We noticed that the use of native language made the interaction process very smooth; the interviewees felt very much comfortable to share their detailed personal experiences and challenges. To conform to the values of the community, women respondents were interviewed by a woman researcher.

Data was collected from six randomly selected *Kebeles* (smallest unit of government administration, under district) (out of 18) of *Fentale* District; namely *Tututi*, *Ebiti*, *Haro Kersa*, *Metehara*, *Kobo*, and *Gelcha*. Using snowball sampling a total of 42 Karrayyus, of which 28 were women (13 are under 40 years of age) and 14 were men (6 young men; 7 elderly, 1 Abba Gadaa) were interviewed from the six *Kebeles*. Besides, 10 officials from various Bureaus (Health, Agriculture, Education, Culture and Tourism Bureau, Youth and Sport, Women and Children Affairs, Labour and Social Affairs Bureaus) were interviewed. We stopped interviewing more people and going to additional *Kebeles* when the data started getting repeated – saturated. The data was collected in November 2017 which overlapped with the time of seasonal migration of the Karrayyu. Hence, the majority of young people were not in the villages (went on seasonal migration). Thus, the researchers used availability and snowball sampling techniques.

Semi-structured in-depth interviews, Participatory Rural Appraisal tools (like Transect walk, daily timeline and seasonal calendar, resource mapping), focus group discussion and participant observation were used to collect data. The Participatory Rural Appraisal tools were mainly used to uncover the resources, daily routines, season-specific workloads and challenges of the women which helped us to explore their roles and associated tacit knowledge and skills. The in-depth interviews and focus group discussion were conducted at the houses, neighbourhoods and workplaces of the respondents. Market places were observed. Each interview and focus group discussion took at least an hour and half. During interviews and focus group discussions, notes were taken parallel to voice recording.

The data analysis was started during the data collection process. The data collected were analysed using *inductive thematic analysis approach* (Miles and Huberman 1994). The voice recordings and notes taken from the FGD, interview and observation data were transcribed and relevant quotations were extracted, which were then translated into English. Then transcripts were read several times and key themes were identified and categorised by the authors with guidance of experts in the area. All names have been changed to ensure anonymity.

Limitations of the study should be mentioned here. We have not conducted detailed analysis of the existing Ethiopian policy and practice as this was beyond the scope of the paper. Furthermore, the Karrayyu are undergoing several sweeping socio-economic changes; how these changes are affecting women and the impact on their learning is an important area for our future ethnographic studies.

Theoretical framework

We used the concepts of 'communities of practice' and 'situated learning' (Lave and Wenger 1991) to explore the learning process in the community following Lave and Wenger (1991) and Wenger's (1998) notion of learning as 'legitimate peripheral participation in a community of practice'. Their conceptualization of learning establishes participation as the way and the destination of learning. They suggest that learning occurs when a newcomer engages in the practice of a community legitimately and peripherally. Legitimacy can be achieved by being the right kind of person, having the right birth, being sponsored, being useful and being feared. Peripherality is achieved through 'lessened intensity, lessened risk, special assistance, lessened cost of error, close supervision, or lessened production pressures'. Peripherality can involve explanations and stories (Wenger 1998, p.100). We use CoP as a concept to investigate knowledge creation and transfer within the Karrayyu community. Previous researchers have suggested that this conceptual approach is appropriate for societies with strong social structures and sense of community such as the Karrayyu rather than societies where there is strong emphasis on the market and individualism (Roberts 2006, Kerno 2008). But, we are also aware that some researchers have critiqued CoP; we will return to the critics in the *'Exploring the ways in which indigenous skills and knowledge are learned – Traditional Midwifery through the CoP lens'* section below.

Indigenous knowledge: the Karrayyu community's view on indigenous knowledge and learning

Rogers (2014) suggests that much of our learning is informal and results from daily activities related to work, family or leisure. He describes it as situated, tacit, 'all round' and as wide as life itself; and larger, more influential than other forms of learning. Nevertheless, much informal learning in everyday life is not recognized as 'learning'. All the knowledge, skills and attitudes we build up through our day-to-day experience are denoted as 'Funds of knowledge' (Moll *et al.* 1992). Such knowledge constitutes the knowledge, skills and attitudes, both individualised and community related, which are built up throughout an individual's life through unconscious learning. While Moll see skills as 'knowing how to' (see Rogers 2014)', Rogers argues that skills are wider than 'knowing how to' and that we all build up tacit 'banks of skills' as well as 'funds of knowledge'.

Rogers and Street (2012) have made a distinction between the 'tacit funds of knowledge and skills' and indigenous knowledge. They consider that indigenous knowledge refers to a collection of traditional knowledge, belief and practices which are common to a whole community. It covers all forms of knowledge and skills, especially (a) conscious taught knowledge and skills, which can be taught formally in schools or indigenous learning systems, or informally in the family and community and is not seen as 'teaching' but it is conscious knowledge and (b) unconscious informal indigenous knowledge . It is difficult to separate these two as one is never conscious of what one knows until it is drawn to our attention by some event or person. Indigenous knowledge differs both in its beliefs and in its epistemology from the knowledges of Western aid agencies and researchers.

The Karrayyu people made difference between two kinds of knowledge – the indigenous knowledge and the knowledge 'brought by outsiders'. Mr Bekele, a participant in our FGD explained their views on nature and sources of their indigenous knowledge:

> 'Our knowledge is not learnt from school and does not emanate from science; … [it] is from nature and God; [it] is not on a paper but inside our mind and heart … it is knowledge descended from our fore-parents. It is practically tested knowledge'.

As many of our respondents commented, several people in their community can read and write without having attended formal education. Remarkably, unlike many unschooled people who regard themselves as deprived, ignorant, inadequate for daily life (Rogers and Street 2012), the Karrayyu whom we interviewed had a clear stand that an 'illiterate' person is not ignorant. The 'Karrayyu people are sharp minded although not educated' (Mr Roobaa); 'We were not taught to write on paper but we know many things!' (Mrs Lomi); 'we know several things, even more than the educated people although we cannot read and write; we are not empty-headed' (Mrs Halko Woda). Moreover, they valued their own knowledge and confidently said that their knowledge is better than the knowledge acquired from schools.

Indigenous knowledge and skills of Karrayyu women

Against the established policy assumptions regarding the pastoral communities in Ethiopia (for example, MoE 2008, Elias and Abdi 2010), the data obtained through our study showed that the Karrayyu pastoralists have rich indigenous knowledge and skills. Here we investigate some of the different kinds of indigenous knowledge and skills that are considered by the Karrayyu community as having central role in leading/sustaining their pastoral way of life. In the subsequent section we look at the skills and knowledge of traditional midwifery in detail and analyse it through the lens of Lave and Wenger's CoP concept.

Basketry

Basketry is one of the indigenous skills of the Karrayyu women we interviewed. They make baskets of different shapes and sizes for different household uses (milking bucket, milk container and churner) from barks of different trees. Baskets are more suited to their semi-nomadic movements. In other (and neighbouring) societies, clay-made pots are used for similar purposes. In learning the skills of basketry, unless care is taken, there could be injuries to the fingers.

Making leather utensils

Our respondents also disclosed that women in Karrayyu learn the skills of preparing bedding, different clothes, material used to carry babies, curtain, household and personal decorations, and *Gombisa*, (leather used to cover the whole body while there is smoke underneath – for fumigation) from animal skin. Their mothers provide a piece of skin to soften, and play with and prepare something small, imitating their elders. As they grew older, they moved on from making bedding to prepare leather clothes for their own use, though not yet as beautiful as the ones prepared by their mothers. At the time of marriage, the bride-to-be and her mother prepare all the leather clothes and household utensils that the new-wed would need in her new house.

House making

Their housing style is modelled after birds' nest. The respondents said that the house gets cold when the outside is very hot. The traditional Karrayyu housing style is susceptible to rainy and windy weather conditions and it requires frequent maintenance, though this housing style is now being changed. Making a house is one of the exclusive traditional knowledge and skills of the Karrayyu women. They help their mother by collecting and bringing grass for making the house. They also help the mother in constructing the house. Most women whom we interviewed do not remember how and when they started learning to make a house; but most started making little houses and played with these, around age seven. Neighbours passing as they worked would stop to correct them and tell them what and how to do.

Preparing food

The Karrayyu people have their own unique traditional food and drink such as porridge, *Becho*, and *Hojjaa* (a drink made up of coffee and milk). Animal products such as milk, butter and meat play a central role in the preparation of these staples. They prefer these meals than food items consumed by urban dwellers (such as *Injera* (Ethiopian flat-bread) with stew, rice, pasta, macaroni …). They consider these foods to be spoiled quickly. They learn about different ingredients and procedures in the preparation and preservation of foods as well as how to avoid getting burned. A young girl will use a small pot alongside that of her mother and if the food is not good, it is given to goats or consumed by her mother and other children, not to men.

Herding animals

The core of Karrayyu people's pastoralist livelihood is animal husbandry. The Karrayyu people believe that herding is a central part of their identity. They own goats, sheep, cattle, and camels and learn to identify the location of pasture, water and know each of their animals individually. Our respondents said that girls used to learn counting numbers from their mothers. Besides, to differentiate them, they put distinct symbol on their animals by using heated iron. According to our respondents, as children they started learning this skill from age five, starting with herding small goats, and progressing to herding goats and calf (small cattle), cattle, and to herding camels, and migrating with camels during draught. Both males and females passed through this process to get married (the exception being herding camel was confined to males). For the girls, the closely associated skill with animals herding is milking. They start milking goats and pass to milking cows and later on to milking camels.

The following remarks can be culled from the examples presented above. There are commonalities in learning all the five skills described above. Karrayyu girls learn these skills from their mothers, their neighbours and extended family members. They start learning these skills from around age five and get better progressively until they get married. The Karrayyu girls learn these skills informally through observation, imitation, helping, running errands, participation, trial and error, playing, demonstration, practice and sometimes, step-by-step oral instruction (specifically for preparing foods). The motivation to learn these skills emanates basically from fulfilling traditional gender roles that are exclusively girls'/women's. These roles include constructing house, cooking, collecting firewood, fetching water, preparing household utensils, milking animals, processing milk to make butter and cheese, fumigate the milk containers etc. Different from the rest, the skills of herding animals is for both sexes. Beyond materialistic and utilitarian reasons, the motivation to learn these skills also stems from a bigger cultural value attached to marriage and married life. When a Karrayyu woman gets married and moves to live with her in-laws, she will be despised and disrespected if she is not well accomplished in these skills. A woman who has not mastered these skills is considered as a woman unmarriageable; even if married, lack of mastery of these skills became reason for divorce. In most of these skills, marriage is, not only the major motivating factor, but also the milestone at which a beginner/newcomer shifts into an expert (except food preparation and animal herding, whereby expertise does not wait until marriage). From the above remarks, it can be noted that learning the indigenous knowledge and skills in Karrayyu community is mainly gendered.

Exploring the ways in which indigenous skills and knowledge are learned – Traditional midwifery through the CoP lens

One of the most widespread areas of indigenous learning and knowledge within this Karrayyu group of women was traditional midwifery. For this reason, we will focus on the ways in which these skills were learned, practised and passed on within the community.

All of the interviewed women gave birth to all of their children (number of offspring ranges from 4 to 13) at home by themselves and/or with the help of traditional birth attendants. All the women interviewed said they have the traditional midwifery skills; but, they pointed out that some are more experienced and skilled than others. We noticed that the Karrayyu's prefer home delivery with the assistance of traditional birth attendants than the hospital delivery. In Karrayyu traditional midwifery seems a wide-spread skill as all women reportedly possess some skill of traditional midwifery, unlike other parts of Ethiopia (Mr Teferi, expert at Fentale District Health Bureau and authors' context knowledge). When it comes to how traditional midwifery knowledge, skills, and judgements are formed, apprenticeship has long been the dominant answer (Dietsch *et al.* 2011, Rishworth *et al.* 2016, Abdul-Mumin 2016, Ohaja and Murphy-Lawless 2017). However, in some places (for example in rural part of northern Honduras), becoming traditional birth attendants is considered as a result of 'religious calling', which means that their ability to attend birth is a 'gift from God' (Low *et al.* 2006).

We now turn to look at how, why, when and where Karrayyu women learn and practice traditional midwifery skills through a CoP lens, a perspective that considers learning mainly as a social practice embedded in culture and day-to-day lives of people. In Lave and Wenger's account, newcomers are said to develop a dynamic 'general idea' as to what their community of practice is composed of and this includes … who is involved, what they do, what everyday life is like … what learners need to learn to become full practitioners … (Lave and Wenger 1991, p. 95)

Becoming a traditional birth attendant: How?

Describing how she learnt the midwifery skills, Mrs Lomi said that ' … we observe carefully and critically. We learnt by observing others. To learn, it requires attention and devotion. It needs observing every detail and comprehension … .'. In line with this, Wenger (1998) indicates that observation can be used in the learning of competence, as long as it leads up to actual engagement in the practice. On the other hand, Lave and Wenger (1991) argue that legitimate peripherality provides newcomers 'with more than an "observational" lookout post, it crucially involves participation as a way of learning – of both absorbing and being absorbed in – the "culture of practice"' (P.95). The midwifery knowledge and skill is not confined to a few individual masters; it is rather participatory and distributed skill among the wider community, although of varying levels of competence. In relation to this, Mrs Galle said that when a pregnant woman starts to labour, 'all the neighbours will gather and they will do what they can'.

Regarding learning pattern/order, as reflected in learning skills of basketry, house-making, and leather-making cases, newcomers started their learning at the stages that seemed less complex for them. This is in keeping with a CoP approach whereby ' … the ordering of learning and of everyday practice do not coincide … less intense, less complex, less vital tasks are learned before more central aspects of practice' (Lave and Wenger 1991, p. 96).

In the process of moving from peripheral to core participation in the CoP of traditional birth attendants, an important milestone is giving birth. Although females participate in the process of child birth practice since childhood, they attain a proficient skill of midwifery and the confidence to attend birth after they gave birth to a child themselves. This has been confirmed by several interviewees; for instance, Mrs Dumbushe said that 'I observe when my neighbours work as traditional birth attendants. I also observed how the traditional birth attendant was working when I gave birth twice. On my third delivery, I delivered on my own, without calling the traditional birth attendants.' Learning is, therefore, part of being a Karrayyu woman helping family, participating in everyday life and socializing with neighbours. That is why Mrs Lomi and the other interviewees said that 'There is no one who teaches us midwifery skills'. With this regard, Lave and Wenger (1991, p. 65) confirm that learning is not just 'the internalization of knowledge by individuals but … a process of becoming a member of a sustained community of practice. Developing an identity as a member of a community and becoming knowledgeably skillful are part of the same process.'

Peripherality and legitimacy are the heuristic tools that Lave and Wenger use to analyse their CoP approach to learning. In almost all our examples, learners are expected to master skills at or after marriage. Before marriage, playing, learning and working are mixed-up; and learners' participation has been mostly peripheral, an essential condition for learning in CoP: '… peripherality requires less demands on time, effort, and responsibility for work than for full participants. A newcomer's tasks are short and simple, the costs of errors are small … It is also true that the initial, partial contributions of apprentices are useful' (Lave and Wenger 1991, p. 110).

In traditional midwifery, as with the other examples given, young girls learned skills from their parents, neighbours, relatives or other members of their community. This provides them with legitimacy, an important condition for learning in CoP. 'Legitimate participation comes diffusely through membership in family and community … the issue of conferring legitimacy is more important than the issue of providing teaching' (Lave and Wenger 1991, p. 92).

In most of our examples, the mastery of skills was reported to result from observation, participation or other forms of learning, not from didactic teaching. This is in accordance with the CoP approach whereby '… learning can take place where there is teaching, but does not take intentional instruction to be in itself the source or cause of learning' (Lave and Wenger 1991, p. 40).

Our respondents also provided accounts of self-evaluation. In this regard, Lave and Wenger (1991, p. 111) state that 'As opportunities for understanding how well or poorly one's efforts contribute are evident in practice': legitimate peripheral participation provides a ground for self-evaluation.

Moreover, it is difficult to identify how long learning the midwifery skills takes for a woman due to the blurred border between learning the midwifery skill and growing up of girls into adulthood. However, we noted that Karrayyu girls start learning the midwifery skill since childhood and requires giving birth oneself before developing the confidence of attending birth. During the interview with Mrs Dumbushe, a girl of about 10 years old came with a message. 'Her mother is an experienced birth attendant,' she said. 'This girl has been observing how her mother performed her midwifery skills'. The girl responded, 'Yes, when I grow up, I can work as birth attendant. When we play with other children, I play the role of a birth attendant. Now, I am afraid of working as a birth attendant; but I will do it when I grow up.'

Becoming a traditional birth attendant: contents of learning

The contents that a peripherally participating Karrayyu woman need to learn in becoming a fully and centrally participating traditional birth attendant can be divided into three phases (pre-, during and post-partum elements) which encompass knowledge, skills, and beliefs. All of these are informed and guided by the society's overarching philosophies.

One of the overarching philosophies of the Karrayyu relevant to learning to become a traditional birth attendant is that nature is inherently good and that it is the role of human beings to understand nature and go with it, not against it. For example, the Karrayyus' hands-off approach to midwifery is grounded on this philosophy. They strongly believe that human beings, like all other animals, can go through the natural process of pregnancy and birth with no or little intervention. Underlining this, Mrs Lomi said that ' ... no animal in this world has ever been attended by a birth attendant. What is so unique about human beings? We have the innate capacity to naturally pass through pregnancy and birth. That is why we give birth alone under tree shade.' The Karrayyu believe that if there is intervention in the natural process of child birth, there will be complications. They strongly associate the sharp rise in cases of stitching and caesarean section in hospital delivery with the unnatural process and manner of birthing there.

One area of knowledge for Karrayyu women to learn in becoming a fully participating traditional birth attendant and mother is counting pregnancy due dates. Karrayyu women do so 'by observing the size of the moon when we realise our period has stopped. When the moon is seen eight times afterwards, we recognise that the delivery time has approached' (Mrs Dumbushe). Thus, in the absence of formal literacy skills, Karrayyu women understood and used nature (the lunar cycle) to count birthing due dates. Such knowledge is used for making the necessary preparations for the delivery.

Another area of knowledge for them is elements of healthy meal and lifestyle and how to continue to practise it. Karrayyu, who led a pastoralist life for centuries, had their own conceptualization of healthy food and life style. They relied, especially in the past, on animal protein-, specifically dairy-based diet. As well as consuming butter, the Karrayyu (women and men alike) used it for anointing their body. They believed that their digestive system and physiology was accustomed to such meal and lifestyle and that their resilience in face of different challenges emanated from their practice of a healthy diet and life style. Several respondents suggested that any deviation from this healthy diet and life style would have negative repercussions in everyday life, including in child birth. For instance, Mrs Adile compared the natural and healthy Karrayyu lifestyle with the currently changes and said ' ... our body used to shine like a glass; it was soft. Our body was strong. We did not face challenges during child birth as our body was soft and elastic. But now, our body has dried like a piece of wood. The oil we eat dried our body ... '

During child birth, one of the essential knowledge and skills of Karrayyu women (and traditional birth attendants) is collaborative participation and division of labour. Everybody contributes something based on their ability. The role of traditional birth attendants is 'praying to God, cutting the umbilical cord, and facilitating the coming out of placenta and if there is any problem, with the help of God, correcting the position of the baby [during breech presentation] by massaging the pregnant woman's belly gently' (Mrs Halko Woda).

Another competence area for a centripetally participating Karrayyu traditional birth attendant includes knowledge about postpartum care and nutrition. In the past, a woman used to get a lot of care and treatment after delivery. For example, she would 'eat porridge with butter, drink butter, drink milk; a fattened goat (even an ox, in the past) would be slaughtered and she would drink its blood and eat its meat' (Mrs Halko Woda and Mrs Lomi). This facilitated the mother's speedy recovery from the delivery pain, enhanced breastfeeding, and facilitated faster growth of the newborn. The experienced traditional birth attendants strongly believe that the change of diet is jeopardising the health, recovery and growth of both the mother and the baby.

Becoming a traditional birth attendant: where does learning take place?

As an instance of informal, unintentional, unorganized learning, learning to become a traditional birth attendant takes place in the sites where actual childbirth takes place. That is, midwifery skills are learnt mainly at home, and sometimes the learning takes place under tree sheds. This is confirmed, for example, by Mrs Halko. 'I delivered my six children at home and the remaining two under tree-shed while herding cattle. I cut the umbilical cord with a sharp stone when I delivered under tree shed.' Distinguishing between the different modes of learning to become a birth attendant, Mrs Lomi said that ' … learning about child delivery is not confined to the hospital and educational institutions; the Karrayyu people learn from each other and work as birth attendant.'

Becoming a traditional birth attendant: continuity and change

Learning traditional midwifery skill, although under pressure, is still continuing. Today, with the growing availability of health facilities and free ambulance service traditional birth attendants are often criticised for attending births, they are undermined and threatened with a ban on their midwifery practice. Nevertheless, the Karrayyu women still prefer traditional birth attendants and while the practice of traditional midwifery continues, so does the learning of traditional midwifery skills.

From the discussion so far, although we do not want to suggest that CoP is the only approach to look into indigenous knowledge and ways of knowing, we believe that it helps to explain better the ways in which a community learn indigenous knowledge and skills of different kind informally. However, we are also aware that some critics have been labelled against the CoP, among others, (1) downplaying the role of teaching in the learning processes, and (2) not having adequately explored on how power and control of resources facilitates or hampers learning of newcomers (Fuller *et al.* 2005, Hodkinson and Hodkinson 2004, Roberts 2006). For example, regarding the role of teaching in indigenous learning, the CoP approach clearly downplays it although the data indicated the presence of step-by-step oral instruction in learning the skills of preparing Karrayyu meals. The other critics against the CoP, such as (1) overemphasizing legitimate peripheral participation as the major learning process; (2) treating newcomers as 'tabula rasa', implicitly, although they seem to agree that people come to a workplace already formed with beliefs, understandings, skills and attitudes; (3) not describing or analyzing communities of practice that are spatially or socially fragmented (Fuller *et al.* 2005, Hodkinson and Hodkinson 2004, Roberts 2006) do not seem to hold water in the context of the Karrayu community.

New ways of learning – Learning beyond indigenous knowledge and skills

In addition to the indigenous knowledge and skills, the Karrayyu are also engaged in non-indigenous learning. While this is mostly informal, some is organized and delivered by external providers.

The District Integrated Functional Adult Literacy/Education (IFAL/E) programme coordinator indicates, in 2017, 859 people have attended IFAL of which 341 were women. It was reported that the women did not attend regularly and often withdraw. The programme includes literacy, numeracy, family planning, balanced diet, avoiding home delivery and personal and environmental hygiene. As the coordinator said, these contents are externally provided as the 'community does not know about a balanced diet...' We noted that the IFAL programme being offered is informed by an 'instrumental and deficit approach' to learning (See Rao and Robinson-Pant 2006) as it does not consider the indigenous knowledge and skill that the women accumulate over time and as it starts from what the people lack. The IFAL programme is instrumental in a sense that instead of aiming to impact on the lives of women themselves, it is delivered to help them perform their reproductive roles.

The needs and challenges of women in the IFAL programme were indicated by an adult literacy facilitator, Mr Mohammed. As he said, not only the content, curriculum and methods that the adults seek to learn were different from what is taught in the programme but also the learners have diverse needs. He also confirmed that women's participation is very low due to the presence of males in the class. When asked why, the interviewed women gave different reasons including lack of awareness on the programme; being ashamed of going to school as they think they are too old to go to schools where their children learn; being busy with household chores; unsuitable place and time and lack of female facilitator.

Though the women were not participating in the formal literacy programme, they were engaged in learning literacy and numeracy from their friends, children and husband. For instance, Mrs Adile learnt ways of mobile phone usage from her children and literacy facilitator. To save contact numbers and make calls, many of them use different symbols in the phone like star symbol, flower, sun, ball, heart, etc. 'Although I do not know the numbers,' said Mrs Adile, 'when I see the symbols, I recognize who is calling.' From the experiences of these women, we can understand that they do learn literacy and numeracy skills informally and they use these skills in their everyday lives. Moreover, it is also evident that the literacy and numeracy skills they are engaged in are part of 'everyday literacies' which are applicable in their day to day lives; not 'school literacy' which is less applicable in their everyday life, and which is taught in IFAL programme (see Rogers and Street 2012 to distinguish different types of literacy).

Health extension workers teach the women to use latrines, the importance of delivering at a health institution, family planning, pregnancy follow-up, and infant vaccination. Although women made the latrine to please the health extension workers, they never used it. The Karrayyu women also learn agriculture-related knowledge and skills by critically observing from the hired labourers and from the agriculture extension experts. We asked if the agriculture office tries to link its content with what the people already know. He said: 'We recognize that they have traditional knowledge. However, their knowledge is not scientifically proven. So, we are teaching them the science-proven knowledge … their traditional knowledge is useless. There is no traditional knowledge that we accepted from them and apply.' We noted that this is a clear illustration that agriculture extension service delivery practice, divorced from the knowledge, tradition and values of Karrayyu people, is informed by deficit approach.

Conclusion

The study has provided empirical evidence which illustrates something of the wide range of knowledge and skills that indigenous/pastoral women acquire informally, of which the knowledge and skills of traditional midwifery are very important. Taking a communities of practice approach we have identified that individual Karrayyu women become traditional birth attendants through different pathways and used this approach to understand the learning process of traditional midwifery skill in Karrayyu. The learning process not only includes the midwifery skills per se, but is grounded in their values, traditions, norms and beliefs of healthy pregnancy and delivery. Learning is embedded in the culture and tradition of giving birth in the Karrayyu community. Traditional birth attendants in Karrayyu are considered by their community members as wise, proficient, considerate, culturally sensitive, and women-friendly; the confidence in their contribution towards the safe birth of Karrayyu babies, their acceptance and reputation emanate from the way they learn their skills. On the contrary, trained health professionals view them as unskilled, unscientific and inferior and they are often despised, ignored, banned, criminalized, frightened, and undermined. Some traditional birth attendants understand the areas where they can make a difference and their limitations and are open to learn and to collaborate with professional birth attendants.

These women resisted knowledge that contradicted their indigenous knowledge. On the other hand, they welcomed new skills that seemed relevant to them. For instance, many of the women involved in this study would like to have mobile phones and watches; and, they have a plan to learn literacy. But, it should be underlined that the literacy skill they demanded is not school literacy, but functional and everyday literacy skills, digital literacy skills which have not so far been included in the IFAL programme.

This article has discussed how women mostly learn their indigenous knowledge, such as traditional midwifery, through informal practices from their neighbours, mothers and skilled traditional birth attendants through critical observation and participation in the child delivery process. They also learn new skills such as cooking non-traditional foods informally from neighbouring Oromo tribes, cafeteria and restaurant owners in the town, relatives living in a town, some NGOs etc. through critical observation and trial and error. Moreover, the pastoral women learnt how to use mobile phone from their husbands, children, siblings, friends and neighbours informally. They have also created their own ways of using mobile phones such as using different symbols to represent contacts. Induced by the changes in their ways of life, farming has become another common informal learning area of new skills. Though they learn new knowledge and skills about cultivation from agricultural extension workers, they mostly learn from labourers hired by the people who contract their land.

This article stressed that the dominant approach to adult literacy and skills training – modelled on schooling and based on a pre-planned curriculum and 'correct' methodology – gives little emphasis to other forms of knowledge and learning and ignores the multiplicity of knowledges and the social nature of literacy. We believe that this 'deficit approach' (Rao and Robinson-Pant 2006) hinders pastoral women from exercising their rights as citizens, as women and as pastoralists. There is a need to not only revisit the contents and approaches of the current education and training programmes intended for indigenous women, but also a strong critique of the way teachers/facilitators are trained.

The Karrayyu have lived as pastoralists for centuries through their highly developed indigenous knowledge and skills. However, due to misguided assumptions about the values of pastoralism and questionable measures of development (MoE 2008, Engidasew 2012, Elias and Abdi 2010), they are being pressured to abandon their way of life. Our study suggests that adult education (including health and agriculture extension) policies and strategies in Ethiopia need to recognize and build on the indigenous knowledge and skills of the pastoral women themselves and thereby facilitate the improvement in their lives instead of changing their identity and way of life.

All educational provision – the formal or informal – for pastoral women should be built on their prior learning. To this end, all people engaged in teaching/providing any training and education to/with the Karrayyu need to learn understand the culture, values, indigenous knowledge and skills of the women and community. In this way Karrayyu women can use their accumulated knowledge and skills as a base to build the new knowledge and skills for their changing society. This way, the learners will feel respected, understood and valued. This calls for participatory action research and ethnographic research to work with and alongside the pastoralist women. Furthermore, learners should participate in the designing of their own learning, rather than being imposed by the providers (extension workers or the literacy facilitators) alone. Pastoral women have distinct educational needs and experiences and although pastoralists are often considered as homogenous groups, they are diverse. The Karrayyu have specific bodies of knowledge and skills and ways of learning that call for diverse education and training programmes which address their needs as a particular group of pastoral women.

Acknowledgements

The authors would like to express their heart-felt gratitude to Professor Anna Robinson-Pant, Dr Sheila Aikman, and Professor Alan Rogers for the mentoring support, and commenting on the drafts. The authors are also very grateful to Mr. Demelash for the guiding service during the fieldwork.

Disclosure statement

No potential conflict of interest was reported by the authors.

ORCID

Turuwark Zalalam Warkineh (iD) http://orcid.org/0000-0001-8121-0007
Abiy Menkir Gizaw (iD) http://orcid.org/0000-0002-6528-0977

References

Abdul-Mumin, K.H., 2016. Village midwives and their changing roles in Brunei Darussalam: a qualitative study. *Women and birth*, 29, 73–81.

Aikman, S., 2011. Educational and indigenous justice in Africa. *International journal of educational development*, 31(1), 15–22.

Barume, A. K., 2014. *Land rights of indigenous peoples in Africa (with special focus on Central, Eastern and Southern Africa)*. Second edition – revised and updated. Copenhagen: IWGIA.

Dietsch, E., *et al.*, 2011. Learning lessons from a traditional midwifery workforce in Western Kenya. *Midwifery*, 27(3), 324–330.

Elias, E., and Abdi, F., 2010. *Putting pastoralists on the policy agenda: land alienation in southern Ethiopia*. London: IIED.

Engidasew, Z., 2012. Functional adult literacy for the pastoral community in Ethiopia – challenges and prospects. *Journal of adult education and development*, 78. https://www.dvv-international.de/en/adult-education-and-development/editions/aed-782012/benefits-of-adult-learning-and-social-inclusion/functional-adult-literacy-for-the-pastoralist-community-in-ethiopia-challenges-and-prospects/

Federal Democratic Republic of Ethiopia Population Census Commission. 2008. Summary and Statistical Report of the 2007 Population and Housing Census. Addis Ababa: UNFPA.

Fuller, A., *et al.*, 2005. Learning as peripheral participation in communities of practice: a reassessment of key concepts in workplace learning. *British educational research journal*, 31 (1), 49–68.

Gebre, A., 2001. *Pastoralism under pressure: land alienation and pastoral transformations among the Karrayyu of eastern Ethiopia, 1941 to the present*. Thesis (PhD). The Netherlands: Institute for Social Science.

Hodkinson, P., and Hodkinson, H., 2004. A constructive critique of communities of practice: moving beyond Lave and Wenger. Seminar Paper Presented at 'Integrating Work and Learning – Contemporary Issues' Seminar Series, 11th May. Oval Research Working Paper 04–02.

International Work Group for Indigenous Affairs (IWGIA). 2016. The indigenous world 2016. Copenhagen, Denmark: IWGIA.

Kerno, S.J., 2008. Limitations of communities of practice: a consideration of unresolved issues and difficulties in the approach. *Journal of leadership & organizational studies*, 15(1), 69–78.

King, L., 2000. *International survey on adult education for indigenous people's country study: the Philippines*. Hamburg, Germany: UNESCO Institute for Education

King, L., and Schielmann, S., 2004. *The challenges of indigenous education: practices and perspectives*. Paris: UNESCO Publishing

Lave, J., and Wenger, E., 1991. *Situated learning: legitimate peripheral participation*. Cambridge: Cambridge University Press.

Low, L.K., *et al.*, 2006. Challenges for traditional birth attendants in northern rural Honduras. *Midwifery*, 22(1), 78–87.

Malifu, E., 2006. *The environmental consequences of dependent development in the upper Awash Valley and the predicaments of the Kereyu*. Thesis (MA). Addis Ababa University.

Miles, B. M., and Huberman, A. M., 1994. *Qualitative data analysis: an expanded source book.* (2nd Ed.). Thousand Oaks: Sage.

Ministry of Education (MoE) 2008. *Pastoralist education strategy in Ethiopia.* Addis Ababa.

Moll, L.C., *et al.*, 1992. Funds of knowledge for teaching: using a qualitative approach to connect homes and classrooms. *Theory into practice*, 31(2), 132–141.

Morrison, S.L., and Vaioleti, T.M., 2011. Inclusion of indigenous people in CONFINTEA VI and follow-up process. *International review of education*, 57(1-2), 69–87.

Ohaja, M., and Murphy-Lawless, J., 2017. Unilateral collaboration: the practices and understandings of traditional birth attendants in southeastern Nigeria. *Women and birth*, 30(4), 165–171.

Rao, N., and Robinson-Pant, A., 2006. Adult education and indigenous people: addressing gender in policy and practice. *International journal of educational development*, 26(2), 209–223.

Rishworth, A., Bisung, E., and Luginaah, I., 2016. It's like a disease": women's perceptions of caesarean sections in Ghana's Upper West Region. *Women and birth*, 29(6), 119–125.

Roberts, J., 2006. Limits to communities of practice. *Journal of management studies*, 43(3), 623–639.

Robinson-Pant, A., 2016. *Learning knowledge and skills for agriculture to improve rural livelihoods.* Paris, France: UNESCO Publishing.

Rogers, A., and Street, B., 2012. *Adult literacy and development: stories from the field.* England: NIACE.

Rogers, A., 2014. *The base of the iceberg: informal learning and its impact on formal and nonformal learning.* Opladen: Barbara Budrich Publishers

Schmelkes, S., 2011. Adult education and indigenous peoples in Latin America. *International review of education*, 59, 89–105.

Takayanagi, T., 2016. Rethinking women's learning and empowerment in Kenya: Maasai village women take initiative. *International review of education*, 62(6), 671–688.

Takayanagi, T., 2017. *The power of informal learning and literacy for women in the Maasai community, Kenya.* Thesis (PhD). University of Sydney.

UIL (UNESCO Institute for Lifelong Learning) 2010. *Belem framework for action.* Hamburg, UIL.

Usman, L. M., 2010. The indigenous knowledge system of female pastoral Fulani of Northern Nigeria. *In* D. Kapoor and E. Shizha, eds. *Indigenous knowledge and learning in Asia/Pacific and Africa: perspectives on development, education, and culture.* New York: Palgrave Macmillan, 213–225.

Wenger, E., 1998. *Community of practice: learning, meaning and identity.* Cambridge: Cambridge University Press.

Negotiating indigenous identities within mainstream community livelihoods: Stories of Aeta women in the Philippines

Gina Lontoc Ⓘ

ABSTRACT

Livelihood participation among members of indigenous communities necessitates redefining of gender roles in indigenous communities. Utilising participatory rural appraisal (PRA) anchored on the principles of Social Identity Theory and Critical Race Theory (CRT), this article draws on a study about adult Aeta women, one of the largest indigenous groups in the mountainous regions of the Philippines. It looks into the perspectives of Aeta women on how livelihood practices address the integration of indigenous communities into mainstream societies. Through seasonal calendars, topical mapping and discussion circles, the study examined Aeta women's negotiation of their identities as they participate in livelihood practices in mainstream communities. Their community participation indicates how intergroup conflict and social categorisation led to marginalisation and resistance to oppressions to strengthen their will to survive and achieve positive social identities.

Introduction

Many indigenous communities around the world continue to suffer social, cultural, economic, and political exclusion and marginalisation. The United Nations Declaration on the Rights of Indigenous Peoples (United Nations 2007) states that "Indigenous peoples and individuals are free and equal to all other peoples and individuals and have the right to be free from any kind of discrimination ... " (p. 4). However, many indigenous peoples (IP) communities still lack access to quality social services, such as housing, healthcare and education, as compared to their non-indigenous counterparts.

As observed by Rodriguez and Carruthers (2008), indigenous people often face regional development and institutional conflicts which often create divisions even within indigenous communities. This also holds true in the Philippines where some IP communities were forced to leave their territories due to natural disasters, development activities, and armed conflicts. Data from the study conducted by the Indigenous Peoples' International Centre for Policy Research and Education (2020), show that IPs who left their ancestral domains experience extreme poverty as characterised by food shortage and high dropout rates among children. IP communities who migrated to lowlands have to deal with the norms of the mainstream society. This creates not only a significant challenge in terms of their community participation but also multifarious issues relating to but not limited to, cultural loss, gender mainstreaming, urbanisation, marginalised identities and social cohesion.

Part of the definition of indigenous peoples formulated by the Indigenous Peoples Rights Act (IPRA) in 1997 is that they:

> refer to a group of people or homogenous societies identified by self-ascription and ascription by others, who have continuously lived as organised community on communally bounded and defined territory, and who have, under claims of ownership since time immemorial, occupied, possessed customs, tradition and other distinctive cultural traits, or who have, through resistance to political, social and cultural inroads of colonisation, non-indigenous religions and culture, became historically differentiated from the majority of Filipinos... include peoples who are regarded as indigenous on account of their descent from the populations which inhabited the country, at the time of conquest or colonisation, or at the time of inroads of nonindigenous religions and cultures, or the establishment of present state boundaries, who retain some or all of their own social, economic, cultural and political institutions, but who may have been displaced from their traditional domains or who may have resettled outside their ancestral domains.(National Commission on Indigenous Peoples 2019. IPRA Chapter 2, Section 3H).

This definition contains major concepts which are pivotal in investigating issues on the challenges that indigenous people have to deal with. These are the concepts of identity, territory, history, and displacement. Though these concepts are tightly woven together, this study focuses on the IP's negotiation of identities as they participate in livelihood practices in the mainstream society. These concepts resonate with findings that indigenous people take efforts to be in sync with government agenda (Li 2000). They also make representations to voice out articulation of themselves, their needs, and aspirations. However, it seems that, still, their voices have been silent in government discourses.

This study involves one of the largest indigenous communities in the Philippines, the *Aetas*. They commonly dwell in mountainous areas in Cagayan Valley or Region 2 and in Central Luzon or Region 3. They are known as Agta in northeastern Luzon, Ati in Visayas and Mamanwa in Mindanao (Padilla 2013) with distinct physical features as short, with curly hair and dark skin. Two communities of Aetas in Tarlac are involved in the study. They used to live on the slopes of Mt. Pinatubo, a volcano which marked one of the largest eruptions in the country in 1991 and which forced the Aetas to relocate to the lowlands. Though most of them have maintained their traditional hunter-gatherer mode of living, their contact with lowlanders introduced them to swidden farming and trading.

Selected women from these two Aeta communities are the participants of the present study. For a period of six (6) months, they have been observed by the researcher in their market areas where they engage in trade by selling their agricultural products. They also participated in discussion circles which gave them the opportunity to discuss community issues. Through the use of these visual participatory methods and women's narratives this study aimed to examine how Aeta women negotiate their identities as they integrate into the mainstream community through engaging in livelihood activities. Furthermore, the study addresses the following questions:

1. What challenges do Aeta women experience in participating livelihoods in the mainstream society?
2. How do they negotiate their identities in engaging in community livelihood practices?
3. How does their negotiation of identities impact their self-determination and community participation?

Negotiation as a continuous process of identity construction

Social constructivism supports the view that an individual creates multiple identities in a particular social context and allows himself to be created by that context (Shen and Dumani 2013). This accounts for how an individual functions in the society; thus, reflecting the notion of identity as a "kind of person" in a given context, as suggested by Gee (2001, p. 99). Though he notes that there is a "core identity" that holds uniformly for one's self and others across contexts, there exists the multiplicity of identities an individual can possibly embody in relation to his performance in the society. He puts forward four ways to view identity construction.

The first perspective is the *nature perspective* or N-identity which pertains to one's state or condition. N-identity is developed from forces of nature and is biological and genetic. Thus, this form of identity is beyond the control of the individual or the society. In the second perspective labelled as *the institutional perspective* or I-Identity, identity is seen as a position invested by institutions. Examples of this are being a student, a professor, a priest, etc. Thus, authorities bear the power created by and within the institution wherein process of authorisation constitutes traditions, laws, rules and principles.

The third perspective is known as *the Discursive identity* or the D-Identity which is recognised by the discourse or dialogues with other individuals. The process refers to an individual trait which is achieved by the individual or ascribed by other people. To illustrate this, social interactions with other people can reinforce one's traits such as being courageous, enthusiastic, courteous, funny, and so on. The fourth perspective, *the affinity perspective* or A-Identity, involves an affinity group composing of people dispersed across large geographical boundaries. The process is the sharing of practices among members of the affinity group and the practice itself is considered as the power. Gee (2001, p. 105) notes that what members share in the affinity group "*is allegiance to, access to, and participation in specific practices* that provide each of the group's members the requisite experiences". These ways of looking at identity forms the dynamics of negotiating one's identities by revealing how one's identities function for him/her in a given context.

In the similar vein, in the essay, *Cultural Identity and Diaspora*, Hall (1990) draws our attention to the conjunction between identity and culture. He posits that "instead of thinking identity as an already accomplished fact, we should think, instead, of identity as a 'production', which is never complete, always in process, and always constituted within, not outside, representation" (p. 222). This draws the link between cultural identity and representation.

Hall claims that cultural identity can be defined in terms of "one shared culture, a sort of collective 'one true self', hiding inside the many other, more superficial or artificially imposed 'selves', which people with a shared history and ancestry hold in common" (p. 223). This means that cultural identities lie beneath the historical experiences which provide the people with "unchanging and continuous frames of reference and meaning" (p. 223). However, he also proposes another notion of cultural identity which subscribes to "critical points of deep and significant *difference* which constitute 'what we really are'" (p. 225) or with the intervention of history, "what we have become". This offers insights about how a person would relate or would or would not be identified with a particular group. Thus, identity construction involves identity negotiation which account for the process of examination of dynamics that exist in social interactions which mediate an individual's state of "being" and his/her state of "becoming".

Critical race theory, social identities and Aeta women narratives

As part of legal studies, Critical Race Theory (CRT) originated in the United States in 1970s in order to address the issues of race, racism, and power particularly in relation to experiences of people of colour. As Writer (2008) points out, the goal of CRT is to construct realities through narratives and storytelling; thus, providing voice for the marginalised. Though popularised in white-dominated territories such as Britain (Hill 2009), Canada (Kubota 2015), and Australia (Nelson 2007), this study provides perspectives on how principles of CRT operate in Asian context and how these principles coincide with theoretical and methodological principles of identity construction.

Torre (2009) suggests that CRT expands forms of narratives to weaken dominant discourses and ideologies. Through stories, testimonies, biographies, etc., CRT challenges social hierarchies by unravelling alternative perspectives and compelling insights on social structures which preserve social positioning. As highlighted by Delgado and Stefancic (2001), one of the strengths of CRT is that it pushes the multiple, overlapping, and conflicting identities of individuals.

At this juncture, the nature of what counts as *indigenous* is crucial in order to understand negotiating identities with mainstream community participation. Although the United Nations has not offered a single definition of *indigenous*, the Department of Economic and Social Affairs (DESA 2009) stated the most cited concept of *indigenous* drawn from the work of José R. Martínez Cobo as follows:

> Indigenous communities, peoples and nations are those which, having a historical continuity with pre-invasion and pre-colonial societies that developed on their territories, consider themselves distinct from other sectors of the societies now prevailing on those territories, or parts of them. They form at present non-dominant sectors of society and are determined to preserve, develop and transmit to future generations their ancestral territories, and their ethnic identity, as the basis of their continued existence as peoples, in accordance with their own cultural patterns, social institutions and legal system (p. 4).

In relation to this definition, DESA (2009) adds that on the level of the individual, there are two components that make up his/her indigenous identity, i.e., group consciousness and group acceptance. Therefore, "an indigenous person is one who belongs to indigenous populations through self-identification as indigenous … and is recognised and accepted by these populations as one of its members … " (p. 5).

Taking the CRT lens, the description of what counts as *indigenous* argues for the centrality of race beyond skin colour but a concept embedded with socio-political dimension and with the notion of knowledge as a political construct which problematises the nature of knowledge created, the knowledge producer and knowledge user. In analysing socio-political participation of Aeta women, this study combines CRT with analysis of narratives about Aeta women's participation in the mainstream society.

Community participation could create tensions arising from conflicting processes of negotiation and transformation. This is perceived to be inevitable as they are part of social groups which identifies one's membership in the society, thus, termed by Tajfel (1981) as *social identity*. He further emphasises that social identity derives from "a comparative and 'relational' manner from an individual's group membership" (p. 227). He conceptualises social identity as "the individual's knowledge that he belongs to certain social group together with some emotional and value significance to him of the group membership" (Tajfel 1972, p. 31 as cited in Turner 1982, p. 18). This component also takes on in-group bias or the tendency to favour the in-group over the out-group thus, leading to favouritism and discrimination, reflective of *social comparison,* which, as suggested by Tajfel and Turner (1979), involves the evaluation of an individual's own group with reference to other groups in terms of value-laden attributes and characteristics.

This issue of social stratification provides the intersection between CRT and Social Identity theory – the theoretical traditions unearth marginalisation of racial groups and the control and oppression from dominant groups. Thus, this reflects how social and political dimensions of participation overlap with gender, which may forge antagonism between social groups.

The role of Aeta women in livelihood practices

In the Philippines, the International Labour Organisations (ILO) (1995) made a survey to collect and analyse the indigenous knowledge systems and practices among primary tribes. They found out that the Atis (Aeta) of Panay were knowledgeable and practicing farming, hunting, handicrafts, fishing, and livestock farming. This reflects their strong connection with the environment and natural resources through the utilisation of their traditional skills as they engage in their traditional forms of livelihood such as swidden agriculture, charcoal production, and honey collection (Balilla et al. 2013).

As previously mentioned, Aetas had to leave their ancestral lands due to volcanic eruption. Relocation to resettlement sites exposed their livelihood practices in mainstream communities. Various non-governmental organisations (NGOs) and faith-based groups extended support to Aeta communities particularly in terms of livelihood programmes. Aetas learned other forms of livelihood like resin extraction (Ella 2008) in case of Aetas in Palawan, another province in the Philippines. As observed by Tindowen (2016), Aetas learned poultry production, and making and selling brooms. They also engage in seasonal paid labour opportunities such as performing traditional dance in events and tour guiding.

Most of studies conducted about Aetas pertain to their conventional livelihood activities and farming system such as those I previously mentioned. Other studies relate to their healthcare needs (Balilla et al. 2014), Indigenous Peoples education and migration (Ličen et al. 2012). More recently, there has been a shift to focussing on their tribal system, ethnic identities, media engagement and self-determination (Austria 2008, Balilla et al. 2013, Rosales-Viray and Versoza 2018). With the exception of the study on healing practices of Aeta women (Torres 2012), there is a scarcity of studies conducted which focus on Aeta women's rights, roles, and identity negotiation within mainstream community livelihoods.

These studies have shaped the present study as to the observed ways of living in Aeta communities, how they use their traditional knowledge in modern-day farming, how their social roles and their role within their own families have influenced how they participate in trading, and how their environment help or impedes their expression of their cultural identities. Therefore, the present study looks into gender dimension of livelihood practices and the changes in nurturing roles of Aeta women. It challenges the view that these women should be confined with nurturing duties of looking after family members, which, in turn, restricts their participation in community development agenda.

Methodology

Narrative inquiry and research participants

The sociocultural nature of qualitative research drawn up from the works of Denzin and Lincoln (2005) guided the methodological approach of this study. They describe qualitative research as a situated activity that transforms the world through interpretive and material practices that make the world visible. This denotes that a qualitative researcher, through interpretive, naturalistic approach, studies "things in their natural settings, attempting to make sense of, or interpret phenomena in terms of meanings people bring to them" (p. 4). As a specific type of qualitative inquiry focussing on the narratives of Aeta women, *narrative inquiry* is used in the present study.

Clandinin (2013) describes narrative inquiry as the study of human lives which honours lived experience where essential knowledge and understanding come from. Here, narratives are regarded as account of events and actions which serve as collection of stories of individuals, reporting their experiences and ordering the meaning of these experiences (Creswell 2007).

This study was conducted over the period of six (6) months and was participated by two (2) groups of women, with a total of thirteen (13) participants, from two *sitios* or areas within barangays (the smallest administrative unit in the Philippine government). Their ages range from 23–50. Through the long standing facilitation of my university in these sitios, through university community extension projects, enabled me to gain access to these communities. There are Aeta women coordinators or group leaders who coordinate their activities with the university. These women served as my key informants who invited other Aeta women to participate in the study. This reflects the concept of *snowballing sampling* in identifying participants.

As suggested by Cohen et al. (2007), snowball sampling is useful if access due to, for instance, topic sensitivity and communication networks, is difficult. Thus, it is the task of researchers to identify informants who could put them in touch with other participants.

Data collection procedure and PRA tools

Apart from Aeta women's narratives, I used empirical materials that "describe routine and problematic moments and meanings in individuals' lives" (Denzin and Lincoln 2008, p. 4) such as *participatory rural appraisal (PRA)* tools. PRA has been popularised in the late 1990s and are visual methods performed by small groups of people. As the name suggests, it has three main components (Dixon 2003). The first component is *participatory* which subsumes the involvement of people and members of project staff; thus, employing the bottom-up approach in community development. Another component is *rural* which means that this technique can be used with various groups in both urban and rural areas. The last component is *appraisal* which denotes generating information about needs, problems, as well as potentials of communities. Sessions using the PRA tools in this study were documented using video and audio recording. Photographs were also taken every session. Data were analysed based on transcriptions from the recording.

One of the PRA tools I used was *seasonal calendar*. This gave information about the changes not only in terms of seasons but also workload and work patterns of both Aeta men and women. In the study, participants were asked to accomplish this chart to illustrate their agricultural activities and to draw up some possible opportunities during lean seasons. Since they belong to the same barangay and follow the same farming pattern, they agreed to create only one seasonal calendar.

To be familiar with the environment of the participants, I asked them to create *topical maps*. These maps revealed information about the geographical features of their environment, the infrastructures built by the government and by the non-governmental organisations (NGOs) which assist them, and the agricultural yields of the area. In doing topical mapping, participants were able to identify the strengths and weaknesses of their environment and the needs of their communities.

Lastly, participants formed *discussion circles* composing of six (6) or seven (7) participants per group. This gave them the space to analyse the situation in their communities. Discussion circles also generated information about their cultural practices such as their rituals and ceremonies, the ways how they learned farming and trading, and social rules they need to consider as they participate in the mainstream society. Apart from challenges, they also shared best practices that they find beneficial to their livelihoods. Three (3) discussion circles where conducted which became venue for the participants to work on their PRA outputs and narrate their stories. However, it is interesting to note that to gain a wider understanding of the participants' contexts, informal conversations were conducted during random visits and their home and trading/market places. These practices fostered trust and narrowed the gap between participants and I, as an outsider and researcher, which has implications to ethical dimension of the study.

Ethical concerns

Informed consent and voluntary participation, confidentiality, and protection from harm are areas of ethical consideration that researchers take into account across fields of study and were also observed in the present study.

After submitting research documents to the Community Development Unit of my university which facilitates Aeta communities, I had meetings with them, followed by meetings with tribal leaders, Aeta women coordinators, and research participants. Before I was granted access to the community, I explained to them the purpose of my study, what their participation entails, and that their participation was purely voluntary. I also maintained regular contact with the community development officer in charge of these Aeta communities to give updates on the research project.

Aware that recording their stories might pose potential risk to privacy of participants, I took on board the proposition of *confidentiality* provided by David and Sutton (2011, p. 47) who state that "confidentiality refers to the situation where that information is known and recorded by the researcher, but is not disclosed in the reporting of the research". Therefore, I assigned pseudonyms to my participants which were then used in coding and filing of data. I also assured my participants that no *sitios* nor individuals would be identified by name in reports and publications.

There is the possibility of emotional harm that might stem from sensitive issues from Aeta women's narratives such as political participation, reclaiming ancestral domains, or even domestic violence. This necessitated me to be conscious and cautious about my comments and be sensitive to experiences and subjectivities of my participants. This demonstrated a high level of understanding, and respect in dealing with issues about their community, religion, gender, and ethnicity.

However, there is another ethical dimension which Social Science researchers have to deal with in conducting indigenous research. In the present study, being a member of the mainstream society belonging to a large educational institution in the capital city of the country, I had to resist the "outsider" identity ascribed to researchers conducting research in poor rural areas. This could spring from being perceived as aid provider or mission worker. Thus, I had to reflect on how I position myself in my research, how I have presented myself in the field, how I have conducted the research, and how I have retold the stories of participants. The dichotomy between being an "outsider" or "insider" in my target communities brings the notion of *reflexivity*, which, according to Subedi (2006, p. 575), makes researchers more "attentive to how we see – and how others see us seeing them".

Data analysis

In order to analyse the data, I employed *content analysis* (Hsieh and Shannon 2005) which entails immersion in the data to allow patterns and categories to emerge. This means that initial stage of my data analysis involved transcribing of audio recordings and reading and rereading of transcribed documents. This is followed by condensing the extracts that captured the key concepts. I, then, made some annotations which formed my initial analysis. Concepts are then grouped into categories leading to coding or labelling . Codes which were generated were further grouped into categories forming

meaningful clusters (Patton 2002). The clusters were analysed and reorder into hierarchies reflecting the relationship between major concepts and their subcategories. This
enabled me to make inferences and summarise the significant points of the study.

It is important to note that before content analysis was applied to transcribed data, a
form of participatory analysis of topical maps and seasonal calendar took place between
me and the participants during discussion circles. The interactions between us, which
involved probing, categorising, and exploring, enabled me to bring the participants'
ideas and insights to the surface. These verbalisation of insights were captured in video
and audio recording and composed the transcribed data of the study.

Results

Aeta women's livelihood practices

The nature of livelihood activities of Aeta women participants reflect their indigenous
identities as hunter-gatherers. This means they maintain their link to environment and
resort to farming as their main form of livelihood.

In one of the discussion circles, the participants developed a seasonal calendar with
me, the researcher, acting as a note-taker who wrote down relevant information shared
by the participants. This seasonal calendar (Figure 1) illustrates their economic activities throughout the year. This was populated by agricultural activities such as preparing the land, planting the crops, harvesting them, and marketing their farm produce.
There were specific crops designated in each month which demonstrates their practice
of crop rotation system, which, according to them, keeps the fertility of the soil and
maximises land use. Being aware of the lean season in farming, they carry out alternative forms of livelihood such as charcoal making and selling seedlings.

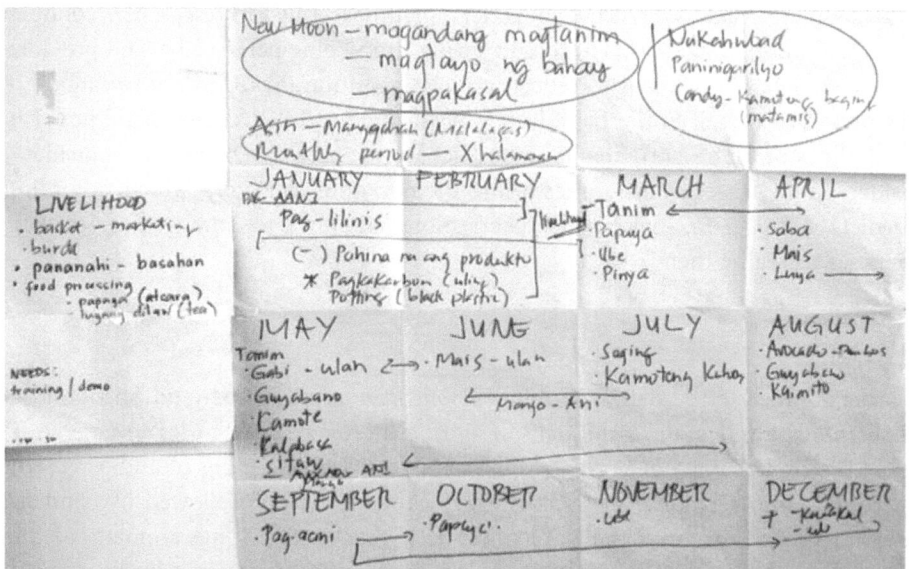

Figure 1. Seasonal calendar illustrating economic activities in selected Aeta communities.

Aeta women also safeguard their indigenous knowledge system by applying this until the present. As revealed by the seasonal calendar, they still consider the phases of the moon in farming. They believe that *new moon* or *dark moon phase* as the best time to plant and sow their fields. Moreover, they believe that women should not engage in farming activities during their monthly period. Aetas believe that when a woman who is menstruating touches the plant, the plant will not bear fruit or the crops will die. They also subscribe to the belief that farmers should be very careful in bringing salt in areas where mango trees are grown because salt halts the growth and development of the tree.

Although most of their children have attended formal schooling, Aeta women have been exposed to the benefits of information technology which they tried to integrate into their farming. This includes selection of crops, land preparation techniques, processing of crop yields and marketing their products. Despite their knowledge of new technology, they still strongly uphold the indigenous knowledge that their ancestors passed onto them.

Community maps as visualisation of marginalisation

As previously mentioned, topical mapping (Figure 2) was used to gain information as to the physical features of the area, the crops people grow, people that occupy the space and facilities which are present in the area.

During discussion, the women articulated that they needed additional infrastructures such as library for the younger generation, health centre, water pumps, vehicle to transport their goods, barangay/village post, trading centre and better road condition. They expressed the perceived needs of the community which may directly impact their livelihoods. These are the basic social services the government should have provided them with.

In spite of the challenges illustrated in their topical maps, these Aeta women capitalised on the richness of their communities. They indicated that the three major community assets they have are their crop yields, the churches and the river. They took pride that their land produces quality crops such as extra large winter melons, sweet papayas,

Figure 2. Topical maps of the sitios.

good quality bananas and smooth and firm root crops such as yams, sweets potatoes and turmeric.

Another community asset they have are churches (*simbahan*) built by several faith-based organisationss. They consider these churches as representation of God's love for them and of unity among members. Also, they use these churches for social gatherings and for welcoming visiting organisationss.

Lastly, they considered the river (*ilog, tubigan*) as one of their communities' greatest assets for two reasons - the river provides the community with valuable source of food for their families and water for their plants and that the riverside has become the site for adult literacy and numeracy classes. My university has been helping these Aeta communities for several decades. Literacy facilitators from my university transmit lessons through radio broadcasts. An Aeta woman who finished secondary education served as the coordinator of literacy and numeracy classes. As emphasised by the chieftain:

> Hindi na po nila pwedeng lokohin ang mga Aeta ngayon dahil marunong na kami magbasa, magsulat at magkwenta.

> (Tr: Aetas cannot be fooled nowadays because we already learned how to read, to write and to compute.)

The stories that resist the oppressions that exist

Living in the mainstream society enabled these women to realise and to voice out the pressing issues in their communities which needed to be addressed as shown in Table 1. Two themes emerged from the extracts - the lines pertaining to Mt. Pinatubo where they used to live before it erupted in 1991 and the struggles they experienced as they trade their harvest and deal with the *unat* or members of the mainstream communities who have straight hair.

For the first set of extracts, the participants expressed the reasons behind their decision to stay in the lowlands. Due to volcanic eruption, it became difficult to reach the

Table 1. Issues relating to ancestral land and dealing with members of mainstream communities.

Filipino	English translation
Pertaining to Mt. Pinatubo	
... hindi na. Sobra na ang layo, pati buhanginan ho sa dinadaanan.	... not anymore. It is too far, even the road is sandy (lahar)
Hindi mo maabot kasi ma-ano na. Hindi na dati.	You can no longer reach it. Unlike before.
Tibag-tibag na.	It has been partitioned.
Kinuha na ko ng mga Koreano.	The Koreans claimed it (their land).
Hindi na mapakinabangan	It is of no use.
Pero puti na yan, nagpantay na.	It is now all white, levelled out
Dealing with the unat	
Hanggang sa magsawa ka hindi ka na babalik. Didiskarte ka na lang kung paano ka mangtitinda. ... pinapalitan na lang ang saging isang kape at asukal	Until you get tired, you will never go back. You will just find your own strategy how you will sell (your goods).
Ayun, nagreklamo sila, "Wala na bumibili sa amin ngayon".	(we are just) trading bananas for one coffee and sugar.
Hindi na kami magkaintindihan saan kami magbebenta ...	They complained, "Nobody buy from us now". We are now confused as to where to sell ...
Kapag hindi n'yo ho tinubos, kanila na yon pati mga lamesa ganon.	If you refused to redeem your goods, they (the policemen) would get even your tables.

place where they used to thrive. They also found it difficult to reclaim their land as foreigners have partitioned it, owned it and, as claimed by one of the Aetas, have converted it into a resort.

They also expressed difficulties participating in trading and dealing with the unat who were seen to have better access to economic opportunities. The unat are considered more favoured as they were given better spaces where they could sell their goods, and are given priority in terms of market location. They often buy the best harvest of the Aetas in cheaper rate and sell the harvest in much higher prices, leaving the Aetas with the rejected low quality produce which are often difficult to market.

However, their immersion in the mainstream society, also allowed them to counter circumstances and past situations which contribute to their marginalisation as depicted in Table 2.

It is apparent from the table that they also recognised how livelihood programmes and school literacies have contributed in improving their living conditions. They gained knowledge in identifying strategic locations for better chances of marketing their harvests. They learned about pricing of goods instead of trading them for commodities such as coffee and sugar. Lastly, they could afford to send their kids to school and provide for their college education.

The foregoing observations support the strong conviction these Aeta women possess about what they think would be best for their livelihoods. During one of the discussion circles, they shared stories about marketing one of their most in-demand crops which is turmeric. They narrated that they were offered by businessmen to produce turmeric as raw materials for soap bars and turmeric powder. They said that they were pleased that people acknowledge them for the quality of crops they produce. However, they asserted that more than selling their crops to big corporations, what would be more useful for them would be training and machinery so that they themselves could produce soap bars and turmeric powder as their direct response to market needs. They also emphasised that in order for them to achieve this, they needed to form women's groups which will be responsible in organising training sessions to enhance their livelihoods, to improve financial management of earnings and draw up plans to empowerment women and the community at large through livelihood practices. With the

Table 2. Expressions of countering past circumstances.

Filipino	English Translation
Changes in their practices	
… pero ngayon hindi na, alam na naming kung saan.	… but it is no longer like that now, we already knew where (to sell).
Ang mga Aeta nagtitinda na sila.	The Aetas are now engaged in selling.
D'yan na kami unti-unting natuto.	We learned from that little by little.
Marketing ho. Sa pagtatanim, okay na kami.	(We need training on) marketing. We are okay with farming.
Kung konti tapos na po ng 10, pero marami po ngayon …	If we have only a few goods, we're done by 10 (AM), now we have a lot.
Sa bayan na po Ma'am. Pag marami na.	In the city, Ma'am. If there's a lot. (referring to harvest)
Nagturo na po sila ng food processing dito Ma'am.	They already taught us food processing, Ma'am.
Alam mo, mga lalaki ngayon, nagtitinda na sila	You know, men nowadays engage in trading.
Ako ho parehong teacher na ang anak ko.	My daughters are both teachers already.
… nakakapagtinda na kami, nakakapagtrabaho pa kami sa lupa.	… now we can sell , and we can also work in our farms.

formation of women's groups, both men and women will be educated in terms of their rights to participate in decision making and political affairs, to have equal rights with men in the labour force, and to make personal choices.

Struggles of Aeta women in safeguarding their livelihoods

In their account of events, they conveyed frustrations and discontent in terms of the government's assistance to their livelihoods. Data sources reflected not only Aeta women's strong desire for commercial spaces where they could sell their harvests and compete with other traders, but also their plea to pay attention, not on their weaknesses but on the skills they possess as stated in the following:

> Kasi kaming mga Aeta eh hindi naman nag-aral. Yung kakayahan namin eh yung bumili at magbenta ng kalakal. Yun po ang irequest namin sa ano (munisipyo). Yung pirmihan talaga kaming tinda sa pwesto.

> (Tr: Because we, Aetas, are uneducated. We only know how to do buy and sell. That is the reason we requested from the municipal office to designate a permanent space where we can sell our products.)

Moreover, they felt the lack of protection from the government and expressed concerns regarding their safety as reflected by the following excerpts:

> Kapag dumarating ang mga manghuhuli, kabado na kami. Paano namin mabubuhat yung paninda namin? Hindi ko kaya. Hindi ako makalakad.

> (Tr: Whenever policemen arrive, we become anxious. How do we carry our products? I cannot. I cannot walk.)

> Kapag hindi n'yo ho tinubos, kanila na (ang produkto) pati mga lamesa.

> (Tr: If you do not reclaim and pay for your products, they will keep them including the tables you are using.)

Lastly, excerpts demonstrate social comparison in two forms – first, with outsiders such as the *unat*; second, within their own Aeta community. This is illustrated in the following translations:

> Kahit dito sa ayaw namin, ibigay sa ganung presyo.

> (Tr: Even if we do not like it, we have to give in to their asking price.)

> Kapag nanadyan mga unat, kita mo wala na sila.

> (Tr: When the straight haired arrives, you will notice that they will leave.)

> Gusto n'yo magpalimos kami?

> (Do you like us to beg for alms?)

The extracts revealed difficulties Aeta women had to go through. As they have noted, trading was controlled by members of mainstream communities. Aetas were forced to sell their products in spite of unjust market prices, putting them in a more disadvantaged position. They were also threatened by the presence of mainstream traders that Aeta women had to leave their space whenever they arrive. In consequence, failure to secure their livelihoods would result to a negative identity as beggars, the previously ascribed identity to them.

Another striking result of the study is the comparison existing within their own community of Aetas. To illustrate this, consider the following excerpt:

Nahiya po sila, Ma'am. Basta Aeta, nahihiya na magtinda.

(Tr: They are ashamed, Ma'am. Aetas are ashamed to sell.)

The previous excerpt was from the narrative of the Aeta women about the roles of their husbands in their livelihoods. They narrated that men usually work in farmlands and marketing of products are left with the women. Due to this role that women take in trading and training, they were perceived by their fellows as stronger and more privileged. They were regarded to be more courageous, enterprising and assertive.

Discussion

Indigenous women take substantial role in production and management of resources of their families and communities. Given proper attention and support, this could directly impact agricultural growth and advancement in trading practices relevant to sustainable livelihoods, food security, and poverty reduction. However, the road to creating sustainable communities for and by indigenous people is a challenge that most indigenous women are facing. Adding up to this, is the struggle to negotiate their identities to survive their (non)membership in mainstream communities.

In the context of agriculture and livelihoods, technological advancement is necessary. However, the study also acknowledges that it is relevant and vital to take into account the indigenous knowledge system of indigenous communities. Aeta women tried to integrate information technology into their farming practices without disregarding the local knowledge passed on to them by their ancestors. Aikenhead and Ogawa (2007) argue for the interconnectedness between *knowledge* and the *knower* which translates to living in harmonious relationship with nature for the survival of the community. It involves respect for indigenous peoples' process of discovery and journey from knowing to imparting wisdom through action.

NGOs and faith-based organisations in Aeta communities have been initiating programmes which aim at preserving indigenous knowledge. This does not equate to depriving the Aetas of the potential benefits of technology in farming and trading such as increase of women's economic stability, awareness of safety and sanitation practices and improvement of their knowledge in business (Pascual and Estolano 2017). Consequently, indigenous knowledge can be integrated into formal training which can bridge the gap between IP and mainstream communities and which can address issues on how relevant and responsive formal and non-formal training programmes are in the community.

The present study supports the findings of existing studies (May and Aikman 2003, Gelade and Stehlik 2004, Trujano 2008) about the adversaries and plight of indigenous people to reclaim their land rights, to have their cultures valued, and to have equal access to government services like their non-indigenous counterparts. However, one interesting theme that emerged from the study was Aeta women's focus on the strengths of their communities generated through community mapping. This went beyond physical assets of the sitios. Their narratives uncover leadership potentials of their members, the sensitivity, the aspirations they hold for younger generation of Aetas, respect for local traditions, and the values they embrace as a group with a deep sense of togetherness and commitment to their indigenous community. Thus they see themselves as the solution to the challenges they identified.

Affirmative statements from participants in the midst of their marginalised position in the society have implications to how indigenous research can be conducted. This counters the deficit model in conducting research and in designing development programmes which perceive communities as sites of problem-solving that in order to improve the system, obstacles and deficits have to be removed (Moore and Charvat 2007). However, they underscore that this does not exclude negative, critical and radical constructs and only privileges positive voices. As the present study suggests, through engaging in retelling their stories, they tend to pay attention more to the process of generating new discoveries and of understanding the components of (re)constructing their identities as indigenous peoples.

In the field of identity studies, Aeta women's narratives offer insights on social positioning through their conformity, resistance and assertion, which, in most instances, have led to their marginalised social identities, at the same time, have enabled them to find the voice to resist oppressions. Aeta women in this study demonstrated a strong communal identity which reflect the concept of *social identification* of Tajfel and Turner (1979). This provides the member with an identification of herself/himself in social terms. It comprises the aspects of the member's self-image deriving from the social group to which one perceives himself belonging.

Furthermore, membership to social groups creates *social categorisation*, "a system of orientation that creates and defines the individual's own place in a society" (Tajfel 1981 p. 258). This provides the distinctions between one's own group (in-group) and the out-group - the dichotomy between "us" and "them" which leads to prejudices experienced by indigenous people and is reflected on the divide between the *kulot* (curly hair) who are the Aetas and the *unat* (straight hair) who are members of the mainstream society. The intergroup conflict "segments, classifies, and orders the social environment, and thus enables the individual to undertake many forms of social action" (Tajfel and Turner 1979 p. 40).

With concepts such as *social identification, social categorisation*, and *identity (re)construction* emerging from the present study, the notion of what constitutes as *indigenous* needs to be problematised. This does not entail a reconceptualisation of the term, but more on looking at the process by which indigenous people have reimagined themselves. This moves from Gee's (2001) N-Identity which is biological, to identity ascribed by institutions and communities, and goes beyond affinity groups which a person has formed allegiance with. As I previously mentioned, identities have histories and undergo constant transformation as a product of the continuous interplay of history, culture and power. Therefore, this could an interesting inquiry for future study. (Re)constructing identities among indigenous groups necessitates an examination of existing social interactions which might contribute to *hybrid identities* of participants and which might address the gap between who they are and what they have become because of their histories.

Conclusion

The study set out to examine how selected Aeta women negotiate their identities as they participate in livelihood activities in mainstream communities. From a sociocultural perspective, the study supports the view that negotiating identities situates the participants in their social contexts and that interactions shape their participation and membership in communities. Using visual participatory approach utilising Participatory Rural Appraisal (PRA) tools, it has argued that engaging in livelihood activities and weaving their narratives are forms of social practice that unpacks resistance, power relations and identity construction.

There are four major findings that emerged from the study. First, Aeta women were regarded as gatekeepers of indigenous knowledge systems. Though they had been exposed to information technology, they still upheld their traditional values and integrated them into their livelihood practices. Second, these women had a strong awareness about the neglect in basic services that the government should have provided them with. However, they utilised the strengths of their communities to find solution to economic challenges that they need to confront. Third, they demonstrated a strong communal identity keeping them aware of the dichotomy between them and members of mainstream communities and served as a weapon against prejudices that they experienced. Lastly, their negotiation of their identities as they integrate in mainstream communities created the possibility of producing hybrid identities of indigenous peoples.

The findings from this research provided some insights for refining indigenous research methodology. It also offered theoretical and methodological contributions in designing community development projects geared towards shifting from deficit to a more transformative approach. The study also attempted to move forward the debate on issues surrounding indigenous peoples' identities. Developing a critical awareness of how these indigenous women experience the world and how these experiences are reproduced in their participation in the mainstream community could shed light for policy recommendations.

Disclosure statement

No potential conflict of interest was reported by the author(s).

ORCID

Gina Lontoc (iD) http://orcid.org/0000-0002-6724-4304

References

Aikenhead, G.S. and Ogawa, M., 2007. Indigenous knowledge and science revisited. *Cultural studies of science education*, 2 (3), 539–620.

Austria, J.D.C., 2008. *Expanding the envelope: the convergence of indigenous Aeta organisations and an external issue-based community organizing model in Tarlac, Philippines* (Master's thesis). University of Florida. Available from: http://etd.fcla.edu/UF/UFE0022467/austria_j.pdf [Accessed 18 October 2019].

Balilla, V.S., *et al.*, 2014. The assimilation of Western medicine into a semi-nomadic healthcare system: a case study of the Indigenous Aeta Magbukun. *EcoHealth*, 11 (3), 372–382.

Balilla, V.S., *et al.*, 2013. Indigenous Aeta Magbukún self-identity, sociopolitical structures, and self-determination at the local level in the Philippines. *Journal of anthropology*, 2013, 1–6.

Clandinin, D., 2013. *Engaging in narrative inquiry*. Walnut Creek: Left Coast Press Inc.

Cohen, L., *et al.*, 2007. *Research methods in education*. London: Routledge.

Creswell, J.W., 2007. Five qualitative approaches to inquiry. *Qualitative inquiry and research design: choosing among five approaches*, 2, 53–80.

David, M., and Sutton, C.D., 2011. *Social research: an introduction*. Thousand Oaks, CA: Sage Publications.

Delgado, R. and Stefancic, J., 2001. *Critical race theory: an introduction*. New York, NY: New York University Press.

Denzin, N.K. and Lincoln, Y.S., 2005. *Handbook of qualitative research*. Thousand Oaks, CA: Sage

Denzin, N.K., Lincoln, Y.S., and Smith, L.T. (Eds.). 2008, *Handbook of critical and indigenous methodologies*. Los Angeles, CA: Sage.

Department of Economic and Social Affairs (DESA). 2009. *State of the world's indigenous peoples*. Available from https://www.un.org/esa/socdev/unpfii/documents/SOWIP/en/SOWIP_web.pdf [Accessed 14 July 2019].

Dixon, A., 2003. The Indigenous Evaluation of Wetlands Research in Ethiopia. *Development in practice*, 13 (4), 394–398.

Ella, A.B., 2008. Almaciga resin gathering by indigenous people of Palawan province in the Philippines. *IUFRO world series*, 21, 46.

Gee, J.P., 2001. Identity as an analytic lens for research in education. In W.G. Secada, ed. *Review of research in education*, vol. 25, pp. 99–126. Washington, DC: American Educational Research Association.

Gelade, S. and Stehlik, T., 2004. *Exploring locality: the impact of context on indigenous vocational education and training aspirations and outcomes*. Adelaide, Australia: National Centre for Vocational Education Research Ltd.

Hall, S., 1990. Cultural identity and diaspora. *In:* J Rutherford, ed. *Identity: community, culture difference*. London: Lawrence and Wishart, 222–237(2), 1–40.

Hill, D., 2009. Race and class in Britain: A critique of the statistical basis for critical race theory in Britain. *Journal for critical education policy studies*, 7. Available from http://www.jceps.com/ [Accessed 5 September 2019].

Hsieh, H.F. and Shannon, S.E., 2005. Three approaches to qualitative content analysis. *Qualitative health research*, 15 (9), 1277–1288.

International Labor Organisations 1995. *Indigenous knowledge system and practices among selected Philippine ethnic groups and their promotion through cooperatives*. Retrieved from: http://www.ilo.org/manila/publications/WCMS_542426/lang–en/index.htm [Accessed 18 July 2019].

Kubota, R., 2015. Race and language learning in multicultural Canada: toward critical anti-racism. *Journal of multilingual and multicultural development*, 36 (1), 3–12.

Li, T., 2000. Articulating indigenous identity in Indonesia: resource politics and the tribal slot. *Comparative studies in society and history*, 42, 149–179.

Ličen, N., Lihtenvalner, K., and Podgornik, V., 2012. The non-formal education and migration of the Aeta, an indigenous tribe in the Philippines. *Anthropological notebooks*, 18 (3), 25–40.

May, S. and Aikman, S., 2003. Indigenous education: addressing current issues and developments. *Comparative education*, 39 (2), 139–145.

Moore, S., and Charvat, J., 2007. Promoting health behaviour change using appreciative inquiry: Moving from deficit models to affirmation models of care. *Family & community health*, 30 (15), S64–S74.

National Commission on Indigenous Peoples. 2019. Rules and regulations implementing Republic Act No. 8371, otherwise known as "The Indigenous Peoples' Rights Act of 1997. Administrative Order No.1 Series of 1998. Retrieved from https://www.wipo.int/edocs/lex-docs/laws/en/ph/ph083en.pdf [Accessed 28 August 2019].

Nelson, A., 2007. Seeing white: a critical exploration of occupational therapy with indigenous Australian people. *Occupational therapy international*, 14 (4), 237–255.

Padilla, S.G. Jr., 2013. Anthropology and GIS: temporal and spatial distribution of the philippine negrito groups. *Human biology*, 85 (1–3), 209–230.

Pascual, P.A.L., and Estolano, C.N., 2017. The Leyte Normal University (LNU) extension project: empowering rural women through entrepreneurship. *International journal of multidisciplinary approach and studies*, 4 (3), 1–11.

Patton, M.Q., 2002. *Qualitative research and evaluation methods*. Thousand Oaks, CA: Sage.

Rodriguez, P. and Carruthers, D., 2008. Testing democracy's promise: indigenous mobilization and the chilean state. *European review of Latin American and Caribbean studies*, 85, 3–21.

Rosales-Viray, K., and Versoza, S.M., 2018. Media engagement and ethnic identity: the case of the Aeta Ambala of Pastolan Village. kss-v3i6, IRCHE 2017, 2018 Bali, Indonesia, 23-26 January.

Shen, W. and Dumani, S., 2013. The complexity of marginalized identities: The social construction of identities, multiple identities, and the experience of exclusion. *Industrial and Organizational Psychology*, 6 (1), 84–87.

Subedi, B., 2006. Theorizing a 'halfie' researcher's identity in transnational fieldwork. *International journal of qualitative studies in education*, 19 (5), 573–593.

Tajfel, H., 1981. *Human groups and social categories: Studies in social psychology*. CUP Archive, Cambridge, England: Cambridge University Press.

Tajfel, H. and Turner, J.C., 1979. An integrative theory of intergroup conflict. *The social psychology of intergroup relations*, 33 (47), 74.

Tindowen, D.J.C., 2016. The economic life of the Aetas of Northern Philippines. *Khazar journal of humanities and social sciences*, 19 (4), 97–109.

Torre, M.E., 2009. Participatory action research and critical race theory: Fueling spaces for nos-otras to research. *The urban review*, 41 (1), 106–120.

Torres, R.A., 2012. *Aeta women Indigenous healers in the Philippines: lessons and implications* (Doctoral dissertation), University of Toronto, Canada.

Trujano, C.Y.A., 2008. *Indigenous routes: a framework for understanding indigenous migration*. London: Hammersmith Press.

Turner, J.C., 1982. Towards a cognitive redefinition of the social group. In: H. Tajfel, eds. *Social identity and inter- group relations: 15–40*. Cambridge: Cambridge University Press.

United Nations. 2007. *Declaration on the rights of indigenous peoples*. Available from http://www.un.org/esa/socdev/unpfii/documents/DRIPS_en.pdf [Accessed 17 June 2019].

Writer, J., 2008. Unmasking, exposing, and confronting: critical race theory, tribal critical race theory and multicultural education. *International journal of multicultural education*, 10 (2), 1–15.

Indigenous adult women, learning and social justice: Challenging deficit discourses in the current policy environment

Sushan Acharya, Catherine M. Jere ⓘ and Anna Robinson-Pant

ABSTRACT

Indigenous education engages directly with an overtly politicised process of knowledge construction, recognising and building on existing skills and informal learning practices within communities. Given the 2030 Sustainable Development Agenda's emphasis on social justice and gender equality, this paper sets out to explore what indigenous movements can offer in terms of developing an alternative approach to adult learning based on a rights perspective. The article compares the documentary analysis of policy on indigenous women and adult education internationally with a case study of indigenous movements and government policy in Nepal. The analysis reveals that international policy recognises indigenous women as a particularly marginalised group, but is not informed by a transformative notion of empowerment nor consideration of the implications of indigenous knowledge for mainstream education. In Nepal, indigenous federations and the government non formal education programmes similarly aim to impart skills for a modernised economy. However, women's indigenous movements are committed to developing capabilities and creating new spaces for indigenous women to engage in political debate and representation. This politicised informal learning offers insights for developing the cross-sectoral rights-based adult education envisaged in the 2030 Sustainable Development Agenda.

Introduction

International education policy has long been framed around a deficit discourse – that certain groups lack and need to 'catch up' on the skills and knowledge essential for a successful modern economy – and policy responses to indigenous communities have often taken a similar starting point (Aikman *et al.* 2016). The 2030 Sustainable Development Agenda (UN 2015) offers an opportunity to look again at how indigenous women are addressed within current educational policy discourses, particularly in relation to gender equality and social justice. Does the sustainable development paradigm signal alternative values – such as a belief in sustainable lifestyles – informing educational policy and how does it mediate between an instrumentalist approach and rights perspectives on adult education? Is there now greater policy recognition of the role that education can play in strengthening valuable cultural practices and indigenous knowledge – and of the assets that indigenous people, particularly women, can bring to society?

Overall, the 2030 SD Agenda gives a strong message that indigenous people need to be brought into mainstream education, particularly schooling and formal adult education, positioning indigenous women as a 'vulnerable group' within SDG4 on education. This could be regarded as an assimilationist approach which also assumes 'indigenous' and 'women' to be homogeneous categories (see Rao and Robinson-Pant 2006: 213), rather than exploring intersecting inequalities within each category. By contrast, in this article, we begin from the position that rather than simply ensuring the 'inclusion' of marginalised adults, indigenous education involves acknowledging and building on gendered knowledge, identities and experiences. Recognising the limitations of focusing only on what kind of indigenous knowledge could be incorporated into mainstream curriculum content or looking at indigenous women as a particularly 'vulnerable' group who have missed out on schooling as children, our aim is to consider the implications for a broader rights-based approach to adult learning. Central to this discussion is the perceived tension between an education that prepares women to engage with global change, yet can also ensure continuity in cultural ways of learning, determine relevant knowledge and support the development of minority languages.

Indigenous movements are actively addressing questions around the meanings, values and relevance of education (Aikman 2011), which are often missing in policy accounts that emphasise a narrow, instrumental view of education. In this article, we set out to analyse international educational policy through the lens of 'indigenous women' and to develop a case study of indigenous movements in Nepal from a gendered perspective. This comparative analysis is intended to help illuminate ways in which adult education could support the empowerment of indigenous women – and help build greater appreciation of the diversity of cultures, and their contribution to sustainable development (as indicated in SDG 4.7).

Research design and methodology

This study was designed to develop comparative analysis in terms of:

- Comparing international and national policy perspectives on indigenous women and adult education (through a case study from Nepal)
- Comparing policy stances/discourses within indigenous movements with international and national official educational policy discourses (in Nepal and internationally)

Our rationale is to develop insights into what indigenous movements might offer to the adult education sector. As well as being academic researchers in this field, we have also played various roles as policy advisers – including working with UNESCO at international and at national level in Nepal – which has influenced our access to and interpretation of policy/programme documentation. The study data consists of policy and programme documentation, including advocacy reports and papers from indigenous movements in Nepal. As a researcher based in Nepal, one of the authors conducted face-to-face interviews with six advocates representing different indigenous forums in Nepal.

This data was analysed using a content analysis approach, similar to that described by Hsieh and Shannon (2005), through generating themes and categories around questions generated by our literature review. For policy documents and educational materials, a discourse analysis approach was adopted [see for instance, Apthorpe and Gasper (1996)], identifying how problems and issues were framed and what appeared to be excluded from consideration within this frame. The latter (i.e. what was not said) was particularly important to take into account in terms of gender – as previous research has indicated that gender is all too often invisible within indigenous adult education (Rao and Robinson-Pant 2006).

Conceptualising literacy, informal learning and gender: a theoretical framework for exploring indigenous adult education

In many contexts in the Global South, adult education is considered synonymous with 'women's literacy' (Robinson-Pant 2016), partly because women make up two-thirds of the world's non-literate population. This is particularly so in Nepal where the government has promoted women's literacy for many decades as a strategy to enhance economic activity and to support women's roles as mothers and carers (Acharya and Robinson-Pant 2017). Such policy is usually based on what has been termed an 'autonomous' model of literacy (Street 1984), where reading and writing are believed to have specific cognitive benefits. By contrast, our study conceptualised literacy as a social practice (Barton et al. 2000), embedded in and shaping everyday relationships and practices – including gendered/indigenous identities and gender relations. This broader understanding of literacy as multimodal and multilingual has particular relevance for indigenous women, offering ways to explore alternative knowledges, skills and literacies. The concept of a hierarchical relationship between 'schooled' or dominant literacy (Street 2005) and indigenous literacy practices is also key to our analysis. The notion of informal learning is integral to these ideas about literacy learning taking place outside formal institutions and classes, through everyday interaction, intergenerational learning and literacy mediators. Tough's (1979) image of an iceberg – where only the formal and nonformal learning is visible above the water level, and the majority of learning is informal learning below the surface – still has resonance with debates about indigenous education where much informal learning is unrecognised and unacknowledged.

Within the field of gender and adult education, we use the distinction between a transformative, rights-based approach and an instrumental, functional approach to analyse the differing policy stances adopted by policymakers and activists. In particular, in development discourse, the term 'empowerment' has often come to refer to economic rather than political aims within an instrumental approach, or as an outcome or destination rather than a 'journey' (Cornwall and Edwards 2014). A view of identities as multiple, shifting and performed rather than given (Butler 1990) is particularly important to our study in order to analyse if or where policymakers and activists are essentialising gender and cultural identities (often for political reasons). Joshi and Ghose (2012, p. 117) suggest that 'gender continues to be largely understood as being a biological category, with girls and women being identified as "target groups"'. In the context of indigenous women and adult education, these ideas point to the importance of interrogating ideologies around both indigenous and gender identities and how these may influence educational programme aims.

Bringing together this conceptualisation of literacy, informal learning and gender, we have developed a framework to expand the debate on indigenous adult women and education from the common focus on vocational skills development and education and employment in the formal sector. Above all, these understandings of literacy and identities as situated and dependent on relationships of power and inequality can help to open up a space to discuss how different actors – including international and national government policymakers and indigenous movement activists – view and define the concept of 'indigenous'.

International policy: indigenous women, adult education and learning

Indigenous rights and education

The right of indigenous peoples to develop and determine their own education systems has been formally acknowledged only relatively recently. This section analyses some of the historical developments by indigenous movements that have influenced educational policy and helped to shape what is considered to be 'Indigenous Education'. The draft Declaration on the Rights of Indigenous Peoples (UNDRIP), as revised by the Working Group on Indigenous Populations in 1993, and only formally adopted in 2007 (Table 1), helped to establish this right, asserting that indigenous peoples have the right to establish and control their educational systems and institutions providing education in their own language (Article 14) (UN 2008).

At around the same time, the Kari-Oca Declaration entitled 'Indigenous Peoples' Earth Charter' (formulated in Brazil in 1992) included similar statements: 'Indigenous peoples should have the right to their own knowledge, languages and culturally appropriate education, including bicultural and bilingual education. Through recognizing both formal and informal ways the participation of family and community is guaranteed' (World Conference of Indigenous Peoples on Territory, Environment and Development 1992, p. 3). As well as emphasising the importance of being able to use indigenous languages and of indigenous people having resources and control over their own education systems, this statement also highlighted the central role of the community, particularly older people, in sustaining indigenous learning and knowledge: 'Elders must be recognized and respected as teachers of the young people. Indigenous wisdom must be recognized and encouraged' (ibid, p. 7).

These early statements led to the preparation of the Coolongatta Statement on Indigenous People's Rights in Education at the World Indigenous Peoples' Conference

Table 1. Recognition of indigenous women in international treaties.

Treaties	Approaches to adult education		Recognition of indigenous women	Recognition of indigenous peoples, knowledge and learning	
	Adult education, learning and literacy	Knowledge, skills and capacities promoted	Aims for indigenous women and education	Representation of indigenous women and their knowledge	Indigenous language needs
International Convention on Economic, Social and Cultural Rights (1966)	Human rights stance, declaring the right of everyone to education (Art 13) Fundamental (basic) education for those not completing primary education encouraged	Concerned with 'full development of the human personality' reiterating the UN Declaration of Human Rights (Art 26) Life-long learning introduced in GC 13	No mention of indigenous women in Articles, but referenced in General Comments	No specific mention of indigenous peoples/women, or IK Notes education has value in passing on cultural values, religion, customs, language and other cultural references... and respect for cultural values	Calls for non-discrimination on basis of language. Reference to language barriers, needs of minorities in GC 20
Convention on the Eradication of Discrimination against Women (1980)	Focus on rights and equal access to education for women/men, at all levels of education & training, including adult and functional literacy	Limited mention of knowledge and skills. Health and family planning information prioritised	No mention of indigenous women	No specific mention of indigenous peoples/women Recognition of the influence of culture and tradition, but only in terms of restricting women's rights	Calls for non-discrimination on basis of language (Art. 2.2)
Rio Declaration on Environment and Development (1992)	Instrumental role of education – catalyst for environmental awareness and sustainable development; Halve 1990 levels of 'illiteracy'	Calls for introduction of environment and development issues into all education programmes	Incorporate indigenous peoples' experience and understanding of sustainable development into education, training	Calls for recognition & application of indigenous values, traditional knowledge and resource management to support sustainable development	No mention of language(s)
Beijing Platform for Action (1995)	Education as a human right and instrumental for achieving equality Focus on gender equitable access to – and treatment in – education, eliminating gender gap in literacy Literacy, life-long education & training for women recognised as means to achieve economic growth & sustainable development	Promotes non-formal education for adult women, to acquire skills in: health, micro-enterprise, agriculture and legal rights Promotes vocational training, leadership & management and STEM	Recognizes the right of *indigenous women and girls* to education Acknowledges indigenous women as underserved group Promotes a multicultural approach responsive to the needs, aspirations and cultures of *indigenous women*	Extensive reference to *indigenous women* Acknowledges traditional knowledge as a form of life-long learning Calls for respect for artistic, spiritual and cultural activities of *indigenous women* Calls for protection and use of the knowledge, innovations and practices of *indigenous women*	Promotes development of appropriate education programmes, curricula & teaching aids in indigenous languages

(continued)

Table 1. Continued.

Treaties	Approaches to adult education		Recognition of indigenous peoples, knowledge and learning		
	Adult education, learning and literacy	Knowledge, skills and capacities promoted	Aims for indigenous women and education	Representation of indigenous women and their knowledge	Indigenous language needs
UN Declaration on the Rights of Indigenous Peoples (2007)	No specific mention of adult education Education as a reflection of the dignity/diversity of cultures, traditions, histories and aspirations	Traditional knowledge and cultural expressions, their sciences & technologies: inc. human and genetic resources, medicines, knowledge of fauna/flora, oral traditions, literatures, sports, visual and performing arts (Art 31)	Indigenous peoples have the right to establish and control their education systems/institutions providing education in a manner appropriate to their cultural methods of teaching and learning (Art 14)	Recognises indigenous peoples' right to protect and develop their traditional knowledge, cultural heritage and intellectual property Respect for indigenous knowledge, cultures and practices contributes to sound environmental management & sustainable, equitable development *Indigenous women as disadvantaged group*	Call for states, alongside indigenous peoples, to ensure that indigenous individuals – when possible – have access to education in their own language and culture (Art 14)

on Education in Hilo, Hawai'i, 1999. Giving the background of indigenous peoples' oppression under colonialisation and the purpose of (non-Indigenous) education being 'to assimilate Indigenous peoples into non-Indigenous cultures and societies' (WIPCE 1999), this statement outlined in greater detail an alternative approach to Indigenous Education. Emphasising that drop-out rates or poor educational results should be seen as 'rejection rates' and a failure of the system rather than of an individual, it argued that non-Indigenous education systems 'have failed to provide educational services that nurture the whole Indigenous person inclusive of scholarship, culture and spirituality' (ibid). There is recognition of the challenge of how to 'promote, protect and nurture Indigenous cultures in an ever-changing modern society' and that Indigenous people should be free to decide whether they prefer to participate in non-Indigenous Education systems. The role of non-verbal communication is highlighted, and the notion that 'indigenous learning is clothed in the medium of spirituality' (ibid).

What comes across strongly in the Coolongatta Statement is the different form and purpose of Indigenous Education (as opposed to 'education for indigenous people') and the difficulty of developing and sustaining these alternative ways of learning, knowing and being through mainstream education systems. The problem is around being evaluated within a system with conflicting values: 'Invariably the nature, and consequently the outcome, of this education has been constructed through and measured by non-Indigenous standards, values and philosophies' (ibid). The Statement outlines the right to self-determination in indigenous education through principles that include 'to establish schools and other learning facilities that recognize, respect and promote Indigenous values, philosophies and ideologies'; and 'to promote the use of Indigenous languages in education'. The statement recognises that Indigenous Peoples are not homogeneous in terms of different philosophies and values in different parts of the world, but there is no mention of differences *within* indigenous communities – apart from generational. Though women are singled out as a specific target group – 'particular attention should be given to indigenous women, children and youth' (ibid) – this seems to be more in terms of their particular needs, or perceived vulnerabilities, rather than different knowledge or gendered experiences or identities.

Moving forward to 2017, the 61st Commission on the Status of Women (CSW61) convened at the UN Headquarters in New York, included a session challenging the stereotypical portrayal of indigenous women as victims rather than agents of change. Indigenous women leaders stated 'their need for rights to economic empowerment, education and their right to be part of decision-making processes for solutions to worldwide problems'. Aminatu Samiratu Gambo (Mbororo) of the Indigenous Information Network Kenya and Cameroon argued that indigenous men needed to give women the space so that 'we can be heard and our situations will be resolved'. As well as the need for more decision-making powers within their communities, this forum highlighted the important role of indigenous women as 'champions of sustainability', being profoundly affected by climate change; more akin to an instrumental perspective on the role of indigenous peoples for sustainable development, a perspective also upheld by the Rio Declaration of 1992 (Table 1).

Clearly, indigenous education is a highly politicised field and the demands of indigenous movements go beyond the right to access education. The inclusion of indigenous people within non-indigenous education systems is regarded as problematic in terms of sustaining indigenous values, cultures and languages. Although no distinction is made between adult education and schooling in the Coolongata Declaration, the issues around the promotion of informal, intergenerational learning, indigenous languages, and the need for resources to develop indigenous education curricula, all link clearly to the notions of literacy as a social practice outlined earlier. The stated aspirations for indigenous education above are grounded in an understanding that learning is shaped by hierarchies of languages, knowledges and social relationships – and that these can be challenged through education.

From this account of the developing concept of indigenous education that emerged from indigenous movements, we move now to consider international policy declarations, from the 1960s to the present day. The following section looks particularly at declarations produced by United Nations organisations, with a focus on education, to analyse how and when indigenous women and adult learning have been addressed. Through an historical analysis of these declarations, we set out to identify how the term 'indigenous' has been viewed and defined by different actors within educational policy spaces, and take the instrumental/rights dichotomy to explore the kind of learning and knowledges being promoted in relation to women's empowerment (Table 2).

International instruments: aims and recognition for indigenous women, their knowledge and learning

There is no internationally agreed definition of the term 'indigenous peoples'. The UNDRIP identifies indigenous peoples as those under the protection of the Declaration, without defining the term itself; nor, given the vast diversity of peoples it encompasses, has formal definition been deemed either 'necessary or desirable' (ILO 2009, p. 9). The Indigenous and Tribal Peoples Convention (ILO No. 169) offers criteria to help identify – rather than define – such peoples. These include a historical attachment to ancestral territories, distinct social, cultural, political and economic institutions, and their own languages, knowledge systems and beliefs (Vinding and Kampbel 2012). Self-identification is considered a fundamental criterion (ibid). UN programmes and international agencies, used similar criteria to develop operational coverage of indigenous peoples, eschewing strict definitions.

However, prior to the 1990s, with its flagship Earth Summit in Rio and the emergence of the Education for All agenda, UN conventions made no specific mention of indigenous women, and, whilst indigenous knowledge systems were clearly acknowledged, adult education was not prioritised (Table 3).

The International Committee for Economic, Social and Cultural Rights (ICESCR), in their General Comments (GC) on the 1966 Convention draws intrinsic links between education (Article 13) and rights to a full cultural life (Article 14), seeing education as a means to allow communities and individuals to pass on their values, religion, customs and language. Yet within the Convention on the Elimination of All Forms of Discrimination against Women (CEDAW) framework, culture and tradition are viewed only in terms of its deleterious effect on girls and women's access to

Table 2. International Treaties and Declarations with a focus on Education.

1960s - 1980s	1990s-2000s	2010 +
•Convention against Discrimination in Education (1960) •International Covenant on Economic, Social and Cultural Rights (1966) •Convention on the Elimination of All Forms of Discrimination against Women (1980)	•World Declaration on Education For All (1990) •Rio Declaration on Environment and Development (1992) •Beijing Platform for Action (1995) •**MDGs** (2000) •Dakar Framework for Action for EFA (2000) •Rio +10 (2002) •UN Declaration on the Rights of Indigenous Peoples (2007) •Belém Framework for Action (2009)	•UN post-2015 Task Team •Rio +20 OWG (2012) •SAARC New Dehli Declaration on Education (2014) •**SDGs** (2015) •Beijing + 20 Global Leaders' Meeting on Gender Equality and Women's Empowerment (2015) •Inter-Agency and Expert Group on SDG Indicators (IAEG-SDGs) (2016)

education. There is no acknowledgement of indigenous knowledge and, for women, access to modernising reproductive health information is prioritised (Table 1).

The ICESCR GC 13, published in 1999, extends the requirement of fundamental – or basic – education to all those whose basic learning needs have not been met, without restriction by age or gender. It notes 'Fundamental education, therefore, is an integral component of adult education and life-long learning. Because fundamental education is a right of all age groups, curricula and delivery systems must be devised which are suitable for students of all ages' (CESCR 1999, p. 24). As such, GC 13 places additional emphasis on the 'adaptability' of education provision, curricula and learning methods to meet basic learning needs of all, and laying the groundwork for greater emphasis on non-formal education for adults.

Through our analysis of these international conventions, a dichotomy emerges – and is sustained – between the recognition of the value of indigenous peoples, and their knowledge, for sustainable development, and an education-led discourse that sees indigenous peoples as underserved, disadvantaged and needing to be accommodated within established education systems.

An exception is the Beijing Declaration and Platform for Action, adopted at the 1995 Fourth World Conference on Women, which makes comprehensive reference to indigenous women. It recognises the traditional knowledge innovations and practices of indigenous women in particular as a form of lifelong learning and calls for respect for their artistic, spiritual and cultural activities (Table 1), whilst, at the same time, acknowledging their position as a previously underserved group.

The Dakar statement acknowledges that a key challenge for the goal of Education For All is that of building a more inclusive concept of education, and reflecting this in international and national policies. Whilst the World Education Forum in 1990 highlights indigenous groups as underserved (Table 3), the overall Dakar statement's list of

Table 3. International Commitments to Education and role of Indigenous Women.

International commitments	Approaches to adult education		Recognition of indigenous peoples, knowledge and learning		
	Adult education, learning and literacy	Knowledge, skills and capacities promoted	Aims for indigenous women and education	Representation of indigenous women and their knowledge	Indigenous language needs
Convention against Discrimination in Education (1960)	No specific mention of adult education. Notes 'education' refers to all types/levels of education, but focus on formal institutions of schooling	Concerned with 'full development of the human personality', strengthening respect for human rights/freedoms; promotion of understanding, tolerance and friendship among all nations, racial or religious groups; maintenance of peace (Art. 5)	No mention of indigenous women	No specific mention of indigenous peoples/women	Recognises teaching of 'national minorities' in their language, but dependent on national policy, need for integration etc.
World Declaration on Education for All (1990)	Basic education as foundation for lifelong learning and human development. Acknowledges that basic learning needs of youth & adults are diverse and met through variety of delivery systems[a]	Literacy of intrinsic and instrumental value, as the foundation of other life skills: health, nutrition, population, agricultural techniques, environment, science, technology, family life, inc. fertility awareness	Highlights indigenous peoples as an underserved group in terms of educational access (Article 3). Prioritises access and quality of education for girls and women	Recognises that traditional knowledge/indigenous cultural heritage have value in their own right, and a capacity to define and promote development	Acknowledges that literacy in the mother-tongue strengthens cultural identity, heritage
Dakar Framework for Action for EFA (2000)	Education of intrinsic and instrumental value. Calls for expanded adult/continuing education, and integrated into national education and poverty reduction strategies. Closer linkages among formal, non-formal, informal adult learning	Literacy as fundamental for lifelong learning, sustainable livelihoods, health, citizenship. Literacy and continuing education for women's empowerment and equality	Reiterates stance of EFA: indigenous peoples are an underserved group in educational access	Reiterates EFA stance- that traditional knowledge/indigenous cultural heritage have a value and validity in their own right, and capacity to define and promote development	Acknowledges the importance of local languages for literacy
Belém Framework for Action: Adult Learning and Education (2009)	Adult education positioned within a lifelong, life-wide learning perspective, to address all aspects of human development (economic, social, personal)	Knowledge, capabilities, skills, competences and values to advance individuals' rights and destinies, achieve equitable, inclusive and sustainable societies; skills/competences for new work environments, social organisation and communication	No specific mention of indigenous women. Support for literacy in indigenous languages by developing programmes, methods, materials that value indigenous cultures, knowledge and methodologies	No specific mention of indigenous women. Indigenous peoples represented as highly disadvantaged populations	Multilingual/mother tongue policies necessary for creating a literate environment, especially for indigenous/minority groups

[a]Examples provided include: skills training, apprenticeships, and formal and non-formal education programmes and media (article 3).

disadvantaged groups does not include indigenous groups, a term dropped, but perhaps assumed to be encompassed by 'remote rural dwellers and nomads, and ethnic and linguistic minorities'.

In the regional Frameworks for Action under Dakar, the Sub-Saharan framework makes the most notable reference to indigenous peoples, recognising that, 'African indigenous knowledge systems, languages and values should be the foundation for the development of African education systems (Preamble, p 21)'. As such, the framework and calls for a review of curricula and validation of African indigenous knowledge systems, values and skills, including the development and publication of textbooks in indigenous (African) languages. Yet definitions of indigenous are not clarified, and appear to counterpoint colonial languages rather than concern specific minority groups, pastoralists, or indigenous peoples. Nor does it voice ideas or strategies relating to the validation or uptake of indigenous knowledge systems. In the Americas Regional Framework, indigenous groups are referenced in relation to the full participation and integration of disadvantaged groups, again taking a strong normative stance to inclusion. The Asia and Pacific Regional Framework, whilst acknowledging previous lack of alternative, non-formal approaches to basic education as a key challenge, gives little attention to adult literacy and lifelong learning; the exception being in relation to harnessing media and new technologies. There is no mention of indigenous peoples or knowledge systems.

Where policy indicates an instrumental approach, there is little detail about what kinds of indigenous knowledge and learning might support sustainable development. These international policy declarations rarely defined what was meant by 'indigenous' (other than as an oppositional term to 'colonial'), tended to focus on formal and non-formal, rather than informal learning, and failed to address indigenous women as a distinct group of actors, except in carrying the burden of a deficit labelling. The Belém Framework for Action – with its focus on adult education – whilst acknowledging the importance of literacy and learning in indigenous languages, reiterates a perspective of indigenous women as a 'highly disadvantaged group' (Table 3).

Pertinent to the following Nepal case study, an analysis of the South Asian Association for Regional Cooperation (SAARC)[1] 'New Delhi Declaration on Education', developed to adapt and prioritise EFA areas of action in the run-up to 2015, found no explicit mention of indigenous peoples. Instead, priority areas follow a normative stance, emphasise formal schooling and are indicative of a singularly instrumental approach to education (SAARC 2015).

The post-2015 era and the SDG 2030 agenda

The 2030 Agenda for Sustainable Development starts from the premise that all people, 'irrespective of sex, age, race, ethnicity, and persons with disabilities, migrants, indigenous peoples, should have access to lifelong learning opportunities'. Indicators for SDG4 (the education goal) are in place to monitor access to learning for groups identified as 'underserved' and 'disadvantaged'; at risk of being left behind in the achievement of SDG goals. As with the Jomtien and Dakar declarations, indigenous peoples are mentioned as one such group, carrying a deficit label, but without clarification of what is meant by 'indigenous'.

> By 2030, eliminate gender disparities in education and ensure equal access at all levels of education and vocational training for the vulnerable, including persons with disabilities, indigenous peoples and children in vulnerable situations – Target 4.5

Indicators for target 4.5 of the SDG goal for education include measures for equity to monitor the progress of 'disadvantaged' groups. Global Indicator 4.5.1 sets out a requirement for parity indices for all indicators that can be disaggregated. Indigenous peoples are a candidate for such a parity index, as data becomes available. Currently, one in six national censuses asked about indigenous status (UNESCO 2017), yet data are very limited and may be distorted by definition and perception biases.

The only other target within the SDG Agenda that specifically mentions indigenous peoples is Target 2.3., which relates to increased agricultural productivity and incomes of 'small-scale food producers, in particular women, indigenous peoples, family farmers, pastoralists and fishers': a target that risks returning focus to predominantly instrumental role for indigenous groups and a 'modernising' agenda. There is no clear recognition of indigenous knowledge, nor the rights of indigenous peoples to protect and develop that knowledge, as reflected in earlier international instruments on sustainable development (e.g. Rio Summit and UNDRIP) (Table 1).

The above analysis highlights this disconnect between the previously emerging recognition of the intrinsic value of indigenous peoples' knowledge systems and culture (e.g. in the EFA global framework), and policymakers' insistence that such groups be better integrated into mainstream education and economic systems (what we described earlier as the dominant deficit discourse). Ironically, the move from the broad EFA agenda to today's SDG framework – with its emphasis on 'leaving no one behind' – sees a shift from a fundamentally rights-based recognition of indigenous peoples and their heritage in global education policy (Table 3) to one of assimilation that risks negating agency and a potentially transformative role for women's indigenous knowledge.

Indigenous women, adult learning and education: the case of Nepal

At this point, we turn to our case study of Nepal, to consider how these issues have shaped national policy development. As well as looking at how 'indigenous' has been defined, we investigate how/whether indigenous women's knowledge and learning have been recognised within national policy.

Nepal has embarked on a process of federalisation, whereby seven provinces replaced the former 14 administrative zones with devolved administrative and financial authority. The newly created provincial assemblies are currently engaging with questions around which languages, indigenous values and cultures to recognise and promote within government institutions, including schools. This section draws on interviews and documentary analysis conducted in Nepal at this critical point of national policy development and debate.

A majority of the population still follow the Hindu religion in Nepal. Formerly, Hinduism was widely practised and promoted primarily because this was the religion of the monarchy, so other indigenous religions and cultures were practised within community circles with limited visibility. Since the 1990 People's Movement brought the absolute monarchy to an end, indigenous cultures and languages have been gradually recognised more widely. The interim Constitution in 2007 ensured the right for every religion to maintain 'its independent existence, manage and protect its religious places and religious trusts' (23/2 Right to Religion). This was further strengthened by the Constitution of Nepal 2015, which established Nepal as a secular state and protects religious and cultural freedoms (26/3, Right to Freedom of Religion).

Many indigenous people still celebrate both the Hindu festivals and their indigenous religion and cultures. Conversion to Christianity among the indigenous population is also growing through the concerted effort of missionaries. Indigenous people are finding it economically and physically convenient to visit local churches, rather than to follow indigenous practices such as worshipping the forest. Thomas *et al.* (2012, p. 34) note that 'many Chepang [an indigenous group] are moving from traditional to Christian beliefs, and use of traditional healers is being replaced by belief in prayer to cure ill-health'. In this dynamic situation, the questions 'what is indigeneity?' and 'how can indigenous identity can be preserved?' have gained in importance.

How are indigenous people and indigenous knowledge defined in Nepal?

There are several national level bodies/organisations whose work has helped to inform definitions of 'indigenous'. Three of the most prominent are:

- The National Foundation for the Development of Indigenous Nationalities in Nepal (NFDIN), a government organisation founded in 2002 under the Ministry of Local Development
- The National Federation of Indigenous Nationalities (NFIN)[2], formed in 1991 as an autonomous, non-partisan, national level umbrella organisation of indigenous peoples
- The National Indigenous Women's Forum (NIWF), established in 1998, a consortium of 41 indigenous women's organisations.

According to the NFDIN and NEFIN, indigenous people are those who have a distinct collective identity, their own language, religion, tradition, culture and civilisation, their own traditional egalitarian social structures, traditional homeland and geographical area, written or oral history and the feeling of 'We' (NFDIN 2017; NEFIN as cited by Sherpa 2009). NEFIN has further added two more characteristics – those who have had no decisive role in the politics and government of modern Nepal and those who declare themselves as *'Janajati'* or *'Adivasi'* [3] (ibid). In Sherpa's (2009) research, respondents (both those actively involved in indigenous issues and those not) all identified lack of political representation, educational opportunities and access to health care along with distinct culture, language and religion as important characteristics of indigenous people of Nepal.

Indigenous academics and advocates working for indigenous rights interviewed for this paper suggested that 'indigenous' is related to those who are original inhabitants. A male university lecturer identified them as 'Those who have high adaptation with nature ... though they are modernized, they hold indigenous knowledge'. This notion of indigenous peoples' proximity to nature was seen to shape their knowledge too. A male lecturer from an indigenous group noted: 'Their identity is formed in relation to land and nature. Their corpus of knowledge is not recognized'.

The Nepal research literature has defined indigenous knowledge as knowledge produced, utilised and transmitted across generations by a distinctive cultural group who are resource users of certain area (Maden *et al.* 2008, Limbu 2015). In the policy context, the Ministry of Science, Technology and Environment (MoSTE) also agrees that indigenous knowledge is tacit but practical knowledge accumulated over the years and transmitted orally and through experiences from generation to generation and that it is constantly changing (MoSTE 2015). In reference to indigenous knowledge and practices for climate change resilience MoSTE indicates that Nepali women's knowledge, skills and their capacity to respond to some challenges generated by climate change, and natural resource management are extensive but they lack access to power and resources 'that would enable them to turn knowledge into solution' (p. 36). Indigenous women are recognised as the 'custodians of traditional knowledge and skills' (ILO 2012), particularly in relation to traditional food preparation and preservation, wine-making, weaving and handicrafts, honey gathering and herbal medicine (ibid, Limbu 2015, Rai 2018). Indigenous women's knowledge in natural resource management is also immense (Magar 2009).

The sustaining and development of this kind of knowledge was recognised by our respondents as dependent on power relationships with the State. An indigenous advocate (male) referred to knowledge as 'Customary practices that are different from that of the Modern Nation State' and argued that '... how much that community remains or continues such knowledge and practices determines indigeneity'.

Indigenous knowledge is considered to be both a process and product of knowledge building, and represented through language, as a female linguist from an indigenous community explained: 'Any word or terminology that is not found in indigenous people's language is not indigenous knowledge'.

Thus indigenous knowledge, as defined by our respondents, includes any local knowledge that is used and/or practised by original inhabitants; experiential knowledge in tacit form acquired through interaction with nature; and recognition of the uniqueness of the community's knowledge building process, including differences from that of the modern nation state. However, the characteristics of indigenous people appeared to be challenged in the changing social and economic context of Nepal. Although there is a consensus among *Adivasi* or *Janajati* regarding the definition of indigenous, questions arise around whether the term can still hold if an individual becomes more economically, educationally, socially and geographically mobile. For instance, there is debate currently about whether the characteristics apply to all those who are born into a particular indigenous community, irrespective of whether they later change location, religion, culture or language, or whether individuals can be considered indigenous if they only hold on to one characteristic, such as participating in certain cultural events?

Though many indigenous people are still living in rural areas maintaining many traditional practices, many others have changed practices in their everyday life and culture – due to the long-lasting influence of Hindu traditions, increased migration among young members and conversion to Christianity. Some indigenous intellectuals opined that how much a community remains or continues customary knowledge and practices determines indigeneity, as noted by an activist in relation to her own identity:

'In terms of practising and exercising, I am not an indigenous now due to forceful state mechanisms that never supported indigenous people to live with their traditional knowledge and practice. Since we have ties with that indigenous community who followed indigenous knowledge and practices we are considered indigenous but we are not doing the same.'

She also attributed this situation to the cultural practices brought by indigenous population who have travelled to other parts of the world and the impact of assertive religious conversion. In addition, Thapa Magar (2009) identified the intervention of new technologies as one of the causes of deteriorating indigenous knowledge.

The Nepal case demonstrates the long-standing tension between the indigenous population and the State that surfaced after the restoration of democracy in the 1990s. One of the major areas of tension has been the issue of identity. Changes in sociocultural status also sped up due to increased, improved technology and the inflow of development agencies. Changes in location and socio-cultural contexts bring into question the definition of indigenous and indigeneity in Nepal. This will lead, potentially, to another layer of tension as multiple identities are shaped and indigeneity recognised in different ways in the globalised context.

Indigenous women's movements in Nepal

There are an ever-growing number of organisations actively working to ensure the rights and development of indigenous people in Nepal, including the NFDIN, NEFIN and NIWF. There are also indigenous women's organisations and research/sector-specific organisations such as the Indigenous Women's Legal Awareness Group (INWOLAG). Identity-based Indigenous People's Organisations (IPOs) have been formed in efforts to create shared identities while recognising the differences that exist within ethnic groups (Hangen 2010). This paper reviews the initiatives of NFDIN, NEFIN and NIWF, with a particular focus on how they address gender issues, and recognise indigenous knowledge and women's learning.

NFDIN works in different districts through separate units, which include: programmes for endangered indigenous communities, income generation and skill development, research, publications, community building, construction and Civil Service examination preparatory classes (International Documentation Division 2015). For example, support was provided to Nepal Magar Women's Association for tailoring training for women in Bardia district (NFDIN 2017), training on investigative journalism for indigenous women and men, and an ethnolinguistic survey (NFDIN 2015). Such programmes are either implemented directly or through IPOs.

One of NFDIN's objectives that has potential to enhance indigenous women's knowledge and learning, is to preserve and promote the traditional knowledge, skills and technologies of the *Janajati* and to guide their vocational use (Information, Publication and Scholarship Section 2015 and Academic Division and Research Team 2015).

However, programmes that address the above-mentioned objective are rarely found in NFDIN documents, and NFDIN objectives do not refer explicitly to issues of gender.

The NWIF recognises that indigenous women face distinct and different issues from that of other women, and from indigenous men. The rationale for its formation was that indigenous women's issues were not adequately addressed by established indigenous organiszations or forums – where men tended to dominate. According to a female social worker respondent, intersecting inequalities that indigenous women faced were often hidden:

'Informally *janajati* women have raised their voices that they bear double discrimination as women and being a *janajati* woman. But it has not been raised strongly.'

This view was supported by an indigenous activist, who maintained that,

There is a notion that there is gender equality in *Janajatis* then there is no need to write about gender issues... If someone tries to talk about differences or diversity among Nepali women relating to particular ethnic group, then that person is seen as disturbing the harmony.

This reflects Hangen's (2010, p. 43) observation that 'as in most political sectors in Nepal, gender inequality has been persistent within indigenous nationalities movement. Participation of women in all aspects of movement is limited'.

The NIWF also points out that traditionally indigenous women are decision-makers in the family and society, and contribute to peace building and reconciliation, which the State has not recognised. They have two objectives relevant to addressing gender inequities: (1) to support economic, linguistic, social, religious, political and cultural aspects of indigenous women, and (2) to research and analyse issues related to the social situations of indigenous women and intervene accordingly (NIWF 2017). Their strategies include: promote gender equity and equality; literacy and education campaigns; deconstruction of ideological, political, socio-cultural, linguistic, religious, and institutional barriers against indigenous women, and construction and/or reconstruction of indigenous women's identity, dignity, status and rights[4].

Indigenous movements and adult learning

NIWF has been implementing projects and programmes geared towards the empowerment and development of indigenous communities perceived as those most marginalised and endangered; political and social advocacy to ensure rights of indigenous population in general, and indigenous women in particular, and skill-based trainings for economic improvement. However, a progress report of the projects implemented from 1998 to 2013 (NIWF, n.d.) indicates that the majority focused on transferring modern skills and knowledge related to occupations, advocacy about indigenous people's rights and anthropological studies of the communities. A review of projects that aimed to address gender inequities within endangered indigenous communities revealed that most were not utilising or promoting women's indigenous knowledge as a vehicle to empowerment. For instance, a community literacy programme for endangered indigenous women implemented by NIWF (n.d.) was not that different from other mainstream literacy programmes, focusing only imparting new knowledge, rather than building on participants' indigenous skills.

There have, however, been several projects around securing new spaces for indigenous women to have a voice in the political and social processes of the State. A five year (2001–2006) project for the empowerment of indigenous people funded by German Development Service (DED) included components addressing social discrimination faced by indigenous women and an advocacy programme for increasing the inclusion of indigenous women in the then Constitution Assembly. Two later NIWF projects included capacity-building activities with village and district level democratic fora, such as conducting discussions with service providers and local women politicians in the area of human rights; situation analyses of indigenous women's issues; publication of a training manual, and formation of indigenous women's networks locally. NIWF continues to advocate for indigenous women's rights and political space at the national level. A recent programme has established monthly dialogue groups with young indigenous women on indigenous culture, politics, book reading and art and activism and radio journalism training (NIWF 2017). However, there is little indication that means to integrate and build on indigenous women's knowledge in these projects' processes was considered.

The NIWF recognises that indigenous women retain some or all of their distinctive knowledge, skills, culture, decision-making roles and traditional institutions, and play a vital role in sustainable management of environment and natural resources. Yet, the goal and objectives of NIWF are more inclined towards gaining political rights on the basis of ethnic, linguistic and regional autonomy with the right to self-determination and ensuring space in State structures. Promoting, preserving and utilising indigenous women's knowledge, skills and capacity are not made explicit in their objectives.

This review of indigenous federations reveals that indigenous women's knowledge, skill and capacities have rarely been considered as important resources within their programmes. Instead, the focus has been on creating space and identity for indigenous women in the State structures through advocacy and capacity development, and taking care of their immediate needs through relief work. The indigenous women's movement has also focused on addressing inequalities in formal schooling, rather than advocacy for integrating indigenous knowledge through non-formal education. A social worker from an indigenous group commented that,

> … not much effort has been made to record, promote and link indigenous knowledge with mainstream discourse. Focus has been given to skill promotion and preservation.

As Rai (2016) notes, indigenous nationalities' focused fight against the State's discrimination, and the effect of the State's single policy and Hinduisation, has envigorated their struggle. However, in research literature, indigenous women are mostly presented from cultural and social perspectives alone and other important aspects of their lives are not given space (ibid.).

The indigenous movements have influenced government education policy and programmes through advocacy for literacy in mother tongue languages. NFE is recognised as a mechanism to preserve and promote local cultures, local knowledge and traditional skills (NFEC 2016, 2017). Government-prepared primers (ibid) teach adult learners about their right to use their mother tongue and women's rights. The primers cover the use of local technology and measures to protect water, land, forest, herbs and animals. However, neither the primers nor facilitator's training manual recognise that the learners are mostly women. The emphasis is more on imparting knowledge and skills, than promoting the indigenous knowledge that women come with, and there is no reference to intergenerational learning. The mind-set behind the NFE materials and delivery appears guided by a 'banking concept' of education that gives little room to integrate women's indigenous knowledge and skills into teaching and learning processes.

Indigenous adult women and learning: combining international and national perspectives

Our earlier analysis of international documents reveals a discourse that positions indigenous communities as an underserved and disadvantaged group, alongside increasing recognition of their right to education (particularly schooling) in their mother tongue. Within the 2030 Sustainable Development Agenda, as with previous international instruments on sustainable development, there is still no clear recognition of a role for women's indigenous knowledge. Significantly, it was the gender-focused Beijing Platform for Action that made greater reference to indigenous knowledge as a form of lifelong learning and called for protection and use of the knowledge, innovations and practices of indigenous women. Taking gender rather than education as the starting point may have led to the focus on informal learning and indigenous knowledges rather than formal or non-formal education within the Beijing declarations. Within our earlier review of educational policy instruments, the emphasis appeared to be on ensuring greater access to skills development for indigenous groups (as in the Belem Framework for Action) – what might be seen as an instrumental rather than a transformative approach to women's empowerment.

By contrast, the case study of indigenous movements in Nepal suggests that transformative political goals have largely informed their educational agenda, which focuses on capacity building in terms of indigenous women gaining new spaces for political representation. Although this process involves informal learning, these organisations' explicitly stated educational objectives are framed around catching up on technical skills and formal literacy. The review of skills development and literacy programmes for indigenous women points to a lack of attention to utilising, preserving or finding ways to facilitate intergenerational learning of indigenous knowledges – rather, they tend to replicate mainstream women's education programmes. Seen from the perspective of multiple identities and multiple literacies, such programmes tend to have prioritised 'schooled' literacy (Street 2005) and overlooked such groups' distinct identities and knowledges as indigenous women. Within this context, 'indigenous education' is interpreted in terms of new skills and capabilities to initiate political reform – rather than focusing on how to preserve and sustain indigenous knowledge.

The questions raised by the Nepal case study around notions of changing identities and definitions of indigeneity relate to the tensions identified within international policy between the value of indigenous knowledge for sustainable development and the recognition that indigenous people need to access new knowledge. Does someone cease to be 'indigenous' when they move away and lose indigenous skills/languages? The highly politicised notion of 'indigenous' in Nepal – as embedded in long-standing relationships with the State and religious hierarchies – challenges international educational policy instruments which are only focused on one dimension of empowerment, particularly the economy. Similarly, the invisibility of gender inequality within some indigenous communities and movements in Nepal signals the importance of ensuring political mobilisation is also gendered – rather than only focusing educational interventions on indigenous women as a doubly disadvantaged group.

Significantly, most of the activities conducted by indigenous movements in Nepal were promoting informal learning for women – whether through discussion forums or political awareness raising. It is not clear how far the formal institutions reviewed here have harnessed the potential of social media to support this learning, though use of mobile phones and digital literacy is widespread amongst women in indigenous communities.

Conclusion

This article set out to look at what indigenous movements can offer in terms of problematising and challenging the SDGs to develop an expanded and cross-sectoral approach to adult learning. In particular, the sustainable development paradigm implies a greater recognition of the impact of climate change and environmental degradation, which has long been a central concern of indigenous movements, and exploring what kind of skills/knowledge might be needed. Although there is a greater focus on educational inclusion in the SDGs, there are questions around how far there is an intended space for groups like indigenous women to influence the values and knowledges within mainstream education. This could be seen as the distinction between 'education for indigenous adults', as compared to 'indigenous adult education'. As Morrison (2011) points out, taking an 'indigenous' perspective on education involves interrogating educational content and dominant practices like measuring quality in relation to international 'standards'. In our analysis, we found that education initiatives within the Nepal context and within international policy declarations tended to replicate such dominant models, focusing on development of skills for the modern economy. 'Indigenous education' – in the sense of alternative values and educational approaches – was neither promoted by the indigenous movements (who focused on more formal skill training) nor mainstream educational providers.

Taking a broader lens on adult education as involving informal and intergenerational learning, we could, however, take the indigenous movements' work on political awareness-raising as exemplifying a 'rights' perspective on skills development. Rogers (2013) distinguishes between different kinds of informal learning: incidental, task-conscious, self-directed and/or unintentional. Through this lens, we can see that whilst international policy and indigenous movements may promote new political spaces as a way of supporting indigenous women's informal learning in terms of leadership and voice ('task-conscious' learning), there is less attention given to how to build on established self-directed and unintentional processes of informal and intergenerational indigenous learning. In other words, indigenous education is rarely taken as a different approach to learning – rather, the emphasis is on ensuring the better integration of indigenous women into the dominant discourse, whether that means mainstream political structures or formal educational institutions. By contrast, taking intergenerational learning as integral to indigenous education might involve questioning taken-for-granted hierarchical relationships between teachers and students within formal education or challenging the tendency to teach literacy as a decontextualised skill, rather than as embedded in social and cultural practices.

As the above analysis has revealed, the assumed dichotomies between instrumental and rights approaches cannot be simply mapped onto that of formal and informal learning – as revealed by the case study from Nepal, formal schooling may also be seen as key to indigenous women gaining greater political voice and representation. Similarly, indigenous movements may see strategic reasons for essentialising gender and culture (rather than recognising indigenous women's multiple identities and literacies) in order to strengthen cohesion within the organisation for political mobilisation. Moving towards the 2030 SD Agenda, the challenge is also how to strengthen the connections between informal, nonformal and formal learning and recognise indigenous women's diverse identities and knowledges. This is needed in order to develop the processes for catalysing sustainable development and the expanded notion of knowledge and skills signalled by SDG 4.7 around 'global citizenship and appreciation of cultural diversity'.

Disclosure statement

No potential conflict of interest was reported by the authors.

Notes

1. Consisting of Afghanistan, Bangladesh, Bhutan, India, the Maldives, Nepal, Pakistan and Sri Lanka.
2. NEFIN is a member of the United Nation's Working Group on Indigenous Populations.
3. Leading indigenous scholars coined the terms Janajati (nationality) and Adivasi (indigenous people) to identify populations outside of the Hindu caste hierarchy (Neupane, 2012). These days the two terms are used interchangeably in Nepal and both refer to indigenous people.
4. See http://niwfnepal.org.np/strategies/

ORCID

Catherine M. Jere ⓘ https://orcid.org/0000-0001-7934-3951

References

Academic division and research team, 2015. ElSuN [Ethnolinguistic Survey of Nepal] completed in three districts. Bulletin of Indigenous Nationalities. No. 13. pp. 24–25.
Acharya, S. and Robinson-Pant, A., 2017. Women, literacy and health: comparing health and education sectoral approaches in Nepal. Compare: a Journal of Comparative and

International Education. 49 (2), 211–229. Available from: http://www.tandfonline.com/doi/full/10.1080/03057925.2017.1393622

Aikman, S., 2011. Education and indigenous justice in Africa. *International journal of educational development*, 31 (1), 15–22.

Aikman, S., *et al.*, 2016. Challenging deficit discourses in international education and development in. *Compare: a Journal of Comparative and International Education*, 46 (2), 314–334.

Apthorpe, R. and Gasper, D., 1996. *Arguing development policy: frames and discourses.* London: Frank Cass.

Barton, D., Hamilton, M., and Ivanic, R., 2000. *Situated literacies: reading and writing in context.* London: Routledge.

Butler, J., 1990. *Gender trouble: feminism and the subversion of identity.* London: Routledge.

Cornwall, A. and Edwards, J., 2014. Negotiating empowerment. *In*: Cornwall and Edwards, eds. *Feminisms, empowerment and development: changing women's lives.* London/New York: Zed Books.

CESCR (Committee on ecoomic, Social and Cultural Rights), 1999. *General Comment 13.* New York: UN Economic and Social Council.

Hangen, I. S., 2010. *The rise of ethnic politics in Nepal: democracy in the margin.* Oxford: Routledge.

Hsieh, H.-F. and Shannon, S.E., 2005. Three approaches to qualitative content analysis. *Qualitative health research*, 15 (9), 1277.

ILO, 2009. Indigenous and tribal peoples' rights in practice: a guide to ILO Convention No. 169. Available from: http://www.ilo.org/newyork/publications/WCMS_106474/lang–en/index.htm

International and documentation division, 2015. Civil Service examination preparatory training. . Bulletin of Indigenous Nationalities. No. 13. pp. 11–12.

Information, publication and scholarship section, 2015. Training on investigative journalism. Bulletin of Indigenous Nationalities. No. 13. pp. 9–10.

Joshi, S. and Ghose, M., 2012. India: literacy and women's empowerment, a tracer study. *In*: Asia South Pacific Association for Basic and Adult Education (ASPBAE) *(2012) The power of literacy: women's journeys in India, Indonesia, Philippines and Papua New Guinea.* Philippines: ASPBAE.

Limbu, R. K., 2015. *Limbu indigenous knowledge and culture.* Lalitpur: National Foundation for Development of Indigenous Nationalities.

Maden, K., Kongren, R., and Limbu, T. M., 2008. *Docunmetation of indigenous knowledge, skill and practices of Kirant nationalities with special focus on biological resources. Unpublished Research.* Lalitpur: SNV-Nepal.

Magar, T.S., 2009. Magars and their indigenous knowledge systems and practices in Tanahu district of Nepal. *Occasional Papers in Sociology and Anthropology*, 11, 67–83.

Morrison, S., 2011. *Quality adult education benchmarks for indigenous education, prepared as a discussion paper for ASPBAE, June 2011.* India: Asia South Pacific Association for Basic and Adult Education.

MoSTE 2015. *Indigenous and local knowledge and practices for climate resilience in Nepal, mainstreaming climate change risk management in development.* Kathmandu, Nepal: Ministry of Science, Technology and Environment (MoSTE).

Neupane, F., 2012. Adivasi and Janajati: indigenous people and nationalities in Nepal. Parivartan Nepal. Available from: https://parivartannepal.blogspot.com/2012/01/adibashi-and-janajati-indigenous-people_04.html

NFDIN, 2017a. Cutting and sewing training for Magar women. Available from: http://www.nfdin.gov.np/

NFDIN, 2017b. Introduction and objectives. Available from: http://www.nfdin.gov.np/eng

NFEC, 2016. *Continuing education facilitator's training manual 2073.* [In Nepali]. Kathmandu: Author.

NFEC, 2017. *NFE and continuing education programme implementation guideline.* Kathmandu: Author.

NIWF, 2017. Past to present of National Indigenous Women's Forum. [In Nepali]. Available from: https://drive.google.com/file/d/0B_DP4QnD9yPQOHp5X2QwX2tnLUU/view

NIWF (n.d.). Past to present of National Indigenous Women's Forum. [In Nepali]. Acessed from: https://drive.google.com/file/d/0B_DP4QnD9yPQOHp5X2QwX2tnLUU/view

Rai, I.M., 2018. Identity paradoxes of Kirat migrants in urban context: an Auto/ethnographic inquiry. Thesis. Kathmandu University.

Rai, K., 2016. Indigenous women's social movement. [In Nepali]. *In*: Kailash Rai, ed., In *search of identity. Indigenous women's social, cultural and political contexts.* Kathmandu: Indigenous Media Foundation, 145–160.

Rai, K., 2017. Nepal government's policy and international provisions in relation to indigenous women and children. [In Nepali]. *In*: Thami and Chhantyal, eds. *Indigenous rights in Nepal: policy situation, challenges and opportunities.* Kathmandu: LAHURNIP, 29–52.

Rao, N. and Robinson-Pant, A., 2006. Adult education and indigenous people: addressing gender in policy and practice. *International Journal of Educational Development*, 26 (2), 209–223.

Robinson-Pant, A., 2016. Women, literacy and development: an overview. *In*: Hornberger, N., ed. *The encyclopaedia of language and education. Vol. 2. Literacy.* 3rd ed. New York: Springer.

Rogers, A., 2013. The classroom and the everyday: the importance of informal learning for formal learning. *Investigar Em Educacao*, 1 (1), 7–34.

SAARC, 2015. New Delhi Agreement for enhancing SAARC collaboration for Education 2030: adopted by the participants of the Sub-Regional Conference on 'EFA Unfinished and Post 2015 Education Agendas in SAARC countries, 13–14 October 2015, New Delhi, India.

Sherpa, P. Y. 2009. Indigenous movements: Identification of indigenous concerns in Nepal. A Master's thesis, Department of Anthropology Washington State University. Accessed from: http://citeseerx.ist.psu.edu/viewdoc/download?doi=10.1.1.427.51677&rep=rep1&type=pdf

Street, B. V., 1984. *Literacy in theory and practice.* Cambridge: Cambridge University Press.

Street, B. V., 2005. *Literacy across educational contexts.* Philadelphia, PA: Caslon Publishing.

The Asia Foundation, 2011. *Political economy analysis of local governance in Nepal with special reference to education and health sectors.* Kathmandu: Author.

Thomas, D., *et al.*, 2012. *Voices from the community: access to health services a rapid Participatory Ethnographic Evaluation and Research (PEER).* Kathmandu: Population Division, Ministry of Health and Population.

Tough, A., 1979. *Adults' learning projects.* Toronto: OISE.

UN, 2008. *United Nations Declaration on the Rights of Indigenous People.* New York: United Nations.

UN, 2015. Transforming our world: The 2030 agenda for sustainable development, draft resolution referred to the United Nations Summit for the adoption of the post-2015 development agenda by the General Assembly, 18 September 2015.

UNESCO, 2006. *A 10-year literacy/NFE policy and programme framework.* Kathmandu: UNESCO.

UNESCO, 2017. Accountability in education: meeting our commitments, Global Education Monitoring Report, Paris, UNESCO.

Vinding, D. and Kampbel, E. R., 2012. *Indigenous women workers with case studies from Bangladesh, Nepal and the Americas.* Geneva: ILO Bureau for Gender Equality.

WIPCE, 1999. Coolongatta statement on indigenous people's rights in education. World Indigenous Peoples' Conference on Education in Hilo, Hawai'I, 1999. Available from: http://ankn.uaf.edu/IKS/cool.html

World Conference of Indigenous Peoples on Territory, Environment and Development, 1992. Kari-Oca Declaration and Indigenous Peoples' Earth Charter, Kari Oca 25–30 May 1992.

Index